Microsoft Office 365 – Exchange Online Implementation and Migration

Second Edition

Plan and execute a successful Office 365 Exchange Online migration with ease

Ian Waters
David Greve
Loryan Strant

BIRMINGHAM - MUMBAI

Microsoft Office 365 – Exchange Online Implementation and Migration

Second Edition

First published: August 2016

Production reference: 1230816

Published by Packt Publishing Ltd.
Livery Place
35 Livery Street
Birmingham
B3 2PB, UK.
ISBN 978-1-78439-552-0

www.packtpub.com

Credits

Authors
Ian Waters
David Greve
Loryan Strant

Reviewers
Richard Diver
Vadim Gremyachev
Yvette Watson

Commissioning Editor
Amarabha Banerjee

Acquisition Editor
Ruchita Bhansali

Content Development Editor
Kajal Thapar

Technical Editor
Deepti Tuscano

Copy Editors
Alpha Singh

Project Coordinator
Shweta H Birwatkar

Proofreader
Safis Editing

Indexer
Mariammal Chettiyar

Graphics
Disha Haria

Production Coordinator
Nilesh Mohite

About the Authors

Ian Waters is technical director for Southern IT Networks Ltd, a managed service provider in the UK. He has built up over 15 years of training and experience using Microsoft products and provides expert technical advice to businesses across the UK. Ian is Microsoft certified in Windows Server, Exchange, SQL Server, and Active Directory but over the last few years he has focused his efforts on working with Office 365 and Azure.

The majority of Ian's work now involves designing, managing, and implementing Office 365 with his team at Southern IT Networks Ltd. and empowering their clients by utilizing the latest cloud technology.

Ian also offers help, advice, and training to his fellow administrators via the website www.slashadmin.co.uk. There you will find how-to guides and walk-throughs on implementing the latest tools used by IT consultants.

His recent work includes publishing the book entitled *The Office 365 PowerShell Reference Manual for IT Super Heros,* which helps Office 365 administrators manage their environments using PowerShell.

I would like to thank my wife Rebecca and my baby boy Archer for putting up with me working most evenings and weekends during the development of this book. Their support and encouragement has made the experience an amazing one, thank you both!

I also want to thank my development coach Richard Tubb at www.tubblog.co.uk for encouraging me to start writing and sharing my experience and knowledge.

Also thanks goes to Southern IT Networks for their years of support and providing me with some amazing training and development opportunities.

I hope this book encourages IT administrators everywhere to keep on training and learning new skills.

David Greve is a two-year Microsoft MVP in Office 365 and a published author of the first version of this Office 365 Exchange Online migration book. He has over 20 years of consulting experience in the IT industry, solving business problems and designing cloud solutions ranging from mid-size to enterprise environments.

David has expertise designing, developing, and marketing cloud computing solutions with a focus on Microsoft Azure and Office 365. He commonly works in the most complex business environments, both with C-level and technical business leaders, to provide thought leadership for strategic business mapping, integration, and migration planning to cloud solutions.

David works for SoftwareONE, as a Global Cloud Innovation and Strategy Leader, with a focus on enabling a full cloud Software Portfolio Management (SPM) platform and services. SoftwareONE is redefining the technology solutions landscape as the thought leaders in SPM services. By combining commercial, technology, compliance and governance expertise into a balanced SPM service offering, SoftwareONE supports customers by ensuring their IT investments are cost-effectively road-mapped towards their unique business needs. Prior to SoftwareONE, David managed a Microsoft Cloud professional services business, as a National Director, at Perficient.

I would like to thank my family, especially my wife Danielle, for their support as I pursue ways to expand my passion for technology and contributions to the community.

Loryan Strant has been a Microsoft MVP for Office 365 since 2011 and a published author of the first version of this Office 365 Exchange migration book. He has worked in various senior roles in the IT industry over the past 20 years across a number of technologies and sectors.

Loryan is passionate about enabling people and organisations using technology the right way, empowering them to become more productive.

He blogs about the cloud at www.thecloudmouth.com as well as writes articles for a variety of vendors and publications. Loryan has also spoken at many Microsoft conferences and events about Office 365.

Loryan founded Paradyne in 2010 to focus on Microsoft cloud solutions and was acquired by Generation-e in late 2015, where he is now the Cloud CTO of the expanded business and able to provide organisations with a greater range of solutions across cloud and unified communications.

I would like to thank my wife and two beautiful daughters for encouraging me to keep focusing on what I love and for supporting me in my passion to grow and share my knowledge with the community, as well as the fantastic team at Paradyne & Generation-e who help deliver my vision.

About the Reviewers

Richard Diver is a solutions architect with 17 years of experience across multiple industries and technologies, with a focus on Microsoft cloud architecture, enterprise mobility, and identity management solutions. His previous book contributions include topics such as Sysinternals Tools and Windows Intune.

Vadim Gremyachev is a solutions architect based in Finland and works as a consultant at NED Software Consulting Oy. He is one of the top contributors to SharePoint StackExchange and an author of a few open source projects including Office 365 API client libraries for PHP and Python; You can follow him at @vgrem on Twitter.

Yvette Watson is a consultant based in the Philippines and a recognized Microsoft Most Valuable Professional (MVP) for Office 365. Her experience with a Microsoft Partner exposed her to Office 365 deployments and Exchange Online migrations for various large and multinational companies. Among her certifications are Microsoft Certified Solutions Associate (MCSA): Office 365 and Microsoft Specialist (MS) in Administering Office 365 for Small Businesses. Yvette is also a regular resource speaker on Microsoft technologies invited by numerous colleges and universities in Manila. She graduated summa cum laude from Treston International College with a bachelor's degree in computer engineering.

To my loving family, Mama Tina, Mommy Nenita, Papa Peter, Gladys, CJ, Kuya Jay, and Kuya Ritche, for your never-failing love, support, and encouragement.

eBooks, discount offers, and more

Did you know that Packt offers eBook versions of every book published, with PDF and ePub files available? You can upgrade to the eBook version at www.PacktPub.com and as a print book customer, you are entitled to a discount on the eBook copy. Get in touch with us at customercare@packtpub.com for more details.

At www.PacktPub.com, you can also read a collection of free technical articles, sign up for a range of free newsletters and receive exclusive discounts and offers on Packt books and eBooks.

https://www2.packtpub.com/books/subscription/packtlib

Do you need instant solutions to your IT questions? PacktLib is Packt's online digital book library. Here, you can search, access, and read Packt's entire library of books.

Why subscribe?

- Fully searchable across every book published by Packt
- Copy and paste, print, and bookmark content
- On demand and accessible via a web browser

Table of Contents

Preface

The introduction of Office 365 has heralded a new era of productivity for organizations of all types and sizes, wherever they are in the world.

Office 365 provides small businesses with the same level of technology that was previously only affordable to enterprises. For many organizations, this can equate to an increase in competitive advantage.

For enterprises, Office 365 allows them to move operationally important systems such as e-mail out to the cloud with Exchange Online—to be maintained and optimized by Microsoft. This allows enterprises to focus on their line of business-enhancing technologies that will empower the organization to achieve greater levels of productivity and efficiency.

Exchange Online is by far the most popular component of Office 365 as it allows organizations of any size to offload their mailbox functionality to Microsoft and focus on their business—instead of having to worry about keeping servers operational and mail flowing.

While Office 365 also includes SharePoint Online, Skype for Business, Office Web Apps, and Office Professional Plus, this book will focus specifically on Exchange Online.

What this book covers

In this book, we will cover common scenarios for implementing Exchange Online, ranging from simple one-way migrations to hybrid environments for co-existence with existing on-premise mail systems.

Chapter 1, *Getting Started with Office 365*, covers the differences in Office 365 plans and the basics around obtaining an Office 365 subscription.

Chapter 2, *Getting Familiar with the Office 365 Admin Portal*, walks you through the administrative interfaces of Office 365 and how to add your first domain name.

Chapter 3, *Integration Options for Businesses*, explains what options are available for customers of the P1 plan to integrate with their on-premise systems.

Chapter 4, *Integration Options for Midsize and Enterprise Organizations*, explains what options are available for customers of the Enterprise or Exchange only plans and integration with their on-premise systems.

Chapter 5, *Preparing for a Simple Migration*, helps subscribers of the small business plan to prepare their environment and existing mail systems to ensure that their migration to Exchange Online happens smoothly.

Chapter 6, *Performing a Simple Migration*, builds on Chapter 5, *Preparing for a Simple Migration* by explaining the process involved in performing a one-way migration to Exchange Online from a variety of mail systems.

Chapter 7, *Preparing for a Hybrid Deployment and Migration*, focuses on preparation to your Office 365 subscription and the integration components necessary for a Hybrid deployment.

Chapter 8, *Deploying a Hybrid Infrastructure – AD FS*, covers technical tasks required to install and configure AD FS for Office 365.

Chapter 9, *Deploying a Hybrid Infrastructure – Directory Synchronization*, covers technical tasks required to install and configure Directory Synchronization for Office 365.

Chapter 10, *Deploying a Hybrid Infrastructure – Exchange Hybrid*, covers technical tasks required to install and configure Exchange Hybrid for Office 365.

Chapter 11, *Performing a Hybrid Migration*, teaches you the necessary steps to perform a migration to Office 365 from both the user interface and through PowerShell.

Chapter 12, *Post Migration Considerations*, teaches you how to address resources and making a mail routing change by following the implementation and migration to Office 365.

Chapter 13, *Additional Hybrid Solution – Lync Online/Skype for Business*, teaches you how to setup a hybrid configuration with your existing on-premises Lync/SFB servers and leverage the cloud to improve user collaboration.

Chapter 14, *Additional Hybrid Solution – SharePoint Online*, explains how to setup a hybrid configuration with on-premises SharePoint servers and seamlessly work with files stored locally and hosted in the cloud.

References, will show references to further reading or the supporting documentations.

What you need for this book

While the scenarios for small businesses and Enterprise migrations may have different requirements, they do share some common needs.

As the person performing the migration, you will need to ensure that you have administrative access to your existing mail system, a high-quality Internet connection, access to make domain name record modifications, and patience.

Who this book is for

While Office 365 can make administration of enterprise-grade mail platforms simpler, readers of this book will still require an understanding of how e-mail systems work and familiarity with DNS and various mail platforms.

It is expected that readers will have at least basic IT skills in order to perform a migration to small business plans. Readers who will be using the enterprise plans and looking at hybrid environments with Exchange Online will need a far greater level of familiarity with Active Directory and Exchange Server.

Ultimately, this book can be categorized as being useful for small business owners with some level of technical understanding, through to corporate messaging administrators and IT consultants.

Conventions

In this book, you will find a number of text styles that distinguish between different kinds of information. Here are some examples of these styles and an explanation of their meaning.

Code words in text, database table names, folder names, filenames, file extensions, pathnames, dummy URLs, user input, and Twitter handles are shown as follows: "Your SharePoint service URL includes your tenant name (for example, `paradynelab.sharepoint.com`)."

Any command-line input or output is written as follows:

```
$s = New-PSSession -ConfigurationName Microsoft.Exchange -ConnectionUri
https://ps.outlook.com/powershell -Credential $cred -Authentication Basic
-AllowRedirection
```

New terms and **important words** are shown in bold. Words that you see on the screen, for example, in menus or dialog boxes, appear in the text like this: "Enter your number and press **Text me** to receive your verification code."

Warnings or important notes appear in a box like this.

Tips and tricks appear like this.

Reader feedback

Feedback from our readers is always welcome. Let us know what you think about this book-what you liked or disliked. Reader feedback is important for us as it helps us develop titles that you will really get the most out of. To send us general feedback, simply e-mail feedback@packtpub.com, and mention the book's title in the subject of your message. If there is a topic that you have expertise in and you are interested in either writing or contributing to a book, see our author guide at www.packtpub.com/authors.

Customer support

Now that you are the proud owner of a Packt book, we have a number of things to help you to get the most from your purchase.

Downloading the color images of this book

We also provide you with a PDF file that has color images of the screenshots/diagrams used in this book. The color images will help you better understand the changes in the output. You can download this file from http://www.packtpub.com/sites/default/files/downl oads/MicrosoftOffice365ExchangeOnlineImplementationandMigrationSecondEdition _ColorImages.pdf.

Errata

Although we have taken every care to ensure the accuracy of our content, mistakes do happen. If you find a mistake in one of our books-maybe a mistake in the text or the code- we would be grateful if you could report this to us. By doing so, you can save other readers from frustration and help us improve subsequent versions of this book. If you find any errata, please report them by visiting http://www.packtpub.com/submit-errata, selecting your book, clicking on the **Errata Submission Form** link, and entering the details of your errata. Once your errata are verified, your submission will be accepted and the errata will be uploaded to our website or added to any list of existing errata under the Errata section of that title.

To view the previously submitted errata, go to https://www.packtpub.com/books/content/support and enter the name of the book in the search field. The required information will appear under the **Errata** section.

Piracy

Piracy of copyrighted material on the Internet is an ongoing problem across all media. At Packt, we take the protection of our copyright and licenses very seriously. If you come across any illegal copies of our works in any form on the Internet, please provide us with the location address or website name immediately so that we can pursue a remedy.

Please contact us at copyright@packtpub.com with a link to the suspected pirated material.

We appreciate your help in protecting our authors and our ability to bring you valuable content.

Questions

If you have a problem with any aspect of this book, you can contact us at questions@packtpub.com, and we will do our best to address the problem.

1
Getting Started with Office 365

Welcome to the world of Office 365 – a cutting edge way of increasing productivity by harnessing the power of the cloud.

By reading this chapter, you will learn what plans are available for your business, how to decide which option to take, and how to get your Office 365 subscription underway.

Throughout this chapter, we hope to provide you with guidance on how to determine your requirements. We will provide you with information on the choices and the decisions you will need to make. We will also provide you with examples of real-world customers of Office 365.

Let's begin by looking at the different options available under Office 365:

- Office 365 plans
- Office 365 Business – considerations and limitations
- Office 365 Enterprise
- When to use a plan and when to pick a la carte
- Options to start your subscription
- The sign up process

Office 365 available plans

At the heart of Office 365 are two essential subscription paths a customer can go through:

- Office 365 Business:
  `https://products.office.com/en-us/business/office-365-business`
- Office 365 Enterprise:
  `https://products.office.com/en-us/business/office-365-enterprise-e3-bu siness-software`

There are several other variants available to individuals, non-profits, education, and government which include a combination of features from the Enterprise plans at a lower cost:

- Office 365 Personal: `https://products.office.com/en-us/office-365-person al`
- Office 365 Nonprofit: `https://products.office.com/en-us/nonprofit/offic e-365-nonprofit-plans-and-pricing`
- Office 365 Government Pricing: `https://products.office.com/en-us/governm ent/compare-office-365-government-plans`

In this book, we will focus on the Business and Enterprise plans, but check whether you qualify for the Nonprofit or Government Pricing plans to lower your operating costs.

The main difference between the two subscription types is that under the Business plans, the subscription provides high value but no licensing flexibility, and a maximum limit of 300 users. There are also several other limitations, which are addressed further in this chapter.

There are a number of different ways to purchase these:

- Directly on the Office 365 Administration portal
- From a Cloud Solutions Provider (**CSP**) (for example, generally a telecommunications provider or Microsoft partner that resells Office 365)
- From a Microsoft licensing reseller (for example, an IT company that supplies Microsoft Open Business or Open Value licenses)
- From a Microsoft Licensing Solution Provider for those with School/Campus/Select/Enterprise Agreements

Navigating the Microsoft licensing maze can be challenging; most people can get quite confused by all the various plans and licensing models.

The best approach is to write down what features and functionality you want for your organization, including your people plans for the next three years. Then arrange people into groups that require similar feature sets. Users in the office may require an Office 365 Enterprise E3 license which gives them the desktop version of Office with e-mail, but users who work remotely may only require an Enterprise E1 license and utilize the online Office applications.

Once you have grouped your users together, you can then look at the Office 365 subscription plans and make the right decisions. If you're still lost, you may need to work with a Microsoft partner who specializes in Office 365 to help you make the right licensing choice.

Office 365 Business – considerations and limitations

The Office 365 Business plans provide amazing value and functionality for small and growing organizations:

Bundle	Features
Business essentials	Exchange Online Plan 1 (Hosted e-mail) SharePoint Online Plan 1 (Collaboration and document management platform) Office Online (Web-based office programs, Word, Excel, and so on) OneDrive for Business Plan 1 (Unlimited file storage, similar to Drop Box and Google Drive) Skype for Business Online Plan 1 (Instant messaging, video calling, and conferencing) Yammer Enterprise (Social networking for business) Sway (Used to create presentations and interactive content)

Business	Office 365 Business (Office desktop applications) Office Online OneDrive for Business Plan 1 Mobile Device Management (Manage mobile settings, security, and remote wipe) Sway
Business Premium	Exchange Online Plan 1 Office 365 Business Office Online SharePoint Online Plan 1 OneDrive for Business Plan 1 Skype for Business Online Plan 2 (Includes the same options as plan 1 with additional ability to integrate with on-premises PBX systems, and also includes enterprise 24/7 support) Mobile Device Management Sway Yammer Enterprise

For many businesses, it will provide far more functionality than they may ever utilize, but there are some key limitations that must be considered prior to purchase.

User count limited

There is a hard limit of 300 users in the Business plans and there is no way around it. However, if you do need to go above this restriction, it is possible to upgrade to Enterprise plans where there is no user restriction. Switching plans is easy and can be done at any time using the Switch plan wizard available from the Office 365 portal.

Doesn't include e-mail archiving

Unlike the Enterprise plans, Office 365 Business does not allow for the addition of a mailbox archive on top of the existing 50 GB mailbox. What is possible however is to segment the existing mailbox into an archive area (for example, 5 GB of your 50 GB). It is also worth noting that this archive folder is only available when online with Outlook or via Outlook Web App because it is not cached as part of the user's **Offline Storage Table** (**OST**) file, and so it cannot be viewed offline.

Office Suite does not include Access

If you currently utilize Office Professional in your organization, it is worth noting that none of the Business plans include the use of Microsoft Access. If some users require the use of Microsoft Access, you will need to assign an Enterprise E3, E5, or Office Pro Plus license to those users.

Doesn't include Skype for Business Cloud PBX

If your business wants to make the most of cloud technology then you will want to consider moving your on-premises telephone system to a cloud-based solution. None of the Office 365 business packages include Skype for Business Cloud PBX, which allows the users to make and receive telephone calls using Skype for Business.

Doesn't include the rights to install Office applications on servers using Remote Desktop Services

If you are using **Remote Desktop Services** (RDS) within your organization, you will want to install the available Office applications which come with your business subscription. Unfortunately, none of the business level subscriptions include the rights to use shared computer activation, which is required to install Office on RDS servers.

Office 365 for enterprises

The Office 365 Enterprise plans allow for an unlimited number of users and even more features and licensing options.

The key bundles available range from plans E1-E5, and the Kiosk (K1) plan. Let's take a look at the features available in each of the following plans:

Bundle	Features
E1	Sway Mobile Device Management Yammer Enterprise Skype for Business Plan 2 Share Point Online Plan 1 Exchange Online Plan 1
E3	Sway Mobile Device Management Yammer Enterprise Azure Rights Management Office 365 Pro Plus Skype for Business Online Plan 2 Office Online SharePoint Online Plan 2 Exchange Online Plan 2
E4	Sway Mobile Device Management Yammer Enterprise Azure Rights Management (Helps to protect and secure business data within Office 365) Skype for Business Online Plan 3 Skype for Business Online Plan 2 Office 365 Pro Plus Office Online SharePoint Online Plan 2 Exchange Online Plan 2
E5	Same as E4 but includes Skype for Business Cloud PBX
K	Sway Mobile Device Management Yammer Enterprise SharePoint Online Kiosk Exchange Online Kiosk

Individual components can also be purchased. The individual plans are listed here:

- Azure Rights Management Premium
- Azure Active Directory Premium
- Exchange Online Plan 1
- Exchange Online Plan 2
- Exchange Online Archiving
- Exchange Online Protection
- Exchange Online Kiosk
- OneDrive for Business with Office Online
- SharePoint Online Plan 1
- SharePoint Online Plan 2
- SharePoint Online Storage
- Skype for Business Online Plan 1
- Skype for Business Online Plan 2
- Skype for Business Cloud PBX
- Office 365 Pro Plus
- Power BI Pro
- Power BI Free
- Project Lite
- Project Online
- Project Online with Project Pro
- Project Pro
- Visio Pro
- Yammer Enterprise
- Enterprise Mobility Suite Direct
- Microsoft Intune

When to use a plan and when to pick a la carte

Now that you know a bit more about the Business and Enterprise subscription levels, let's delve deeper into helping you make a choice between them.

The Enterprise plans contain similar feature sets to the Business plans, but are able to go above and beyond their limitations.

Some key benefits and features are:

- No limit on the number of users
- Ability to mix and match license types
- Access to more applications and features
- Increased usage rights, such as shared computer activation

Let's look at some scenarios where you might choose one subscription type over the other:

Scenario	Plan choice
Professional services firm of six people: Planning to grow to 30 people within 3 years	Business Essentials
Start-up recruitment firm of 10 people: Planning to grow to 70 within 2 years	Business Essentials
Established audio engineering company of 27 users: Have been operating for 9 years No growth plans	Business Essentials
Architectural firm of 12 people: Have been operating for 6 years No growth plans Need storage space for drawings	Business Essentials SharePoint Storage
Call center company with 40 staff: 10 in the office all day, five remote workers 25 shift-based call center staff who don't have their own PCs and simply need access to e-mail and the company intranet	Enterprise: E1 (15) K1 (25)
Franchise coffee house with 40 staff: 30 staff at head office 10 franchises managers Want to perform Business Intelligence with SharePoint Server 2016 Enterprise on-premises, and let franchise managers access the reports	Enterprise: E1 (10) E3 (30)

Medical services with 120 staff: Exchange 2016 on-premises Using other intranet system 15 staff require video conferencing	Enterprise: Skype for Business Online Plan 2 (15)
Hospitality services company with 700 staff: Exchange 2003 on-premises 300 staff at head office 400 staff spread across eight offices Legacy phone system, want IM and presence, and video conferencing for management SharePoint on-premise, heavily integrated with CRM and other systems	Enterprise: Exchange Online Plan 1 (700) Skype for Business Online Plan 1 (600) Skype for Business Online Plan 2 (100)
Financial services company of 5,000 staff nationwide: Lotus Notes 25 percent of workforce is permanently mobile 10 percent of workforce is primarily limited to Line of Business Application Has Enterprise Agreement which includes Office	Enterprise: E1 (4,500) K1 (500)
Automotive manufacturer of 30,000 staff globally: GroupWise IBM WebSphere for intranet Cisco CallManager telephony with Unified Comms 30 percent of workforce is factory-based Has Enterprise Agreement which includes Office	Enterprise: Exchange Online Plan 1 (17,000) Exchange Online Plan 2 (3,000) Exchange Online Kiosk (10,000)

As you can see, there are quite a number of choices and scenarios available to organizations of all types and sizes. Making the correct choice involves identifying the requirements and which options address them.

Options to start your subscription

There are many ways to get started with an Office 365 subscription. Some of these ways include:

- Working with Microsoft on a license agreement (through a licensing reseller)
- Working with a Microsoft deployment partner
- Signing up for the service directly on the website using a credit card

 If you decide to sign up directly on the website using a credit card then you have two options when checking out your purchase. You can choose to pay monthly or commit to an annual subscription and enjoy a cheaper rate, saving you money.

Let us now explore these options in the following sub-sections.

Working with Microsoft on a license agreement (through a licensing reseller)

Chances are you are only working with Microsoft if you have a large set or a combination of licenses you need to purchase. An example of this would be if you are an Enterprise customer seeking specific contract requirements and a combination of licenses, outside of Office 365, in a suite for your users. Specific contract requirements, and suites of licenses are typically sold as **Enterprise Agreement** (**EA**). The benefit of an EA is that it allows an organization to leverage a number of Microsoft products, for a single per seat cost. If you are an EA customer or plan to be one, the sign-up process is different. When you sign up for an EA, you will typically receive an e-mail with two options:

- The first option is to attach your license to an existing Office 365 trial account
- The second option is to create a new account with your licenses assigned

If you have already purchased licenses in an existing account, it may be difficult for you to have Microsoft attach licenses to this account. Microsoft may ask you to recreate an account in this scenario.

Working with a Microsoft deployment partner

If you are working with a Microsoft deployment partner, there is a good possibility that the Microsoft deployment partner will be able to help you through this process. A Microsoft deployment partner has the ability to send you a customized link. This link can be a trial or a set of licenses to be purchased. The benefits of a Microsoft deployment partner sending you a link are twofold. The partner can help ensure you have the right licenses and the partner obtains benefits while being associated with your subscription. These benefits include subscription notifications for changes/upgrades and there are financial benefits. The notifications/changes are of benefit as the partner can work closely with your organization to ensure you are prepared for upcoming changes. The financial benefits a partner receives are specifically related to the partner being an adviser for your subscription.

Signing up for the service directly

The last option is to sign-up for the service directly. Chances are that you are taking this approach if you are not signing an EA, or are not working with a Microsoft deployment partner, and are planning to trial or move to this service on your own. Often, organizations sign up for the service ahead of working with a partner or Microsoft on licensing. If you have signed up for a trial service, but plan to work with a partner or Microsoft, it is recommended not to purchase licenses until you have requested their advice on how to proceed. The impacts of purchasing license prior to engaging Microsoft or a partner can mean reallocating enabled accounts or a delay in how soon Microsoft can apply the EA licenses.

In all cases, we leverage the Office 365 admin portal, `https://portal.office.com`, in a similar way. Before we get started with the Office 365 admin portal, we need to sign up for the service.

The sign up process

We recently learned about the various subscription options. Now it's time to sign up for the service. In the following steps, we are simply going to sign up for a trial-based subscription. This will allow us the flexibility to choose how we add licenses in the near future.

You now have a decision to make. Do the Enterprise plans include the features you require or do you have more than 300 users or plan to grow to more than 300 users in the near future? If yes, then you need to create an Enterprise trial. Let's take a look at the process to give you its overview.

To get started, let's head over to the Office 365 site. Simply go to `http://www.office.com/` and sign-up for a free **FOR BUSINESS** trial from the home page, as shown in the following screenshot. By default you will be directed to sign up for a Business premium trial. If you require an Enterprise trial follow the link **See all plans and pricing options for Home or Business**. Locate the Enterprise E3 **Free trial** link at the bottom of the page:

1. Click through to create a trial account. Your next page will be a sign up page. This page will require you to enter your business information. You will also be selecting your tenant name, which is important for a few reasons, as follows:
   - Your SharePoint service URL includes your tenant name (for example, `office365laba.sharepoint.com`)
   - It will be your default e-mail address or account name for your users, until you add your own vanity domains
   - You will reference this name for support concerns
   - It will be used to associate your Enterprise Agreement licenses to your subscription
2. Your e-mail address is also a very important field. The e-mail address you add on this page will be the default e-mail address that receives messages from Office 365. In addition, subscription information and errors that may occur with your integration components will be sent to this address. Ensure you add an e-mail address that you plan to monitor.

It's a good practice to create a new e-mail address setup as a group or shared mailbox so that it can be received by multiple people. This is useful when employees go on holiday and you need access to the e-mail to manage the Office 365 account.

In the following screenshot, we enter all the required details and press **Next** to continue:

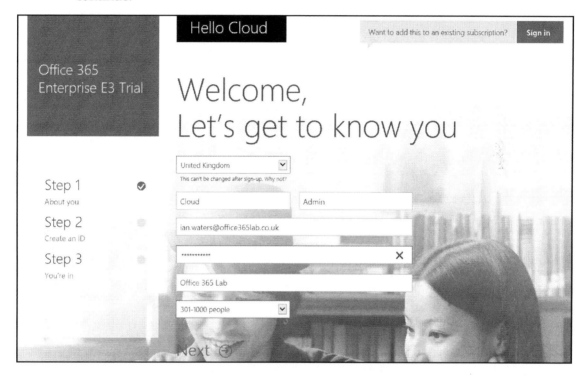

3. The subscription name is important, but in the long term your users may never see it, if you apply a vanity name (a vanity domain is a simple name to mask a more complex domain behind it). During the sign-up portion, you will have an opportunity to check to see whether your subscription name is free. If your name is taken, try a few others until you find the name that fits your organization.

Just remember, once you set the tenant name you can't change it later, so ensure it makes sense and looks presentable. So avoid adding numbers just to move on to the next step.

In the following screenshot, we settled on cloudadmin@office365laba.onmicrosoft.com for our lab environment. Press **Next** to continue:

4. Next you will need to enter and verify your phone number. To prevent fake sign ups, Microsoft has instituted a phone-based authorization process. Ensure you are near a phone for this part. Enter your number and press **Text me** to receive your verification code, as shown in the following screenshot:

5. Once you have received your text message, press **Create my account**, as shown in the following screenshot, to begin the process:

6. The Office 365 environment creation process is relatively quick. Once you have pressed **Create my account**, you will be shown a progress screen with some important details, as shown in the following screenshot. Make a note of these details so you can refer back to them as required:

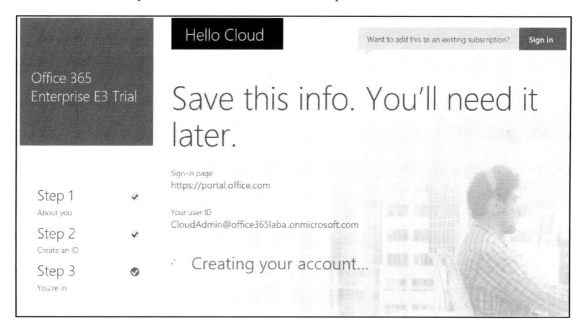

7. Within a few short minutes, you should be shown that the environment setup has completed, as shown in the following screenshot. Click on **You're ready to go...** to continue:

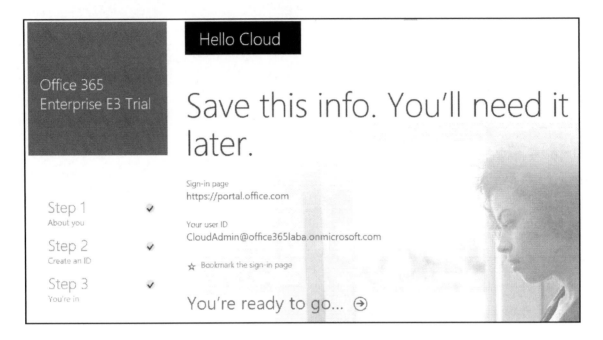

8. After pressing **You're ready to go...**, you will automatically be logged in to your environment and within a few minutes all services will be ready, as shown in the following screenshot; however, provisioning times may vary:

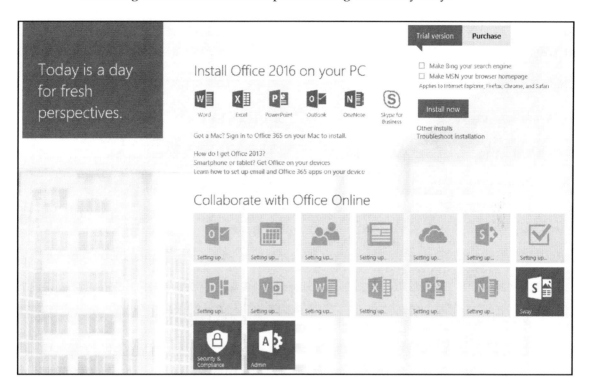

Congratulations! You have created your Office 365 tenant with an Enterprise E3 trial. In the following chapters, we will explore the setup processes required to fully configure your tenant to meet your organization's specific requirements.

Summary

Office 365 offers many ways to subscribe and all sorts of licensing combinations. Whether you're a small business or an enterprise, you have a number of ways to get started. The good news is that you can start a trial subscription and always associate your long-term licenses to the trial, leveraging any method. We learned about the licensing available within the service, which should clarify how you proceed. By this point you should be deciding how these licenses fit your organization and whether you are going to sign-up directly, work with a Microsoft Deployment Partner, or engage an Enterprise Agreement with Microsoft.

As we reflect on the sign up process, you can see how Microsoft designed the process to be greatly simplified. Microsoft focused on minimizing many decision points for a trial. The fact is, it is a trial, so why complicate the sign up process more than it needs to be? Either way, in the end, your team managing and configuring the service will be required to do all the tweaking and tuning, based on business and technical decisions made within the organization.

In conclusion, you should now be ready to start getting more familiar with the service: configuring it to your specifications, starting the integration process, and finally either migrating or starting to use the service full-time. Before your trial ends, you will need to obtain or assign the licensing plan that best fits your subscription.

Now that we have established a subscription, in the next chapter we will focus on using the admin portal. We will also start walking through some key initial configuration steps.

2
Getting Familiar with the Office 365 Admin Portal

Now that we have shown you how to sign up for Office 365, it's important to get familiar with the administration interface as it is the central control point for everything to do with your subscription.

In this chapter, we will walk you through the high-level interface, adding a domain to your subscription, as well as diving deep into the administration sub-interfaces. Topics covered will include:

- First-time login and adding your domain
- Navigating the administration overview interface
- Exchange online administration interface

First-time login and adding your domain

To get to the administration interface you will need to browse to `https://portal.office.com` and log in with the credentials you chose during the sign-up process (as seen in `Chapter 1`, *Getting Started with Office 365*):

1. The first step of utilizing Office 365 for your business requires that you add your domain (for example, `yourcompany.com`) in the portal. This is a necessary place to start, as your domain will be used later in many aspects of the admin portal.

2. Upon logging in for the first time, we will see the provisioning page from when we first signed up:

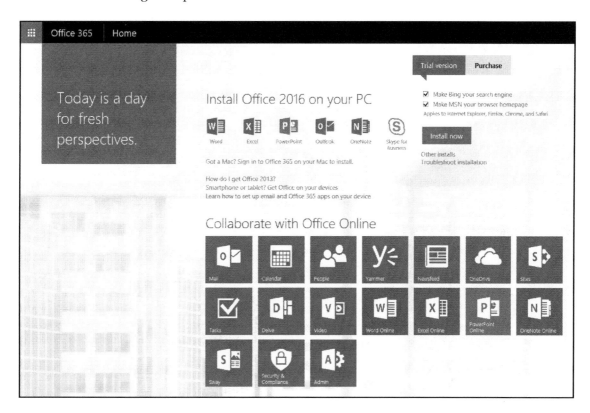

3. To add your domain to Office 365, click the **Admin** tile to enter **Admin Center**. From here, click **Settings** and then the **Domains** menu option on the left:

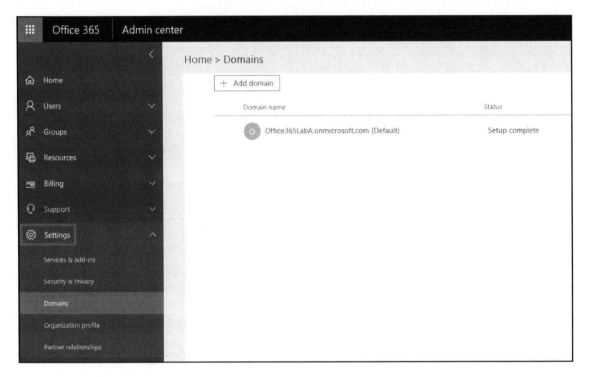

You will see that the tenant domain already exists (for example, yourcompany.onmicrosoft.com) in the listing. This domain cannot be removed, however after completing the next few steps, your Office 365 subscription will be set up in a way that the tenant domain will not be seen by your users.

Important DNS requirements

Office 365 requires two key types of DNS records that are not supported by many domain name hosts or providers: TXT and SRV. Check with your domain host to ensure that they support the creation of these records within your domain name, otherwise you may need to change domain hosts before going further.

Setting up the domain

For setting up your domain, follow the steps mentioned here:

1. Press **Add domain** to take you to the next page where you will be guided by a wizard interface to add your organization's domain name. You will be prompted to enter your domain. After doing so, press **Next** as shown in the following screenshot after the information box.

 You must already own the domain name before starting this process. If you don't already own the domain, it may not be available for use. Use a domain registration service such as GoDaddy to register your chosen domain name.

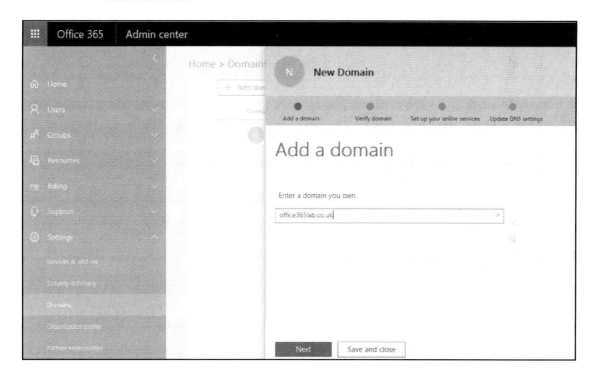

2. The domain wizard will then provide you with a list of popular domain name hosts which can display customized instructions. If your domain name host is not on the list, select **Not your registrar?** as shown in the following screenshot:

3. At this point you will need to create the **TXT record** (or MX record if TXT is not available to you) as instructed within your DNS provider's domain name control panel. The speed at which this DNS addition is visible by Office 365 depends on various factors – you may see it instantly or you may need to wait anywhere from 15 minutes to 72 hours to see the **TXT record** appear. Pressing **Verify** will begin the domain validation process to ensure that Office 365 can see the **TXT record**. If the records have not yet updated, you will receive the following message:

> ⚠ We didn't find the record you added for office365lab.co.uk. If you just added this record please allow 5 to 10 minutes for the change to be replicated through the system, sometime it can take significantly longer depending on your registrar.

4. Once the DNS records have updated and you are able to **Verify** ownership of the domain, you will proceed to the **Set up your online services** section, as shown in the following screenshot:

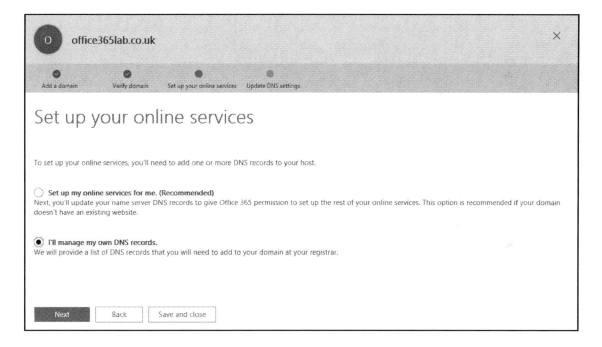

Here you decide if you want Microsoft to manage the DNS of your domain. Although this is shown as recommended, I highly recommend managing your own DNS records. The reasons for this are that Microsoft will point your domain at their own DNS servers and remove any existing records you have setup including an existing WWW record. Using their recommended option will limit your ability to add your own records at a later date and any existing records you have in place will not be copied over to Microsoft's DNS servers.

5. As recommended from the preceding note, select **I'll manage my own DNS records** and press **Next**.

    You will now be guided to configure the required DNS records that allow the domain to be used.

Before adding all the suggested DNS records to your domain name, it is important to consider if there are any existing services that need to remain in place. For example, if you are already using e-mail on `yourdomain.com` then you should not modify the MX record until you are ready (this will be addressed later in the book).

6. The next section is **Update DNS settings,** which will display a list of all the required DNS settings to make full use of all the services within Office 365.

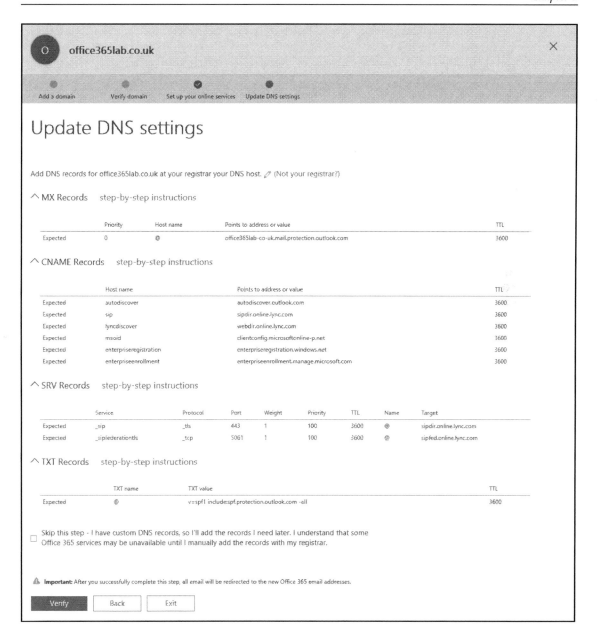

Update DNS settings

Add DNS records for office365lab.co.uk at your registrar your DNS host. ✎ (Not your registrar?)

⌄ MX Records   step-by-step instructions

	Priority	Host name	Points to address or value	TTL
Expected	0	@	office365lab-co-uk.mail.protection.outlook.com	3600

⌄ CNAME Records   step-by-step instructions

	Host name	Points to address or value	TTL
Expected	autodiscover	autodiscover.outlook.com	3600
Expected	sip	sipdir.online.lync.com	3600
Expected	lyncdiscover	webdir.online.lync.com	3600
Expected	msoid	clientconfig.microsoftonline-p.net	3600
Expected	enterpriseregistration	enterpriseregistration.windows.net	3600
Expected	enterpriseenrollment	enterpriseenrollment.manage.microsoft.com	3600

⌄ SRV Records   step-by-step instructions

	Service	Protocol	Port	Weight	Priority	TTL	Name	Target
Expected	_sip	_tls	443	1	100	3600	@	sipdir.online.lync.com
Expected	_sipfederationtls	_tcp	5061	1	100	3600	@	sipfed.online.lync.com

⌄ TXT Records   step-by-step instructions

	TXT name	TXT value	TTL
Expected	@	v=spf1 include:spf.protection.outlook.com -all	3600

☐ Skip this step - I have custom DNS records, so I'll add the records I need later. I understand that some Office 365 services may be unavailable until I manually add the records with my registrar.

⚠ **Important:** After you successfully complete this step, all email will be redirected to the new Office 365 email addresses.

[Verify]   [Back]   [Exit]

7. Upon adding the relevant DNS records in your host's domain name control panel and waiting the required propagation time, press **Verify** to allow the system to check that you have entered all the records correctly. The following screenshot will pop up after the verification:

8. Once the DNS settings have been verified, or if you decided to skip the verification process, press **Finish** and you will then be brought back to the **Domains** listing where your domain should now be listed as **Setup complete**, as shown in the following screenshot:

You have now successfully set up your domain within Office 365 and can begin using your subscription.

Navigating the administration overview interface

In this section of the chapter, we will take you through the high level administrative interface for Office 365. The interface is broken down into several sections:

- **Home**
- **Users**
- **Groups**
- **Resources**
- **Billing**
- **Support**
- **Settings**
- **Health**
- **Admin centers**

Home

The Home section assists you with beginning your journey with Office 365 and gives a quick access to common administrative tasks, such as adding users, managing billing, giving an overview of service health, and displaying any new messages regarding new features and changes.

In this section, you will find other general information about how to get started with your Office 365 subscription as well as links to more information. We will cover most of this information through the rest of this book as it relates to migration and Exchange Online.

The following screenshot shows the **Home** screen with all its menus in the left panel and quick links in the center:

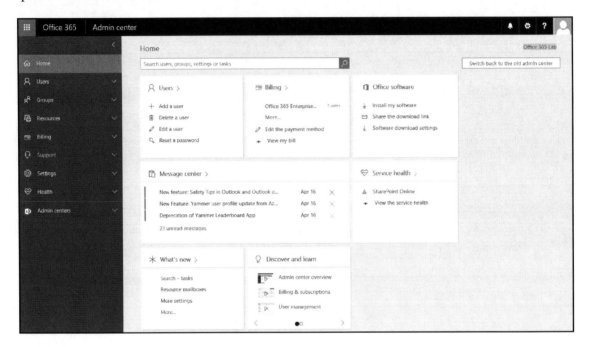

Users

The **Users** page of the management interface allows you to create/modify/delete user accounts as well as allocate and change licenses that are associated with accounts.

Users can be created on a one-by-one basis or imported in bulk by utilizing the supplied CSV file template.

If however you choose to utilize Active Directory Synchronization, either as a standalone solution or as part of Active Directory Federation Services, then all users will already be listed here so the portal is merely used to assign licenses. How to do this is covered in later chapters.

The following screenshot shows users created without Active Directory Synchronization and provides some options for quick actions on the right side:

Groups

The **Groups** section in the admin center is made up of Office 365 distribution and security groups. Office 365 groups are relatively new and not to be confused with e-mail distribution or security groups. Although they perform a similar basic function, the new Office 365 groups offer more functionality by combining e-mail-based conversations with a group calendar, SharePoint file storage, and a group Notebook within OneNote.

Similarly to users, if Directory Synchronization is enabled, it will bring across any groups from your Active Directory, as shown in the next screenshot. Security groups that have been synchronized across can also be turned into distribution groups within the Exchange admin center:

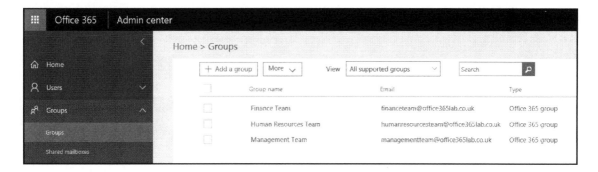

Resources

The **Resources** section allows you to manage **Rooms & equipment** mailboxes, as shown in the following screenshot, which are used if you have shared meeting rooms or projectors and other office equipment which is booked out and used by employees. From here you can also manage your SharePoint sites and configure sharing and access to external users. You can also get information on where to purchase and setup public website hosting. Office 365 doesn't support public website hosting itself but rather links to GoDaddy and WIX for more information. From the **Resources** menu, you can also configure **Mobile Device Management (MDM)** which lets you configure security policies for mobile devices, such as mobile phones and tablets. For example, you may want to enforce the use of a pin code to lock mobiles after X number of minutes or stop users from downloading files for offline use.

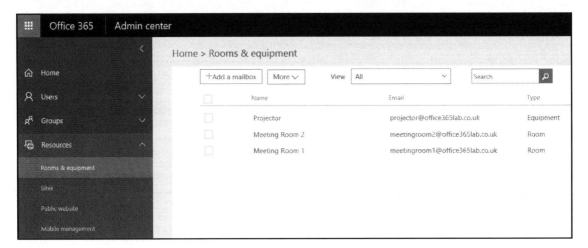

Billing

The **Billing** section is where you can manage your subscriptions, view your billing invoices, view how many licenses you have available, and see how many are assigned to users within your tenant. You can also purchase new subscriptions from the **Purchase Services** menu option. Let's take a look at a few of these options in more detail.

Subscriptions

The **Subscriptions** section of the Office 365 administrative interface allows you to view your current active and deprovisioned subscriptions. Since you signed up for an E3 trial, you will see an active subscription and a number of user licenses, which you can assign to users to activate the associated features.

From here you can add additional user licenses to your subscriptions, add a partner record, edit the service usage address, and add a tax code so that invoices show the correct amount of tax for your country, as shown in the following screenshot:

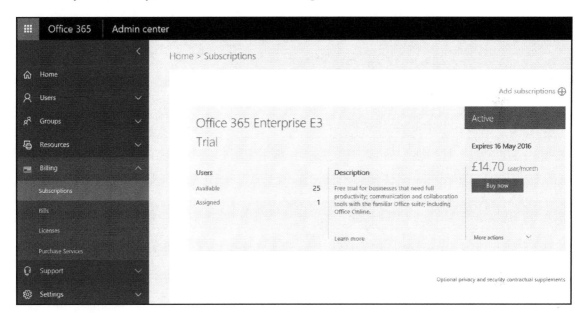

If you are working with a partner, it is important to add their information so that they may assist you in future with support. To do this, you will require their Microsoft partner ID number which you can obtain by asking them. Select the **More actions** drop down arrow and select **Add partner of record** as shown in the following screenshot:

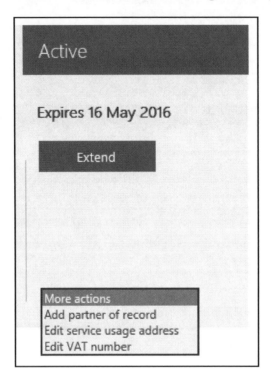

Enter the partner ID and confirm the name of your Office 365 partner by clicking **Check ID**. Check the **Add this partner to all of your subscriptions** checkbox and press **Submit** as shown in the following screenshot:

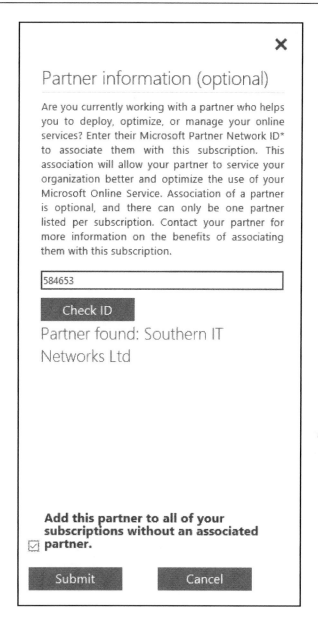

After adding the partner information, ask your partner to verify that they can see your tenant within their partner portal. They will now be able to log support requests on your behalf.

Should you choose to work with a different partner in future, you can easily change this information by repeating the previous steps using the new partner ID.

Bills

Within the **Bills** section, you can view all invoices by month and year, as shown in the following screenshot, and download a PDF copy for your accounts. You can assign members of your accounts department the billing administrator role to allow them access to this information within the portal. We will be looking at how to assign roles later in the book:

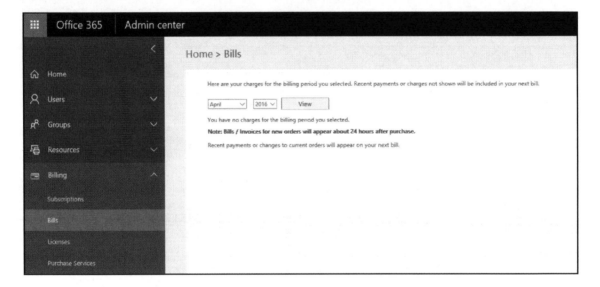

Licenses

The **Licenses** section is quite simple in its function, which is simply to display the number of licenses you are subscribed to and how many are allocated, as shown in the following screenshot:

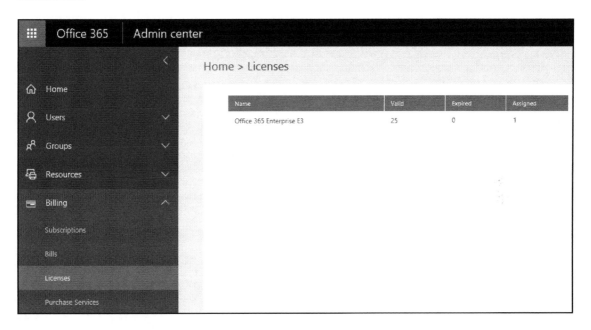

Purchase Services

Clicking on **Purchase Services** will take you to the services catalog page, where you can browse all the available subscriptions, such as Microsoft Dynamics CRM, Exchange Online kiosk, or additional file storage for SharePoint.

Support

The support interface is the first point of call for any technical issues you may be having with your Office 365 subscription. From the support page, you can see a snapshot of all the information and tools available to assist you with your Office 365 subscription:

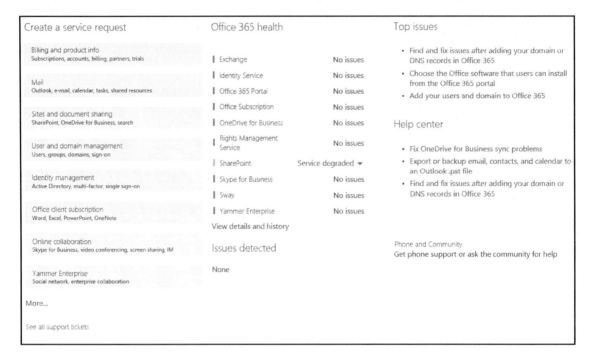

It is the first point any Office 365 administrator should visit to resolve any possible issues as it contains a wealth of information sourced from several areas, such as Microsoft support and the Office 365 community.

Service requests

If you require technical assistance and cannot find the answer in areas such as the Office 365 community site or on the support overview page, then submitting a service request is the next step. The issue identification process is very comprehensive which allows the Office 365 support and escalation teams to deal with your issue with a much faster response time. The window looks like the following screenshot:

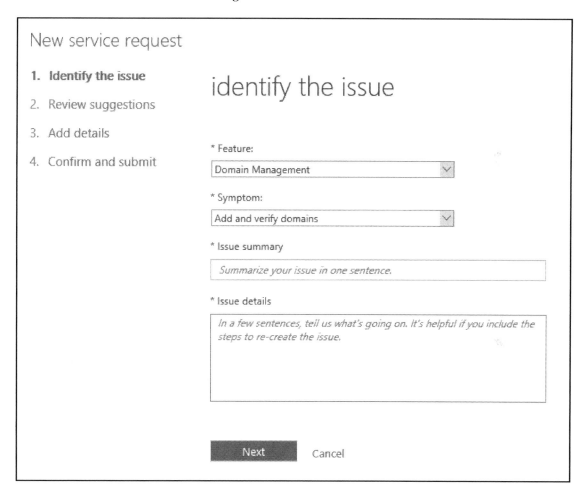

Upon submitting your service request, you will be able to modify its status at any time as shown in the following screenshot, through the process and use it to interact with the support team:

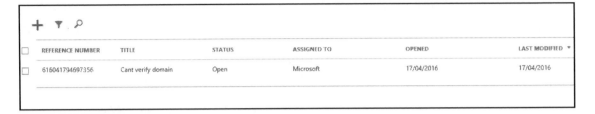

	REFERENCE NUMBER	TITLE	STATUS	ASSIGNED TO	OPENED	LAST MODIFIED ▼
☐	616041794697356	Cant verify domain	Open	Microsoft	17/04/2016	17/04/2016

If you find that you are unable to log support requests then that may be because you have added a partner ID to your subscriptions. When you associate a partner with your subscriptions, they will be responsible for logging support requests on your behalf. Log a support ticket with your Office 365 partner first to see if they can resolve the issue and if they can't they will engage with Microsoft for support.

Settings

The settings menu allows you to configure a vast array of features and options for your tenant. Throughout the book we will spend a lot of time within these sections. Spend some time getting familiar with the available options. We have already seen the *Domains* section earlier in this chapter but you can also configure various services such as Azure multi-factor authentication and Directory Synchronization as shown in the following screenshot:

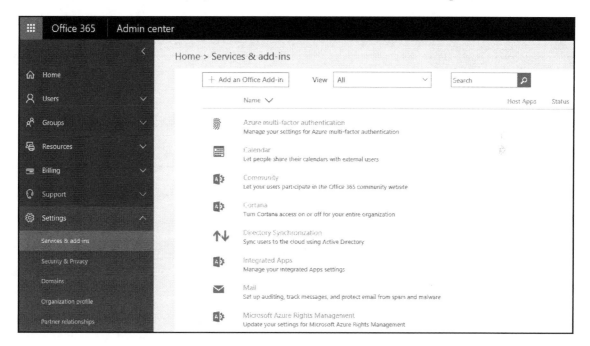

If your company requires a specific password policy, explore the **Security & Privacy** section, as shown in the next screenshot, and configure how often users must change their password. Try and avoid setting the password policy to never expire because users will set very simple passwords if you let them, so ensure they change it as often as possible without becoming an inconvenience, or better still make use of Azure multi-factor authentication. Although not covered in this book, it is very easy to configure so speak to your Office 365 partner if you require assistance with this:

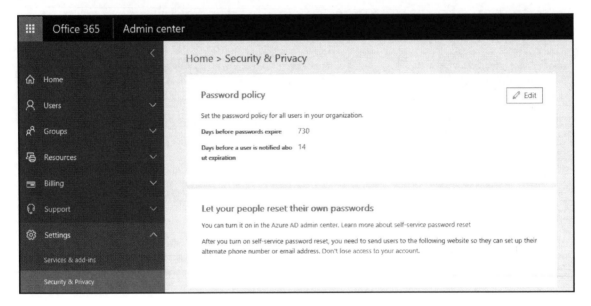

From the **Organization profile** section, you can update your company address and contact information, and set the technical contact for the tenant. As we highlighted in Chapter 1, *Getting Started with Office 365*, in the *The sign-up process* section, it's a good idea to set the technical contact to an address shared by multiple support staff for when people go on holiday or leave the company. From here, you can also set the **Release preferences** which specify how often your tenant receives new features released by Microsoft, as shown in the following screenshot. As you become an advanced Office 365 user you can enable the **First release** option to preview new features before they are released to the general public:

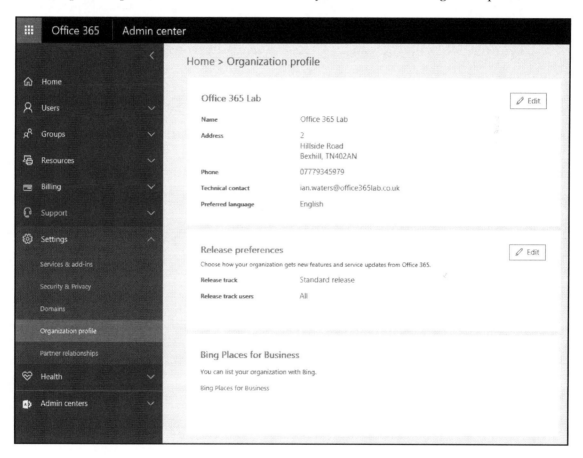

Health

Should you believe that you are experiencing any form of service issue or degradation, the first place to check is the **Service health** page which displays the status of each service which makes up all the Office 365 features. In the following screenshot, we can see there is an issue with SharePoint Online, specifically with the OneDrive for Business app responsible for syncing user files to local devices:

You can also view a history of outages by clicking on **View history** seen in the preceding screenshot. Clicking on any day on the calendar will give details on the outage, what services were affected, and details on resolution times:

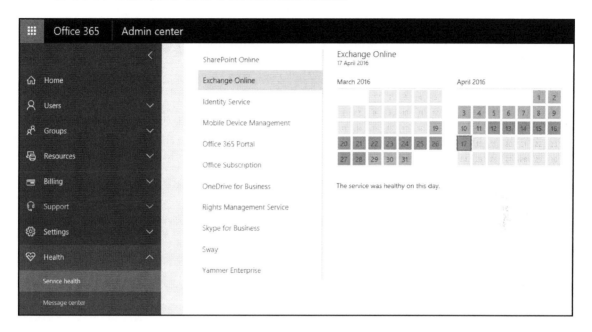

Being aware of what maintenance is scheduled allows you as an Office 365 administrator to better serve your organization by understanding the potential impact to their productivity. Clicking into **Message center** will give you lots of information regarding updates, maintenance, and required changes, as shown in the following screenshot:

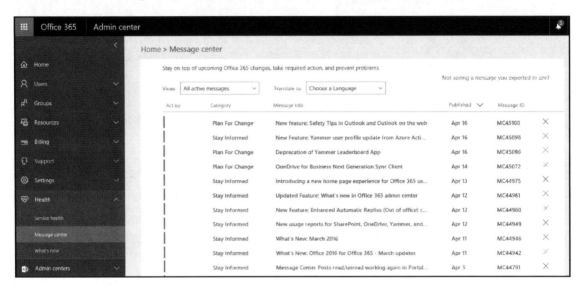

Admin centers

The **Admin center** menu contains links to portal pages specific to the following services:

- Exchange
- Skype for Business
- SharePoint
- Yammer
- Security and compliance
- Azure AD
- Cloud app security

We will spend most of our time within the Exchange admin center, so let's take a close look over this interface but spend some time learning about the others and expand your knowledge to benefit the users of the tenant you are managing.

Exchange admin center interface

Delving deeper into the **Exchange admin center** interface is possible by selecting the **Exchange** option under **Admin Centers** in the left hand menu. This will open a new tab within your browser and provide you with much more granular access to the interface. The following screenshot shows you the intricacies of the Exchange admin center interface:

While a great many features and functions are available through the web-based exchange admin interface, a lot of functions are only available through PowerShell which will be covered later in the book.

Recipients

From within the **Recipients** section of Exchange Online management, you have the ability to:

- Modify properties of user mailboxes
- Create room mailboxes (for example, meeting rooms)
- Create shared mailboxes
- Create distribution groups or mail enabled security groups
- Manage external contacts
- Perform mailbox migrations from Exchange 2007, 2003, 2010, 2013, 2016, and IMAP mail systems

Permissions

From within the **Permissions** section of Exchange admin center, you have the ability to:

- Define administrator roles and permission levels
- Define the level of self-administration available to end users
- Define Outlook Web App policies

Compliance Management

From within the **Compliance Management** section of Exchange admin center, you have the ability to:

- Configure eDiscovery and hold settings, and run searches
- Run auditing reports for:
  - Non-owner mailbox access
  - Litigation hold
  - Administration role group
- Export mailbox audit logs
- Export administrator audit logs
- Configure data loss prevention policies
- Define journaling rules for e-mail retention and archival strategy

Organization

From the **Organization** section, we can configure sharing of free and busy information between federated Exchange organizations. You can also configure what add-ins are available to users from their mailbox. You can add additional add-ins from the Office store, such as Evernote for Outlook or Zendesk, to integrate your own ticketing system to handle customer support requests.

Protection

The **Protection** section allows you to configure a variety of e-mail hygiene options to help protect your users from spam e-mails and spoofing attacks:

- Malware filters
- Connection filters
- Spam filtering
- Outbound spam options
- Quarantine
- Action center
- **Domain Keys Identified Mail (DKIM)**

Mail Flow

The **Mail flow** area of Exchange admin center allows Office 365 administrators to take control of the mail flow at a granular level – both external to/from their organisation as well as internal.

From within this interface, administrators are able to:

- Define rules to control the mail flow within the organisation
- Run delivery reports
- Accepted domains and connectors

This is not to be confused with the **Protection** section of Exchange Online that allows for the configuration of filters, spam, and quarantine settings.

Public Folders

The **Public Folders** area brings back a much utilized feature of Exchange Server over the years (after being absent in previous iterations of Office 365). From this interface, administrators can define both public folders as well as the mailboxes used with them.

Mobile

The **Mobile** section provides the ability to control and manage how mobile devices work with Office 365.

Mobile devices that include the ActiveSync protocol can be managed in great detail, allowing you to:

- Quarantine devices and set appropriate rules and notifications
- Control which devices can connect to Exchange Online (for example, restrict either operating systems such as Android or manufacturers such as HTC)
- Create security policies to control and restrict mobile access to Exchange Online, such as requiring PIN security and specifying how many failed attempts before performing a remote wipe of the device

Unified messaging

Moving beyond the mailbox and on to both mobile devices and unified messaging, Exchange Online can become the cornerstone of organizational communications.

Despite being in the cloud, customers are able to connect their IP telephony systems (such as Skype for Business, Cisco CallManager, Avaya IP Office, and most other SIP-compliant systems) to Exchange Online. This allows for organizations to have a single system for mail – be it voicemail or e-mail (aka unified messaging).

The two key features that facilitate this functionality are the ability to define:

- Unified Messaging Dial Plans which ensure that both Exchange Online and your IP phone system can translate phone numbers to email addresses
- Unified Messaging IP Gateways which allow the conversation between Exchange Online and the IP phone system to speak in the first place

Summary

In this chapter, we have shown you how to find your way around the Office 365 and Exchange Online administrative interface.

We have also shown you how to start customizing Office 365 by adding your own domain to the environment.

From here you should now have the knowledge and tools to begin planning your migration to Exchange Online.

In the next chapter, we will discuss the integration options available when using the Office 365 Business plans.

3
Integration Options for Businesses

For many small businesses, moving to the cloud can be a daunting task and can also be a significant change in how they operate on a daily basis. Decisions need to be made around whether to have a mixture of on-premises and cloud services or to simply go *all in*. Certain advanced features of Exchange Online and PowerShell are often neglected by small businesses due to their perceived complexity. In this chapter, we will aim to simplify this by providing you with information on:

- Business scenarios
- Working with a server
- Managing user accounts
- Working with PowerShell

Business scenarios

Organizations around the world come in a variety of shapes and sizes. Many are not prepared to fully move to the cloud yet or have various reasons to retain on-premises infrastructure.

Businesses that are looking to move to Office 365, they may be doing so for a variety of reasons.

Ageing servers

IT is generally relegated to business support and rarely seen as a revenue generator, with small businesses holding on to their servers as long as possible. As such they are usually reluctant to spend a portion of their capital to fund another depreciating asset. For this reason, Office 365 becomes an attractive option as there is no capital outlay to start using the service.

Remote workforce

With the ready availability of mobile broadband and decreasing cost of portable devices such as laptops and tablets, many organizations are finding that their staff are spending more time out on the road or working from home.

Accessing e-mails, files, and applications from a central office location via VPN can often be a hindrance to remote workers if the server is unavailable for various reasons (for example, office Internet connectivity, server issues, and so on). Users need the flexibility of being able to access their content wherever they are and on whatever device they may be using.

For these small businesses, moving to Office 365 alleviates many challenges and potential issues that may affect business productivity, and ultimately profitability.

Staff expansion

When organizations expand, the IT requirements can often get in the way. Traditionally, businesses would need to purchase (on top of hardware) additional server licenses and obtain the services of an IT professional to connect and configure the systems.

Office 365 greatly simplifies this by reducing the requirements to the procurement of hardware and a new user subscription – everything else can be done by the user.

Working with a server

When moving to Office 365, customers are faced with the question: do I still need my server? For many, the requirement to continue using a server is negated based on the functionality that Office 365 provides and as such they are able to remove their server after their migration is complete.

However, some businesses may still require the services of an on-premises server for a variety of reasons, such as filesystems, databases, and line of business applications.

If companies do keep an on-premises server, they would now be faced with the challenge of maintaining two disparate systems (their server and Office 365).

Generally, a business can maintain a single set of usernames through the implementation of directory synchronization. Historically, in the Office 365 small business plans that was not possible however in late 2014 the plans were changed to accommodate a variety of synchronization functionalities.

Integration options for directory synchronization are covered in `Chapter 4`, *Integration Options for Midsize and Enterprise Organizations*.

Utilizing the username and password synchronization solutions allows businesses to at least keep passwords the same for the users, both on the server and within Office 365, facilitating an improved user experience.

Windows Server 2012 R2 Essentials

Microsoft Windows Server 2012 R2 Essentials (W2012R2E) is the continuation of the small business server solution to natively support Office 365 through the integration module.

By utilizing this server solution and module, businesses can have a seamless user management experience between the on-premises server and Office 365.

It is important to note that a limitation of W2012R2E is its restriction to 25 users, whereas Office 365 Business has no limitation.

Connecting your Windows Server 2012 R2 Essentials to Office 365

Before being able to manage Office 365 via the W2012R2E Dashboard, we must complete the integration steps outlined here:

1. Enable Office 365 integration.
2. Choose existing subscription.
3. Enter cloud admin credentials.
4. Accept strong password policy.
5. Verify configuration.

6. Restart Dashboard.
7. Verify subscription.

We will now perform all these steps:

1. **Enabling Office 365 integration**: This can be found under the **Windows Server Essentials Dashboard** by selecting the task under **Services** called **Integrate with Microsoft Office 365**, as shown in the following screenshot:

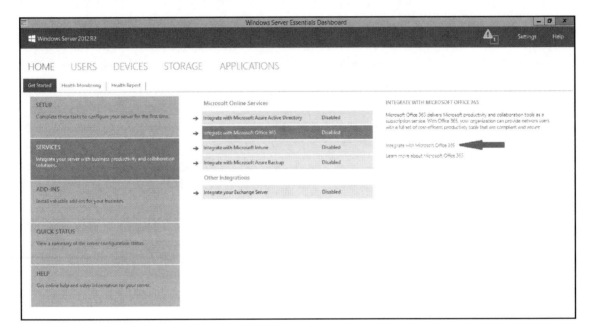

2. **Choosing existing subscription**: As we have already signed up for an Office 365 subscription, we can select this option and move on to provisioning our service, as shown in the following screenshot:

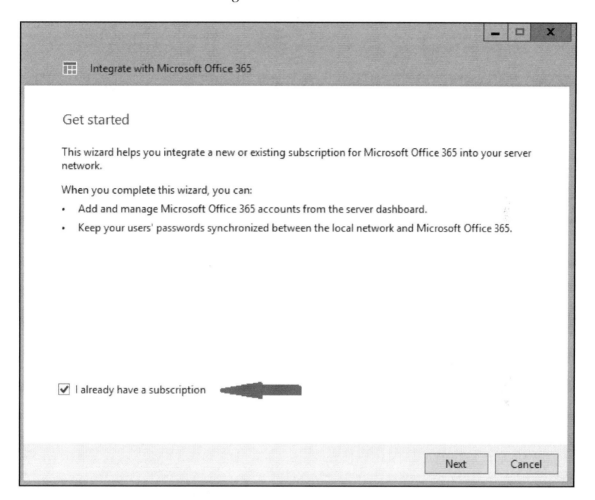

3. **Entering cloud admin credentials**: We must now enter the username and password of an account that is used to administer Office 365, as shown in the following screenshot:

It is recommended that you do not use your own account for this and instead use the provided admin account, as your password may change. You may also wish to set the password to never expire, which will stop the integration from working.

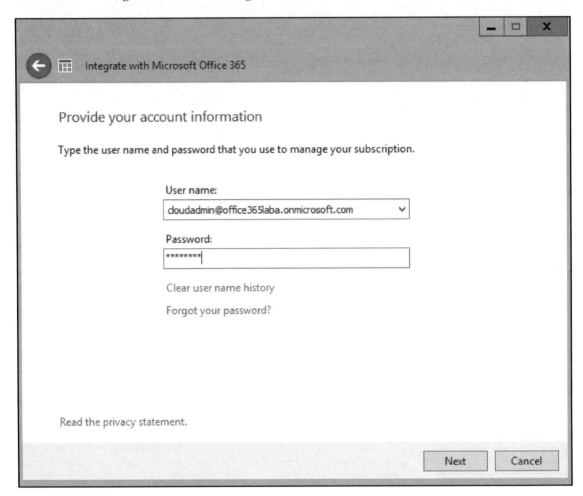

4. **Accepting strong password policy**: At this point you will be asked to adhere to the Office 365 strong password policy, as shown in the following screenshot:

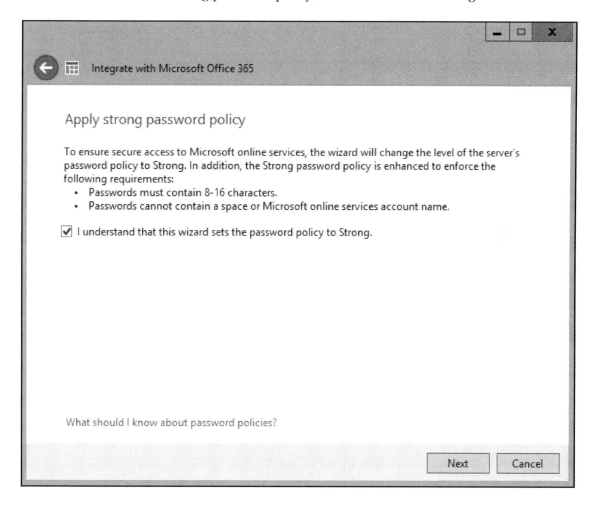

5. **Verifying configuration**: The server will then take a few moments while it connects to Office 365 and verifies your credentials:

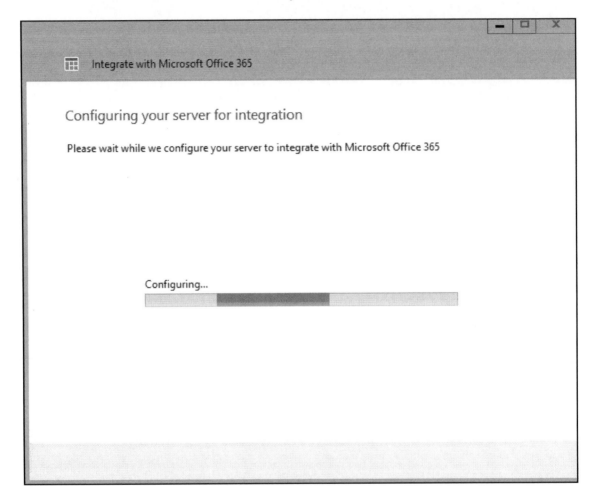

6. **Restarting Dashboard**: Upon completion of the module configuration, the server will need to be restarted, as shown in the following screenshot, in order to show up on the Small Business Server Dashboard:

7. **Verifying subscription**: Upon rebooting, you should now see the Office 365 icon appear in the Dashboard, as shown in the following screenshot:

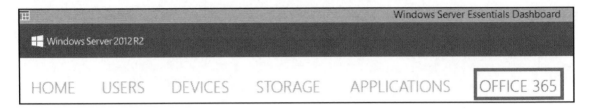

Clicking on the **Dashboard**, you will be taken to the Office 365 interface which obtains information about your **Organization**, **Domain**, **Subscription** details, and **Exchange Online** mailbox usage, as shown in the following screenshot:

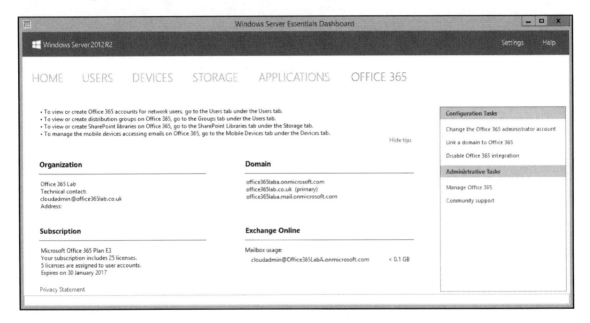

As we have already verified the domain in the previous chapters, we will now see it displayed under the *Domain* section on the screen without having to follow the **Link a domain to Office 365** process.

Managing user accounts

There are three options available to Office 365 administrators for managing user accounts:

- Microsoft Online portal
- W2012R2E Dashboard
- Windows PowerShell

Microsoft Online portal

To manage users via the Microsoft Online portal, the first step is to log in to `http://portal.office.com` with your administrative credentials.

Upon logging to the admin interface, you will be able to create new users by using the **Add a user** shortcut link from the main page, as shown in the following screenshot, or by entering the **Users** menu and **Active users** sub menu:

As highlighted in `Chapter 2`, *Getting Familiar with the Office 365 Admin Portal*, the **Active Users** page is also where the existing users can be modified and deleted.

Most businesses will also require e-mail groups (known as distribution groups) so that they may receive e-mails sent to generic e-mail addresses and distribute them among multiple users. An example can be `sales@yourdomain.com` which is received by all the sales people. This can also be used for departmental e-mail distribution, such as `finance@yourdomain.com` going to all members of the finance team.

This functionality can be administered by accessing the **Exchange** link under the **Admin centres** menu, as shown in the following screenshot:

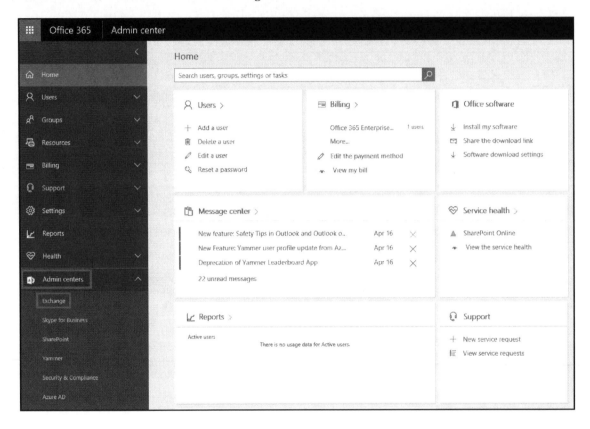

Upon clicking this, you will be taken to the **Exchange admin center**. From here you can then select **Groups,** as shown in the following screenshot, to work with distribution groups:

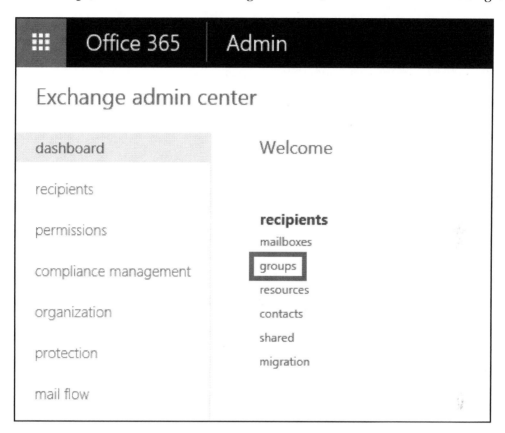

Windows Server 2012 R2 Essentials Dashboard

If you have previously created accounts on Windows Server 2012 R2 Essentials server, you can use the server dashboard to provision these accounts for Office 365 and begin to manage them.

By default, the integration won't query Office 365; this must be done manually to import any users that might exist in Office 365. For the purposes of this exercise we will assume that no users exist in Office 365 as it is a new setup, and we simply want to activate the existing users on the server, so that they also have Office 365 accounts. The process is broken down into the following five easy steps:

1. Add Microsoft online accounts.
2. Select accounts to sync.
3. Assign licenses.
4. Synchronize accounts.
5. Verify synchronization.

We will see all the steps now:

1. **Adding Microsoft online accounts**: In the **Windows Server Essentials Dashboard**, select **Add Microsoft online accounts,** as shown in the following screenshot:

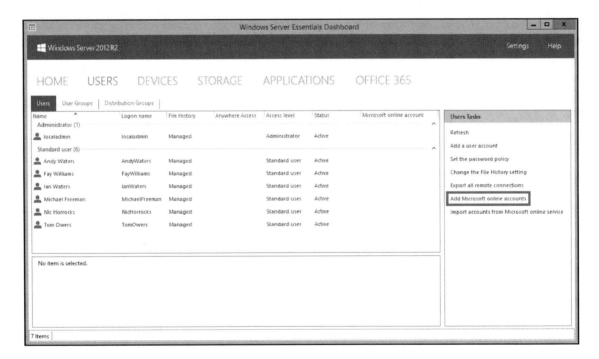

2. **Selecting accounts to sync**: At this point we are able to choose which account we want to have created in Office 365. In general, it is not advisable to create generic accounts from your server (such as admin or service accounts) in Office 365 as they will consume a license. Upon making the selection to create a new Office 365 account, we then have the option of selecting the e-mail address to be used and the domain name to be selected, as shown in the following screenshot:

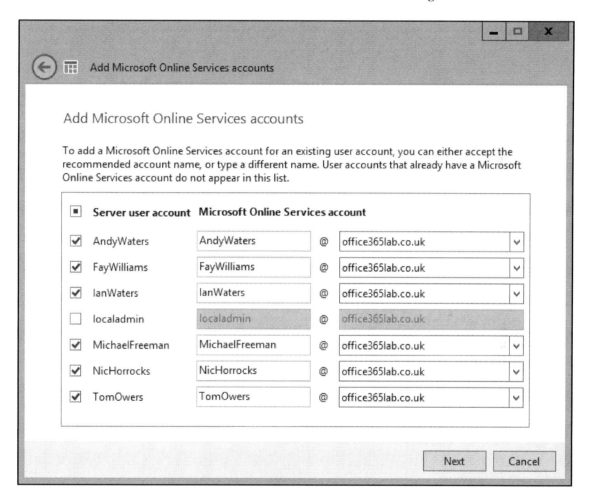

3. **Assigning licenses**: From here we will be prompted to select what licenses to assign to the users, as shown in the following screenshot:

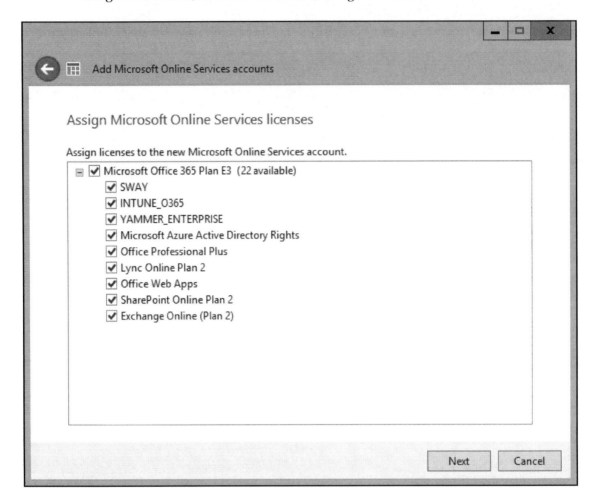

4. **Synchronizing accounts**: This process will then run PowerShell cmdlets behind the scenes, while you get the following screenshot, to create the account and link it to the account in W2012R2E:

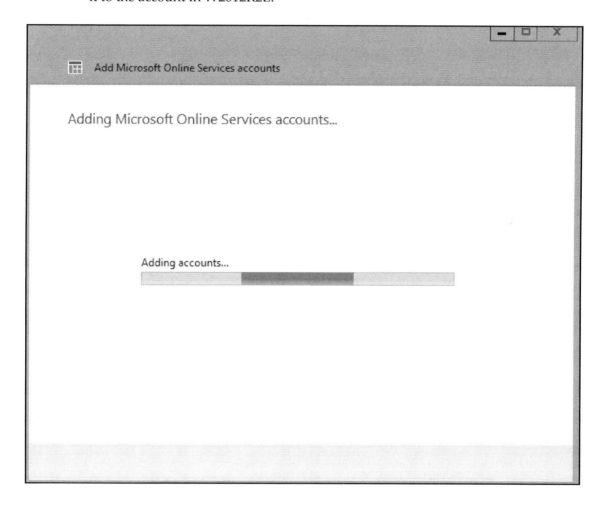

One of the key features of the Office 365 Integration module for Windows Server 2012 R2 Essentials is the built-in password synchronization functionality. To complete the user creation process within Office 365, you will need to change the user's Windows password so that it can perform the initial password synchronization with Office 365, as shown in the following screenshot:

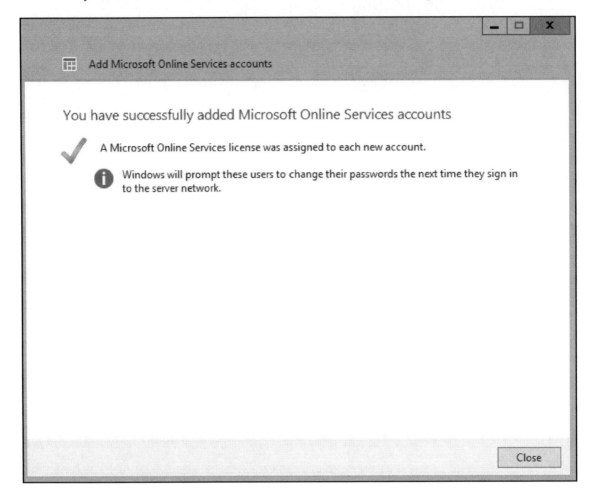

5. **Verifying synchronization**: After completing the account provisioning process, you will now see from the following screenshot that the Office 365 account is now connected to the W2012R2E account:

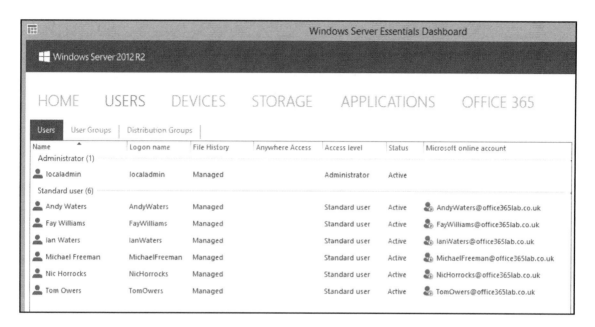

From here you now have the option to manage the accounts in one of the following five ways:

- View the account properties
- Deactivate the user account
- Remove the user account
- Reset the password on both the W2012R2E and Office 365 accounts
- Un-assign the Office 365 account

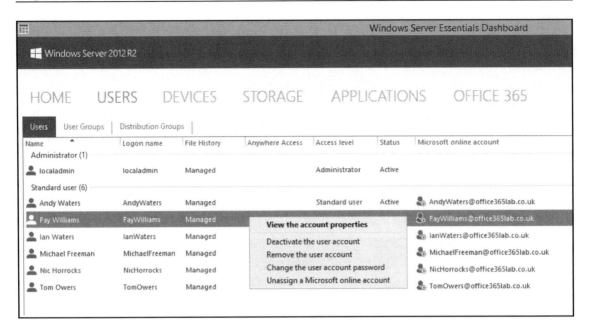

In order to add single user accounts in both Windows Server and Office 365, you simply need to follow these four steps:

1. Add a new user account.
2. Create or assign an Office 365 account.
3. Assign a license.
4. Confirm account creation.

Let us now see how to perform these steps:

1. **Adding a new user account**: Select **Add a User Account** and enter the relevant account information, as shown in the following screenshot:

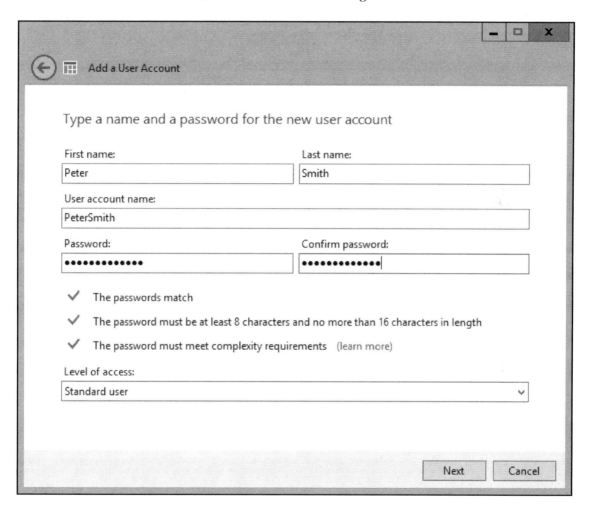

2. **Creating or assigning an Office 365 account**: The next screen will ask if we want to create a new Office 365 account, use an existing one, or not create one at all:

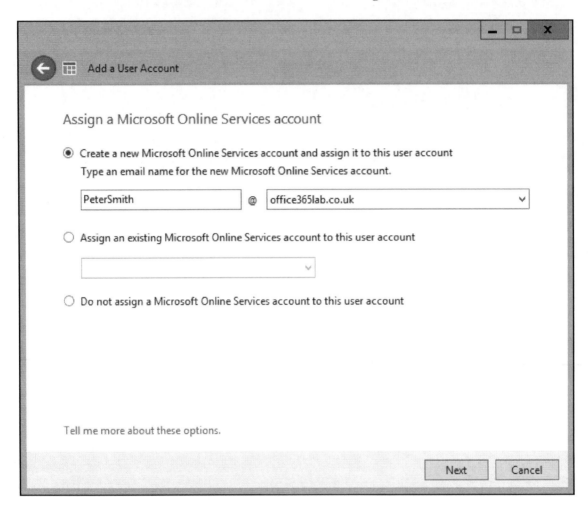

3. **Assigning a license**: On the next page, we will need to select which license or elements we want to provide to the user:

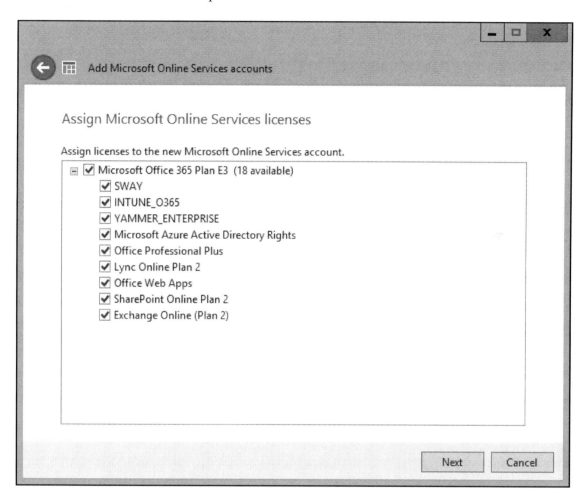

4. **Confirming account creation**: From here, we are prompted for various server settings which do not relate to Office 365 and will not be covered here. Following this, we will see that the account has been successfully created:

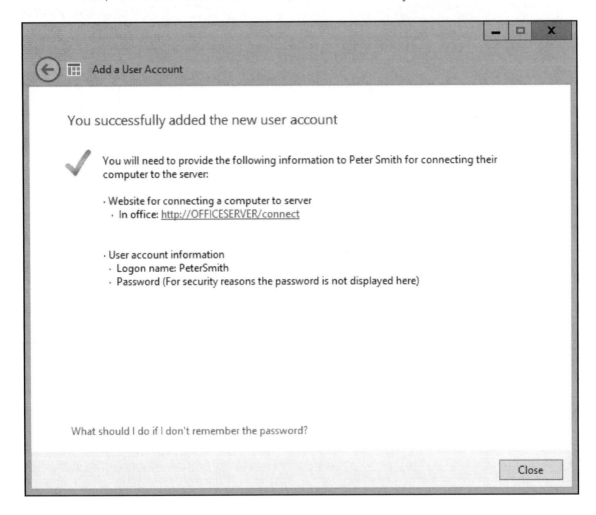

We can now see that the account created has both a Windows logon and Office 365:

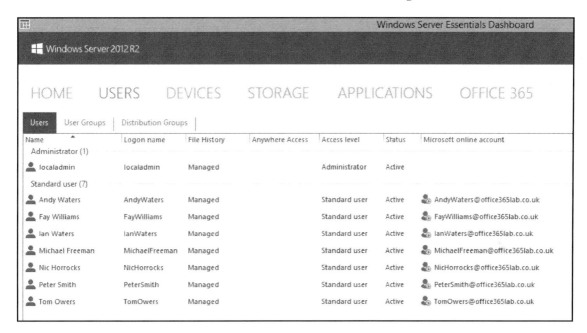

Windows PowerShell

Using PowerShell with Office 365 is broken up into two forms of administration:

- General Office 365 administration
- Exchange Online advanced administration

Connecting to Windows PowerShell for Office 365 requires the installation of the Microsoft Online Services Sign-in Assistant in order to adequately pass credentials through to Office 365. Most of the functions usually performed under Windows PowerShell for Office 365 can be performed through the Microsoft Online portal – therefore this is not really applicable for small businesses.

Working with PowerShell

There are numerous Exchange Online functions that can only be performed through PowerShell, such as:

- Setting mailbox permissions
- Creating a shared mailbox
- Allowing users to send on behalf of other users

Any Windows 7 (or above) computer is capable of running Windows PowerShell commands against Exchange Online. You can also create PowerShell scripts to automate functions and actions if you plan to perform them regularly.

 It is important to note that PowerShell sessions may become inactive after 15 minutes of idle time, so make sure you know what commands you wish to run before creating the connection.

Connecting to Exchange Online with PowerShell involves a few steps:

1. Load Windows PowerShell (search for it via the **Start** menu).
2. Specify your Office 365 administrative credentials:

```
$cred = Get-Credential
```

3. Establish a new PowerShell session with the Exchange Online interface:

```
$s = New-PSSession -ConfigurationName Microsoft.Exchange -
connectionUri https://ps.outlook.com/powershell -Credential $cred -
Authentication Basic -AllowRedirection
```

4. Import the Exchange Online PowerShell cmdlets:

```
$importresults = Import-PSSession $s
```

5. At this point, you are ready to begin running commands to perform your desired functions.
6. `Get-PSSession | remove-PSSession` closes PowerShell's connections with Office 365 when completed.

PowerShell cmdlets follow the path of:

- Verb
- Noun
- Required parameters, inputs, and variables

Some examples would be:

Task: obtain mailbox size for a single user						
Verb	Noun	Parameter	Input	Pipe	Parameter	Variable
Get	MailboxStatistics	`-Identity`	`john@office365lab.co.uk`	`|`	`Select`	`totalitemsize`

Task: grant access to a mailbox							
Verb	Noun	Parameter	Input	Parameter	Variable	Parameter	Input
Add	MailboxPermission	`-Identity`	`john@office365lab.co.uk`	`-AccessRight`	`Fullaccess`	`User`	`sarah@office365lab.co.uk`

As you work with the Exchange Online Control Panel (the web-based admin interface), there will be various functions or actions that you want to perform that are simply not possible. Rest assured, in most cases these can actually be done via PowerShell.

Summary

In this chapter, we have shown you some of the options available for integrating your existing small business environment with Office 365, as well as managing your user accounts.

As has been demonstrated, the different methods available, range in complexity and are suitable based on your comfort levels.

In the next chapter, we will show you how to prepare for a simple migration from an existing mail platform to Exchange Online.

4

Integration Options for Midsize and Enterprise Organizations

Moving to the cloud for some of the services you provide today is a major shift in how you manage both your infrastructure and your users. The key item to focus on when moving to the cloud is what type of experience you choose to provide for your users, whether it's migrating from Exchange and preventing a new download of cached mail or seamlessly authenticating from SharePoint Online while navigating to SharePoint on-premises. To provide this experience, you need to enable some of the core integration options provided by Microsoft Online. Topics covered in this chapter include:

- Directory Synchronization
- **Active Directory Federation Services (AD FS)**
- Exchange Hybrid
- Non-Exchange messaging systems

Directory Synchronization

Directory Synchronization allows organizations with an **Active Directory** (**AD**) environment to synchronize AD users and groups to an Azure Active Directory, which is the identity solution supported by your Office 365 subscription and other Microsoft cloud platforms. The Directory Synchronization tool provided by Microsoft is called **Azure AD Connect** (**AAD Connect**) and synchronizes your local active directory into your Office 365 tenant. If you are currently using depreciated tools such as DirSync and AAD Sync, they must be uninstalled before installing the new AAD Connect.

Once you deploy AAD Connect in your environment, you should consider this server to be a permanent addition to your environment. Azure AD Connect can be installed and managed from an existing domain controller in your environment, but must be installed on a Windows Server 2008 or later with the latest service packs and updates installed. It's worth noting that AAD Connect supports not only single forest but multi forest configurations which can be found deployed in larger organizations.

If you want to read about the installation requirements and supported topologies in more detail, follow up with these links:

Installation pre-requisites: https://azure.microsoft.com/en-gb/documentation/articles/active-directory-aadconnect-prerequisites/

Topologies for Azure AD Connect: https://azure.microsoft.com/en-gb/documentation/articles/active-directory-aadconnect-topologies/

There are many benefits for synchronizing your AD environment to Office 365. These benefits include the following:

- Enabling AD password synchronization
- Enabling a unified address book
- Providing detailed address entries
- Simplifying the provisioning and object management process
- Maintaining a consistent set of groups

Enabling AD password synchronization

Not all organizations will choose to leverage a **Single Sign-On (SSO)** solution to support authentication from Active Directory. For those organizations that choose not to deploy a SSO experience, you do have an option to synchronize the password hash of the AD account and forest/domain you are synchronizing from. For those of you not familiar with SSO, it allows you to configure Office 365 so that it trusts your local Active Directory in such a way that users can automatically log into the Office 365 portal or sign in using their existing domain\user credentials from your on-premises environment. If you don't configure SSO in this way but use AAD Connect to synchronize passwords, then users can login using their office 365 username (user@domain.com) with the same password they use to log in locally.

A password hash is the encrypted form of the password, and since Office 365 knows how the password is encrypted, when you enter your password it encrypts it to generate a hash (a long string of characters). If the two match, then Office 365 knows you entered the correct password. What that means is that the user can use their Office 365 credentials to log on to the service with their AD password.

This greatly simplifies the on-premises infrastructure necessary to connect to Office 365. Password synchronization is a great fit for organizations that want to quickly deploy Office 365 and start realizing the benefits of it early, while still providing a consistent experience for their users. In such a scenario, these organizations can deploy AD FS at a future point. It's also a benefit to organizations that cannot or do not want to support an SSO solution but still want to ensure that the users have a simple way to connect to the service. Password synchronization is not an SSO solution and will not provide an SSO experience.

AD FS can be a very complicated topic but it's basically a secure way of sharing information between two parties over the internet. In this case, it is Office 365 and your on-premises Active Directory. It does require multiple AD FS servers to be setup in your environment and the use of certificates. Apart from allowing you to create a single sign-on experience for users, it can also be used to enable two factor authentication with vendors such as RSA secure ID.

Enabling a unified address book

When you plan a migration of mailboxes to Exchange Online, maintaining a single address book across messaging systems will be critical. This single address book will simplify communications overall.

Directory Synchronization allows for Outlook users to see on-premises mailboxes in the **Global Address List (GAL)**. When an Exchange Online user e-mails an on-premises user, Exchange detects that the mailbox or license for that users does not exist and then routes the mail to the on-premises mailbox. (Setting the primary e-mail domain in Exchange Online to **internal relay** is a critical step for this to be successful. We will learn more about this in Chapter 7, *Preparing for a Hybrid Deployment and Migration*.) The same occurs on-premises, to online; however, in this scenario the mailbox has the forwarder or target address of a service domain within Exchange Online.

Providing detailed address entries

At a minimum, Directory Synchronization requires the following attributes:

- `accountEnabled`
- `objectGUID`
- `userPrincipalName`
- `mail`

The preceding attributes do not provide a great user experience for users leveraging any of the Office 365 services. The mandatory attributes are enough to synchronize on-premises AD, but Office 365 allows you to synchronize so much more. As an example, you can synchronize first names, last names, e-mail address, office locations, manager, phone numbers, and so on. Chances are that if you have Exchange on-premises, you likely have most of these attributes filled in. These attributes offer great benefits for maintaining a simplified address book in Exchange and a more complete directory in SharePoint Online.

If you have another messaging system such as Gmail, Lotus Notes, or GroupWise, then you may not have these attributes filled in. In order to provide a rich user experience, it's highly recommended that you populate these attributes. Many third-party migration tools will help you organize and populate this information. If you maintain this information in an external system (for example, an HR system), then you may want to consider leveraging an identity management solution to keep your AD and external system in sync.

 To learn more about which attributes are synchronized, review the following list provided by Microsoft: `http://social.technet.microsoft.com/wiki/contents/articles/1991.list-of-attributes-that-are-synced-by-the-windows-azure-active-directory-sync-tool.aspx`

Simplifying the provisioning and object management process

By default, the Directory Synchronization process runs every three hours. After the first run, the synchronization process looks for changes within the environment. These changes can consist of attribute changes (for example, manager or title change) or they can consist of adds/deletes within the environment.

The advantage of Directory Synchronization is to prevent organizations from having to manage multiple directories. When you maintain multiple directories, you can cause a significant disconnect in object information. This can also be a security risk to most organizations as you may be leaving access open to individuals who should no longer have it.

Since Directory Synchronization enforces changes within Office 365, during synchronization, you can simplify your provisioning process. As an example, when you want to provision a user, you add them to AD as you normally would. Once you add them to AD, you then license them for the services they need in Office 365 after synchronization. It's even more simplified when you de-provision a user. When de-provisioning a user, all that is required is either disabling or removing their account within your AD environment. Once you remove their account in AD, their license will then free up in Office 365 on the next synchronization and their mailbox will be removed.

Organizations that leverage an existing identity management solution, or plan to leverage one in the future, can take advantage of the simplified provisioning options from Microsoft Office 365. Here is an example of a provisioning process you might consider:

- Provision a user in your HR system
- Your identity management solution creates the account(s) in AD
- Identity management solution forces an Office 365 Directory Synchronization manually (to be executed on the Directory Synchronization server, and if that is not possible, wait for 3 hours)
- Run a PowerShell command to provision a license for the user in Office 365

Maintaining a consistent set of groups

Managing groups apart from AD could be challenging, especially if these groups maintain security for a SharePoint site or a distribution list for company wide-e-mails. Directory Synchronization does synchronize both security groups and distribution lists. The only difference between these groups within Office 365 is that the distribution lists also have a display name and an e-mail address. It is possible to have a security group serve as both a security group and distribution list.

Security groups can only be leveraged within SharePoint Online, unless the security group is mail enabled. It's highly recommended that you continue to maintain security groups within AD; however, your strategy to leveraging SharePoint groups or security groups will depend on your approach for SharePoint Online. There are many advantages to leverage security groups within SharePoint. The biggest advantage may come with a Hybrid deployment of SharePoint Online, while providing a seamless transition from online to on-premises.

Distribution lists, on the other hand, have different pros and cons for being leveraged in AD. The following are some of the common pros and cons for distribution list management in AD.

The following are the pros:

- Continue to manage your on-premises process for groups/lists
- Simplified helpdesk management of distribution lists
- Maintain your existing groups/lists already established within AD
- In Hybrid mode, leverage the same lists for both online and on-premises users

The following are the cons:

- Users cannot directly modify distribution lists, unless the list was created in Office 365 or the authority belongs to Office 365 for that group
- Group membership changes take up to 3 hours, while waiting for Directory Synchronization

The following is an example of how you may position Directory Synchronization in your environment:

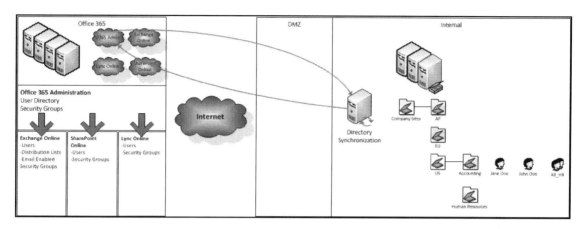

Active Directory Federation Services

With Office 365, Microsoft offers a single account sign-on experience, or Single Sign-On. Microsoft leverages Active Directory Federation Service 2.0, 2.1, or 3.0+ (AD FS) to provide this single sign-on experience. AD FS is not the only SSO solution that works with Office 365. There are many other supported solutions, but those solutions typically come at an additional cost. It's important that you evaluate your future use of SSO to determine whether AD FS or another SSO solution is the right fit for your organization.

AD FS enables organizations to connect their existing AD forest to Microsoft's federation infrastructure, creating a secure trust relationship with Microsoft. Once your organization is connected to this service, you can then allow your users to log on to the Office 365 services you provide, with their Active Directory credentials. There are many benefits to organizations providing this type of access. These benefits include:

- Simplified logon experience
- Less confusion versus maintaining multiple accounts/passwords
- Business control to quickly disable access to AD accounts when an employee leaves the organization
- AD policy adherence defined by the business (for example, password complexity, password attempt limits, and so on)

- Internal/external logon restrictions (for example, allowing users to only connect to the service while on the corporate networks versus externally)
- Enhanced security (for example, two-factor authentication)
- Ability to provide simplified logons for all AD FS services

In order to deploy AD FS within your environment, there are some initial areas to consider:

- Base requirements
- Database requirements
- Authentication strategy
- Infrastructure design considerations

We will consider them in the following subsections.

Base requirements

The following are some of the base requirements you should consider. These base requirements include:

- Active Directory
- Windows Server 2008, 2008 R2, 2010, or 2012 R2 domain controllers
- Publicly routable **User Principal Name** (**UPN**) (for example, a UPN is `%username%@domain.com`, not `domain\%username%`), as you can see from the following screenshot:

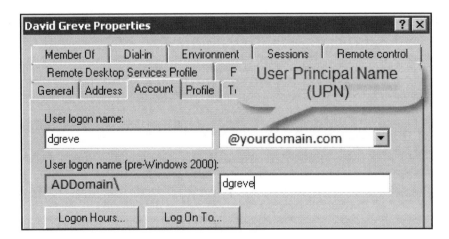

Many organizations have their users log on as `domain\%username%`, which has been a standard practice since the first logon method back when domains where introduced in the Windows NT days. Changing to this standard is not difficult, but it will be an important communication and training exercise for your end users when they leverage the Office 365 service. You do not need to change the computer logon to a UPN logon, just the logon to Office 365 services. If you do not leverage a publicly routable UPN in AD, you can simply add one by following these steps:

1. Go to **Active Directory Domains and Trusts**.
2. Select **Properties** of Domains and Trust.
3. On the **UPN Suffixes** tab, add the UPN you plan to register for Office 365.
4. Now update each user you would like to have this UPN.

It's also important to leverage a UPN that exactly matches the user's e-mail address. The reason why this is important is that a UPN looks like an e-mail address and by providing this to your users, you may cause confusion if it's a different address. There are also some other complexities to services such as Skype for Business, when leveraging a different UPN for a user's logon versus their e-mail address.

Single AD FS farm versus multiple farms

When you deploy AD FS, you essentially create a single AD FS farm. An AD FS farm is a set of AD FS servers that communicate to a single database source. When you assign a UPN to a user, they can only authenticate to one AD FS farm. Most organizations leverage a single farm; however, you may consider multiple farms if you leverage multiple UPNs and you choose to provide local authentication to regional areas that connect to the same Active Directory environment.

You also need to plan to deploy an Office 365 Directory Synchronization server. This service is a key requirement for AD FS. The Directory Synchronization server updates your Office 365 subscription with all the federated versus non-federated accounts. This is important so the service knows not to allow a logon without approval from your Active Directory environment.

Database requirements

In addition to the previous requirements, AD FS also requires a database server to attach to. The out-of-the-box configuration is ready to attach to a **Windows Internal Database** (**WID**). WID is basically a SQL Express deployment within Windows. For most base deployments, but WID is acceptable. WID has some limitations. These limitations include the following:

- WID does not tolerate high latency connections (you cannot deploy multiple AD FS servers in a single AD FS farm and span it across very slow WAN links)
- WID can only support up to five AD FS internal servers
- Only one AD FS internal server will be considered the master read/write server

If you plan to span AD FS across multiple sites with very slow connections, or you plan to deploy more than five servers, you may want to consider a SQL deployment to support the AD FS servers.

Authentication strategy

Another requirement to AD FS is planning out your authentication strategy. The major item you need to know about AD FS is how it routes the user to the AD FS servers. Today DNS is primarily used to refer the connecting client to the appropriate AD FS server. All users have to log on to the service with a UPN, as mentioned earlier it looks similar to `%username%@domain.com`, and that user's logon domain is `domain.com`. Since DNS is used, you are somewhat limited on how you leverage AD FS. Here is an example of the first few steps of authentication:

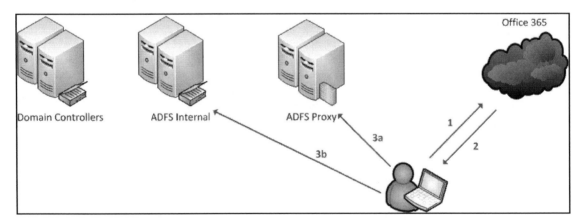

The first step is for the user to request access to the service. Office 365 then determines if the user is an AD FS or non-AD FS user, based on UPN. If the user is an AD FS user, the user is then referred to an address set up within the service. As an example, it may be `sts.domain.com` (based on the user's UPN). The end user then does a DNS lookup for the location of that server (the STS DNS, a record part). If the end user is outside the network (for example, the public IP outside of the internal network where AD FS is located), then the user will likely get a public IP address for the AD FS proxy servers, which will securely traverse to the internal AD infrastructure (see path 3a in the preceding image). If the end user is within the internal private routable network, on the same network as the AD FS internal server, the user will receive the internal IP address for the AD FS internal servers.

The primary limitation with this setup, for all users leveraging the UPN of `@domain.com`, is that you can only have one DNS record to refer the user to a proxy or internal AD FS server. This creates challenges for the companies looking to globally distribute AD FS for redundancy or performance reasons.

For those companies looking for redundancy or local authentication performance, there are some options. Companies that want to maintain the same UPN for all the users, but need to provide global redundancy, can deploy a DNS solution that enables the capability to load balance information between sites. This is based on the location of the user, availability of the services, and general performance of the servers. F5 is one example of a great option to enable this capability. With a solution from F5, you can deploy AD FS server to each of your sites dedicated to AD FS, then rely on the F5 DNS service to direct your users to the appropriate servers.

 Review the AD FS Office 365 guides from Microsoft when scaling AD FS servers. Refer to `https://blogs.technet.microsoft.com/ucando365tal ks/214/4/14/adfs-high-availability-quick-reference-guide-for-a dministrators-implement-single-sign-on-for-office-365/`.

If you are required, or have the ability, to manage multiple UPNs, you have the option to deliver users to a specific site, based on their UPN. Here is an example of how this would work:

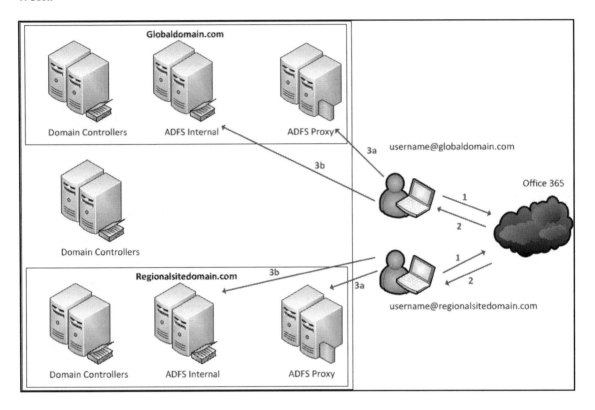

Infrastructure design considerations

Many organizations have various operating requirements or **service-level agreements (SLAs)** when deploying certain types of service within their infrastructure. In most organizations, e-mail is considered a mission critical service for their end-users. With that, AD FS offers organizations a great number of deployment options to support various internal SLAs for the servers hosted by that organization. These requirements often include:

- Base infrastructure
- Base infrastructure with redundancy
- Base infrastructure with redundancy and a disaster recovery site
- Base global infrastructure to support local regional logons

- Azure IaaS as an alternative data center

Let's review what these deployments may look like in your organization.

Base infrastructure

At the core of it, there are minimum infrastructure requirements needed to support AD FS within an organization. These minimum requirements include:

- AD FS Internal server
- AD FS Proxy server
- Directory Synchronization server

The following is an example of a base infrastructure:

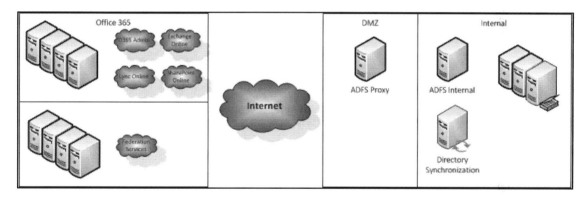

Base infrastructure with redundancy

If the AD FS internal server or AD FS proxy server were to go down, your users would not be able to authenticate to the Office 365 service. What this mean is, your users will not be able to connect to read e-mails online or in an active state. To most organizations, this is unacceptable. To fulfill a base infrastructure with localized redundancy, you may consider the following items:

- AD FS Internal
  - Single primary internal server
  - Redundant internal server
  - Managed by software or hardware load balancing

- AD FS Proxy
    - Redundant proxy servers
    - Managed by software or hardware load balancing
- Directory Synchronization server

The following is an example of a base infrastructure with redundancy:

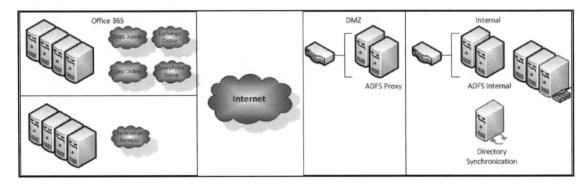

Now you are probably asking, why is there not a redundant Directory Synchronization server? Directory Synchronization only occurs every 30 minutes, out of the box. The purpose of Directory Synchronization is to ensure that Office 365 has the most recent account information from your local AD environment. If this server were to go down, your loss would only be of no updates to Office 365. This server does not need to be up for users to log on (as long as the user's account has already been synchronized). Arguably, you could build a standby server for Directory Synchronization, but you could also rebuild this server in a few hours, if you have a virtual or another readily available server. Your downtime would be pretty limited if you have the options mentioned earlier.

Base infrastructure with redundancy and a disaster recovery site

Many organizations today require disaster recovery sites for all critical services. These disaster recovery sites often mirror their data centers, in the event a core service goes down. Adding a disaster recovery site does add complexity to your base deployment of the Office 365 infrastructure.

AD FS Internal and AD FS Proxy have a single dependency of a Directory Synchronization server, to enable users for authentication. When you install AD FS, you are required to attach it to a database server. The standard configuration for a base AD FS install is to attach it to WID; however, when you plan to span AD FS across multiple sites, you may need to consider a SQL deployment. To create a base infrastructure with localized redundancy and a disaster recovery site, you may consider the following items:

- AD FS Internal
  - Single primary internal server
  - Redundant internal server
  - Managed by software or hardware load balancing
  - Communications with SQL
  - Single or dual internal server at the DR site
- AD FS Proxy
  - Redundant proxy servers
  - Managed by software or hardware load balancing
  - Single or dual proxy server at the DR site
- SQL cluster
  - Two SQL servers at the primary site, supported by Windows Clustering
  - Single or dual SQL servers at the DR site, leveraging geo-clustering, replication, or mirroring
- Directory Synchronization server

The following is an example of a base infrastructure with redundancy:

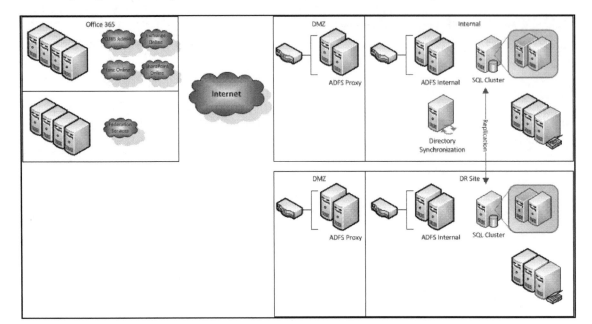

There are a few important items to note in order to support this type of configuration. To start, your SQL environment needs to be able to synchronize changes frequently and read-write will have to take place in the SQL DB, once the AD FS servers are active in the DR site. Another consideration is how you plan to fail-over to the DR site. Consider leveraging a solution that can perform failover for a DNS record. You may deploy a DNS failover solution or an infrastructure solution that enables failover for data centers.

Base global infrastructure to support local regional logons

Some organizations operate independently based on sites or regions, but support the same infrastructure throughout. These organizations may also manage their own existing AD domains and messaging infrastructure. In some cases, it may be necessary to deploy independent AD FS environments to support local management and authentication for those sites.

This may come in two forms: a redundant AD FS deployment covering multiple sites or independent AD FS farms at each site. Redundancy for an AD FS farm allows you to use a single UPN across all these sites; however, having redundancy does not guarantee you can direct users to the appropriate site. To accomplish this, you would need to utilize geo-load balancing.

Alternatively, you can deploy multiple AD FS farms within your organization. The limitation with multiple AD FS farms is that you can only assign a UPN to a single farm and you cannot span a single UPN across multiple farms. To leverage multiple farms, you need to be able to direct specific UPNs to each farm. As an example, you may assign `%username%@region1.com` to AD FS farm 1 in region 1, while `%username%@region2.com` would be assigned to AD FS farm 2 in region 2. To create a base global infrastructure to support local regional logons, you may consider the following items:

Region 1:

- AD FS Internal
    - Single primary internal server
    - Redundant internal server
    - Managed by software or hardware load balancing
- AD FS Proxy
    - Redundant proxy servers
    - Managed by software or hardware load balancing
- Directory Synchronization Server

Region 2:

- AD FS Internal
    - Single primary internal server
    - Redundant internal server
    - Managed by software or hardware load balancing
- AD FS Proxy
    - Redundant proxy servers
    - Managed by software or hardware load balancing

The following is an example of a base global infrastructure to support local regional logons:

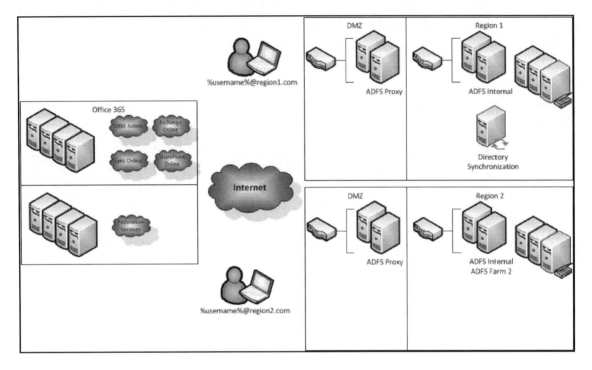

Azure IaaS as an alternative data center

Now you may be asking yourself, if Iâ©©m moving to the cloud, why am I deploying servers on-premises? Certainly there are many reasons why you would not want to deploy servers on-premises. That may include limited physical or virtual space, limited storage, unreliable internet connections, unreliable data center locations, high acquisition growth, and so on. Microsoft has an answer to your concerns. You now have the ability to build AD FS within Azure **Infrastructure as a Service (IaaS)**, which is Microsoftâ©©s infrastructure platform that supports the ability to create a virtual environment, much like one you may create on-premises.

You can simulate many of the scenarios listed previously, within the Azure IaaS environment. The one catch is that you have to build Azure IaaS to work independently in the event your connection to the service is ever broken. What that means is that in addition to the AD FS and Directory Synchronization servers you build in Azure IaaS, you also need to build domain controllers for all the AD domains in your AD forest.

In this book, we will focus on building an AD FS solution in an on-premises environment. To read more about how to deploy AD FS in Azure IaaS, review the TechNet White Paper at `http://technet.microsoft.com/library/dn59539.aspx`.

AD FS summary

At a fundamental level, a simple AD FS deployment does not require much complexity to offer your users a simplified logon to the service. The good news is, if you are planning to pilot the service, a basic infrastructure is all you need to get started. As you start to evaluate Office 365 further, you will start adding complexity to your core infrastructure, in order to support your business. In most cases, this is not significantly more complex than the services you have likely already planned and deployed for your users, meeting your existing general business requirements and SLAs. Additionally, the other side benefits you receive from AD FS is the ability to use AD FS with other applications or cloud based services. For example, you can connect Yammer to your AD FS solution, providing an SSO experience to the Yammer platform.

Exchange Hybrid

Exchange Hybrid is really a rich coexistence option provided by Microsoft, by leveraging existing native Exchange tools. Exchange Hybrid offers customers with an existing Exchange 2010, 2013, or 2016 environments the capability to integrate directly with their Office 365 subscription. Think of the integration as merely an extension of your environment. The integration components can be enabled when a customer deploys Exchange 2010 (SP3), 2013, or 2016 in their environment. Integration is established by creating an Exchange Federation agreement from the on-premises Exchange Organization to the Office 365 subscription. The benefits of Exchange Hybrid are:

- Mail routing through Exchange 2010, 2013, or 2016, leveraging TLS
- Mail routing control (mail flow from/to Office 365 or on-premises)
- Simplified management from Exchange 2010, 2013, and 2016 **Exchange Management Console (EMC)**
- Maintaining a long-term Exchange mailbox presence on-premises and in Office 365
- Calendar free/busy lookup between Exchange on-premises and Office 365 mailboxes

- Simplified mailbox moves between Exchange on-premises and Office 365 mailboxes
- Simplified desktop Outlook 2010+ conversion between Exchange on-premises and Office 365 mailboxes
- Single **Outlook Web App (OWA)** URL between Exchange on-premises and Office 365 mailboxes

As you plan for your deployment to Office 365, there are many areas you need to consider for your Hybrid deployment. The following are key areas that we will review:

- Is Exchange Hybrid the right fit?
- Exchange Hybrid deployment considerations
- Exchange Hybrid design examples
- Exchange Hybrid summary

Is Exchange Hybrid the right fit?

The answer to this question is easier for organizations with a single Exchange Organization consisting of Exchange 2010, 2013, or 2016 in your existing AD environment. The answer to this question gets more complicated if you have a hosted Exchange environment or you are leveraging a non-Exchange messaging system. This is due to the requirements of an Exchange Hybrid deployment. Exchange Hybrid requires the following:

- Office 365 Directory Synchronization in the same AD environment as the Exchange Hybrid server
- Existing AD must be Windows Server 2003 forest functional mode or higher
- Mailbox moves by the Hybrid server have to occur from the existing Exchange Organization, leveraging Office 365 Directory Synchronization
- Multiple Exchange Hybrid configurations in Multiple Exchange Organizations is supported, but it will require the deployment of **ForeFront Identity Manager (FIM)** or the Azure AD Connect to keep things simple, we will only focus on a single AD forest and a single Exchange Organization

If you currently have an Exchange Organization and you can connect the Directory Synchronization server to the same AD environment for long-term, then deploying an Exchange Hybrid server will be to your advantage. Some of the key advantages are:

- By deploying an Exchange Hybrid server, you greatly simplify the mailbox migration process to Office 365
- By simplifying this process, you are cutting down the need to introduce third-party tools for either migrations or coexistence
- It enables the ability to perform a phased migration versus a flash cut-over
- Leads to a greatly improved user experience during a migration by not causing users to re-download their cached mailbox, and you provide them with a rich coexistence experience

If you currently have a disconnected Exchange Organization (hosted or you are being split off from another company), or you have a non-Exchange messaging system, then a Hybrid server may not provide you with a significant advantage. The reasons why you may want to deploy an Exchange Hybrid server, in this scenario, are as follows:

- Plans to maintain an on-premises messaging system and you want it tightly connected to your Office 365 subscription
- You plan to use this infrastructure as a swing infrastructure to speed up migrations from an existing messaging system
- You have applications that depend on connecting directly to an Exchange Organization (not necessarily for open-relaying)

If you choose not to deploy an Exchange Hybrid server or the Exchange Hybrid server does not fit your environment, then you will be dependent on third-party tools to perform the migrations and if necessary to create coexistence with Office 365. Leveraging third-party tools does increase complexity and costs, but there are some great third-party tool options that can simplify this process. We will review these tools in the deployment considerations section.

Exchange Hybrid deployment considerations

An Exchange Hybrid configuration can be deployed in almost any environment connected to Office 365 by Active Directory and the Office 365 Directory Synchronization server. When you plan to deploy an Exchange Hybrid server, you need to consider several items:

- Location and version of your existing messaging system and users
- Migration bandwidth for the Hybrid server
- Scaling your Hybrid server (including availability services)
- Exchange schedule free/busy store
- Public Folder Hybrid

Let's review these items and their importance in the following subsections.

Location and version of your existing messaging system

You may have a centralized or distributed messaging system. Likewise, you may have subscribed to the Office 365 service in one of the three major regions. If you maintain a centralized messaging system, then it may be important to locate an Exchange Hybrid server at that location. By locating the Hybrid server close to your existing centralized messaging system, you will prevent latency and possible corruption when migrations occur. Also, if you have a centralized messaging system, you may have adequate bandwidth to support the query attempts made by end-users when performing user information look ups, like free/busy, and so on.

If you have a distributed messaging system, you may have to consider the following:

- Are the users leveraging the same e-mail name space across all the systems?
- If users are leveraging a different e-mail name space across regions, can you break down the name space and regions, and group them together for a distributed Hybrid deployment?
- Is there a primary site that all the users eventually traverse to, where you could locate the Hybrid server?
- If you are distributed across multiple regions, are there a larger number of users within the region in which you can locate a Hybrid server?

There are many more questions that can be asked when planning your Exchange Hybrid server deployment. In most cases, the Hybrid server will follow existing Exchange 2010/2013 architectural decisions. As we close this section, we will review the various design examples.

Migration bandwidth for the Hybrid server

If you have an existing Exchange Organization, then you are likely planning a migration while leveraging the Hybrid servers. Bandwidth is a critical component when you position this Hybrid server. If your organization has minimal bandwidth, both during business hours and outside business hours, you may need to consider renting additional bandwidth during the migrations. Otherwise, you may have to relocate the Hybrid server. If you have adequate bandwidth, the next step will be planning and testing your migration throughput. We will dive deeper into migration throughput planning in `Chapter 7`, *Preparing for a Hybrid Deployment and Migration*.

Scaling your Hybrid server

Much like the location of your messaging system, a scale out of your Hybrid environment may be necessary. Key considerations for scaling your Hybrid environment are as follows:

- You plan to maintain a long-term Hybrid environment
- You plan to leverage multiple Hybrid servers in multiple environments
- You want to increase migration throughput for the various e-mail name spaces

While scaling out your Hybrid servers may be an advantage, it's important to plan how your users will leverage these servers or if they will be used at all. Currently, the Hybrid servers respond to user's requests based on the services provided. As an example, if you have Auto-discover set up, it's likely that only a load balancer or array will respond to that lookup for the name space specified.

Exchange schedule free/busy store

When a user is migrated to Office 365, they start to leverage the availability service for free/busy lookups, the **Offline Address Book (OAB)**, and other services such as the Out of Office Assistant.

Public Folder Hybrid

In addition to Exchange Hybrid, you are now able to set up Public Folder Hybrid. Public Folder Hybrid is the ability to enable access to Public Folders on-premises when a user is moved to Exchange Online. This is an important component of the Hybrid model, as it enables you to provide access to your on-premises Public Folder store while you are transitioning your users to Exchange Online. If your goal is to migrate all users to Exchange Online, you can finalize your migration with a move of all your Public Folders to Exchange Online.

> To review all the supported Public Folder Hybrid scenarios, refer to the Microsoft TechNet Article at `http://technet.microsoft.com/en-us/lib rary/dn249373(v=exchg.15).aspx`.

Exchange Hybrid design examples

An Exchange Messaging Organization can be deployed in many ways. Likewise, an Exchange Hybrid deployment can follow a similar approach. Optimizing the positioning of your Exchange Hybrid deployment is critical in both migrations and client response times. The following are some examples of a complete deployment, including AD FS integration in the following scenarios:

- Centralized Exchange Organization
- Distributed Exchange Organization
- Disconnected Exchange Organization or non-Exchange messaging environment

Centralized Exchange Organization

The following is an example of a centralized Exchange Organization with the Exchange Hybrid server deployed in the same site. The Exchange Hybrid server maintains the Federation agreement with Office 365 and all mail routing to/from Office 365:

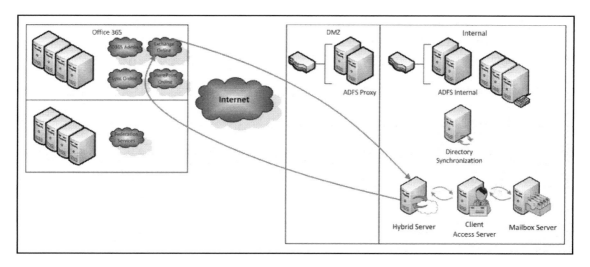

Distributed Exchange Organization

The following is an example of a distributedExchange Organization with the Exchange Hybrid server deployed in multiple sites. The Exchange Hybrid server maintains the Federation agreement with Office 365 and all mail routing to/from Office 365. However, in this example, the additional Exchange Hybrid server manages Auto-discover availability services for the other sites. If the first Hybrid server becomes unavailable, then the Federation Trust needs to be transferred:

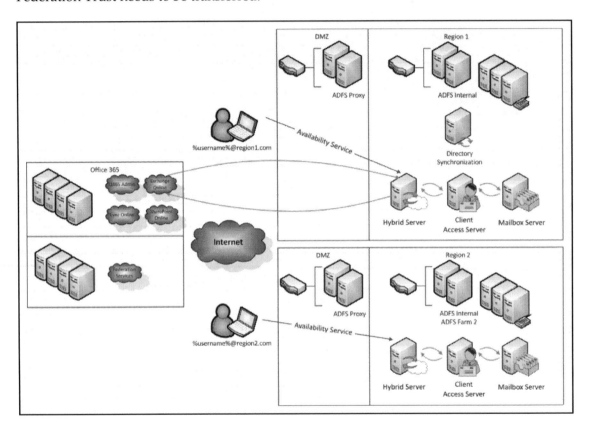

Disconnected Exchange Organization or non-Exchange messaging environment

In this scenario, the Exchange Hybrid server's purpose would only be to manage mailboxes you plan to keep on-premises long-term, or you plan to use the Exchange Hybrid server as a swing server to Office 365. In this case, it's unlikely you already have an Exchange Organization deployed. The following are examples of these two approaches:

- Maintaining Exchange Mailboxes on-premises long-term:

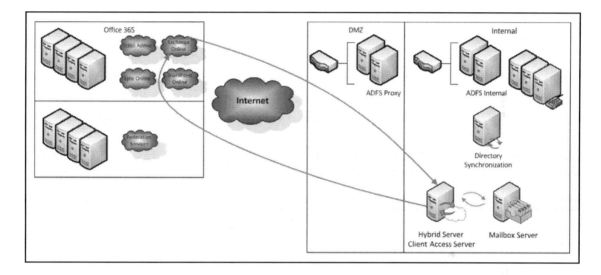

- Use of Exchange Hybrid as a swing migration environment:

Although an Exchange Hybrid server is not required to perform migrations to Office 365, in this example a Hybrid server is used for a number of reasons that include:

- Plans to keep some mailboxes on-premises for long-term
- Increase the performance of a migration to Exchange for the end users, minimizing third-party coexistence requirements
- Third-party coexistence tools do not exist for your messaging system
- Storage is not a limitation
- Bandwidth is a limitation, therefore making a staged migration from Exchange Hybrid is a more attractive solution

Exchange Hybrid summary

There are many options when planning for an Exchange Hybrid server. Whether you have centralized environment, distributed or disconnected environment, there is an architecture that fits your organization. Once you have completed your integration planning for Office 365, you will be ready to start the preparation process.

Non-Exchange messaging systems

Believe it or not, not everyone has a Microsoft Exchange messaging system within their environment. Although we are not focusing on non-Exchange messaging systems, it's still an important topic when working towards an understanding of how to integrate with Office 365. The key items of focus for non-Exchange messaging systems are:

- Active Directory readiness
- Coexistence options
- Migrating from a non-Exchange messaging system

Active Directory readiness

If you are managing a non-Exchange system, then you already know that your Active Directory environment may not match your existing messaging environment. As an example, if you have Gmail, Lotus Notes, or a GroupWise environment, these environments do not depend on Active Directory for authentication. Because of this, it's likely that your messaging users may not be an exact match to your Active Directory users. In fact, even if they are a match, the attributes may not look the same. When you plan to migrate a non-Exchange messaging system, it's necessary that you update Active Directory if you plan to leverage Office 365 Directory Synchronization. When you leverage Directory Synchronization, you create your Office 365 address book for all the services you leverage. This address book is critical, as it provides the following:

- Entries in the Exchange **Global Address List** (**GAL**), providing your migrated users the ability to e-mail users still on-premises
- SharePoint security groups and a general user list
- Lync address book, enabling you to add people within your organization to your contact list

By having inaccurate data within the address book, you risk users not finding who they are trying to address and e-mail messages will **Non-Delivery Report** (**NDR**) due to an invalid or inaccurate e-mail address information in Active Directory.

Having accurate data within Active Directory will enable you to smooth out both your coexistence and migration options. If you leave inaccurate data in Active Directory, then after you start this process you are likely going to cause your users some pain.

Migrating from a non-Exchange messaging system

The Exchange Hybrid server offers a great way to migrate users from on-premises Exchange environments to Office 365. So what do you do when you don't have an on-premises Exchange environment or have a hosted Exchange environment? You leverage one of the following methods:

- Use the simple migration method provided by Office 365 (ideal for smaller organizations)
- Purchase a third-party tool specialized in migrating from your source messaging environment to Office 365

Migrating any mail is certainly not the easiest option; purchasing a third-party tool is likely to be the most ideal option. Third-party tools typically offer the following benefits:

- Translation of e-mail addresses from the source messaging system to Office 365 (for example, converting a Lotus Notes e-mail address to an SMTP address).
- Enable the ability to scale up a number of migration consoles to increase the performance of the migration and number of mailboxes/amount of data you can migrate. You can even use a cloud-based migration tool, which eliminates the need for a large number of on-premises migration consoles.
- Provide reporting, enabling you to proactively repair or notify a user of a problematic migration of their mailbox.

Certainly, migrations from unlike messaging systems are not perfect, but leveraging third-party tools will help streamline and smooth out the process by addressing some complexities with manually moving the users and easing the desktop e-mail transition. In most cases, it's recommended to bring in experts that know how to leverage these tools, if you move forward with them.

Summary

Office 365 provides a nice set of basic and rich integration options for both Exchange and non-Exchange messaging systems. We learned about the base integration options to enable a simplified logon process for users, to an extended integration option, enabling rich coexistence for on-premises and online Exchange Organizations. These options should help you work through your planning process, bringing us to prepare for the deployment of these options.

Based on the integration options for professionals, small businesses, and enterprises, you have a decision to make on which path is the correct path for your organization. If you choose to leverage the professional or small business path, then the next chapter is a right fit for you. If you plan to leverage the enterprise path, you may want to skip ahead to Chapter 7, *Preparing for a Hybrid Deployment and Migration*.

In the next chapter, we will look at how to prepare for a simple migration. We will look at few of the migration options available to us when migrating from Exchange server, Gmail, and other POP3 and IMAP based systems.

5
Preparing for a Simple Migration

So far in this book, we have prepared you for purchasing and beginning to use Office 365. However, a key factor yet to be completed is to migrate mailbox content from your existing mail system.

In this chapter, we will discuss the various options available for performing a migration to Exchange Online and what needs to be done to prepare. This will cover the following topics:

- Overview of a simple migration
- Available migration options
- Differences between source platforms
- The migration process
- Preparing your environment for migration

What is a simple migration?

When an organization looks to migrate mail in a single direction to Exchange Online, it is called a simple migration due to the fact that it is one way.

Organizations looking to retain on-premises Exchange Server functionality as well as utilize Exchange Online would choose a hybrid environment over a simple migration. A hybrid environment is a mixture of both the environments, which is more complex to implement and maintain than a simple migration. We discuss these further in Chapter 7, *Preparing for a Hybrid Deployment and Migration* and Chapter 8, *Deploying a Hybrid Infrastructure – AD FS*.

Migration options

There are really only five main mail platform types used by organizations that wish to migrate to Exchange Online:

- POP e-mail systems
- IMAP e-mail systems
- Hosted Exchange server
- Gmail or Google apps
- Exchange Server 2003 or 2007

Based on these platforms, we have created several scenarios that are reflective of common customer environments and situations.

POP e-mail

Many small businesses currently utilize POP e-mail provided by their domain name or website host. These are the simplest of migrations as the mailbox content is migrated by relying on the PST file import functionality in Outlook. Users simply need to import their existing PST file into the new Exchange Online mailbox.

IMAP

Some organizations may be utilizing IMAP either from a hosted service provider or on an on-premises server (such as Novell GroupWise). These mail systems can be imported natively by using the migration wizard within the Exchange Online Control Panel. It is important to note that IMAP only contains mail objects and folders (not calendars, contacts, tasks, or any other Outlook-based items, as these are stored in PST files).

Hosted Exchange or Gmail

For organizations that have already made a move to cloud services and are using e-mail from either a hosted Exchange Server provider or Gmail (aka Google Apps), they are better off utilizing third-party cloud-based migration systems. An example of this is www.migrationwiz.com, which allows for mailbox content to be moved from the original mailbox directly into the new Exchange Online mailbox.

Exchange Server 2003 and 2007

It is quite common to find organizations still running Exchange Server 2003 or 2007, either as a standalone solution or as part of **Small Business Server** (**SBS**) 2003 or 2008.

Effectively, all that is required is the enabling of RPC over HTTP for any of the versions. However, this can prove to be challenging as the functionality was not native to Exchange Server/SBS 2003.

In Exchange Server 2007/SBS 2008, however, there are more complexities around the provisioning of the actual certificates and utilization of the Autodiscover functionality.

The actual migration is performed by running the migration wizard within the Exchange Online Control Panel.

Staged migration

A staged migration allows you to choose which mailboxes get migrated to Exchange Online and move at your own pace. During this process, however, users of both Exchange Server on-premises and Exchange Online are in separate environments. As a result, these users will not have access to a shared Global Address List or free/busy information.

During the migration, all emails that are routed via the on-premises Exchange Server are also retained locally, which provides for rollback if required.

Cutover migration

A cutover migration simply begins the process of migrating all mailboxes from your on-premises Exchange Server to Exchange Online in a single step.

Migration option comparison

For simple digestion of the preceding scenarios, we have broken down the differences between the options into the following table and listed the requirements for each:

Migration type/requirements	PST migration	IMAP	Third-party tool	Exchange staged	Exchange cutover
Server access	No	No	Possibly	Yes	Yes
Directory Synchronization	No	No	No	Yes	No

Define your own migration schedule	Yes	Yes	Yes	Yes	No
SSL certificate purchase	No	No	Possibly	Yes	Yes
PC access to migrate content	Yes	Yes	No	No	No

The migration process – in a nutshell

The steps involved in the actual migration process will differ depending on the option chosen.

Effectively, they will follow the same basic pattern:

- Creating user accounts
- Activating Exchange Online mailboxes
- Migrating mailbox content

Generally, the **Mail eXchange (MX)** record is cutover after the completion of a successful mailbox migration. However, some administrators prefer to do this beforehand to ensure that no new mail items are left behind.

However, the key to a successful migration is not the actual mailbox content migration itself, but the planning and preparation.

Planning for migration

Several key factors must be addressed when planning the migration to Exchange Online to ensure it is done successfully. These are both technical factors and human factors.

Technical considerations

There are numerous technical considerations that must be taken into account when planning for a migration. Some of the more common questions are as follows:

- Which of the previous example scenarios mirrors yours?
- Have users been informed of the change?
- How much data can you send through your Internet link to Exchange Online (meaning how many gigabytes of mail can be uploaded)?

- Does your monthly Internet download allowance cater for the mailboxes being downloaded back into the Outlook OST file for each user?
- Do you plan to start users on Exchange Online with their full mailbox or just a portion of recent content?
- Do you have access to all desktops so you can configure the new account in Outlook?
- How many computers will you have to re-configure, and do you have the resources to do them all in the timeframe?

Asking questions such as these will help determine your migration plan.

For example, if you have 80 users, each with mailboxes of 5 GB, then it is not likely that you will be able to transfer 400 GB of data in a single weekend. This is especially important as Exchange Online only supports mailbox transfer speeds of 500 MB per hour (higher speeds can be achieved by raising a support request before commencing the migration). Therefore, you would most likely go for a staged migration approach (if using Exchange Server) or alternatively a third-party solution such as `www.migrationwiz.com`, which allows multiple mailbox copy passes.

People considerations

Another key element of any migration plan is change management and a communication plan with a view to ensure that the end user experience is not a negative one.

It is important to notify users of any changes to their day-to-day operations that may impact their productivity, as any disruption could further delay the migration or leave a sour taste in their mouths.

Part of the change management is to inform the users about the migration procedure at a high level so that they are made to feel part of the process.

There will also be an element of having to re-configure the desktops and mobile devices. So the more comprehensive your change management and communications, the more you will be able to empower the users to do the work themselves. However, this can also be simplified by utilizing solutions such as `https://www.bittitan.com/products/deploymentpro/about` (from the same company that makes MigrationWiz) to automate the desktop configuration process.

Preparing your environment for migration

Before beginning the migration process, it is important to ensure that your environment has been prepared and that all requirements have been met.

Due to the varying requirements and processes, we have broken these down between types of migrations.

PST-based migrations are not documented as they are merely a file export/import procedure, which requires little preparation. You may want to document a procedure that states where the PST files are stored and how they are named, and even list the PST file passwords if password protection is required.

IMAP

In order for Exchange Online to access your IMAP server/service, it must be accessible via the IMAP protocol from the Internet—which is generally the case.

It is important that the users be created via the Office 365 administrative interface, either individually or in bulk.

You also need to prepare a listing of the existing IMAP mailboxes in CSV format which is imported into the Exchange Online Control Panel. This CSV maps the IMAP credentials (e-mail address, usernames, and passwords) to the Exchange Online mailbox.

Hosted Exchange/Gmail

When migrating to Exchange Online from a hosted Exchange or Gmail environment, you will generally have less access to the environment and as such less preparation work can be done.

The process will be similar to that of IMAP, whereby users are created in Office 365, followed by you working through the process of the third-party provider to get access to the existing mail system and have the migration provider (for example, MigrationWiz) move the content directly.

On-premises Exchange 2003 or later

A requirement of preparing to migrate to Exchange Online from Exchange Server 2003 or later is to ensure that the server can be reached using the RPC over HTTPS (Outlook Anywhere) method on port 443.

 You must have a valid SSL certificate installed from a trusted root Certificate Authority. Self-signed SSL certificates issued by your server will not work as they are not recognized by external sources as **trusted**.

To ensure your Exchange Server to be accessible by Office 365 and ready for migration, it is recommended that you test Outlook connectivity by using the Microsoft Remote Connectivity Analyzer (`https://testconnectivity.microsoft.com`).

1. Select the **Outlook Connectivity** test to be run:

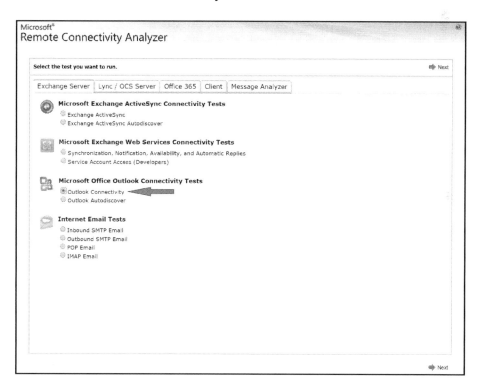

2. If you are using Exchange Server 2007 or later, and already have Autodiscover working, then select **User Autodiscover to detect settings**.

   Alternatively, if you do not have Autodiscover or are using Exchange Server 2003, you will need to input various information to enable the analyzer to connect and interrogate your server.

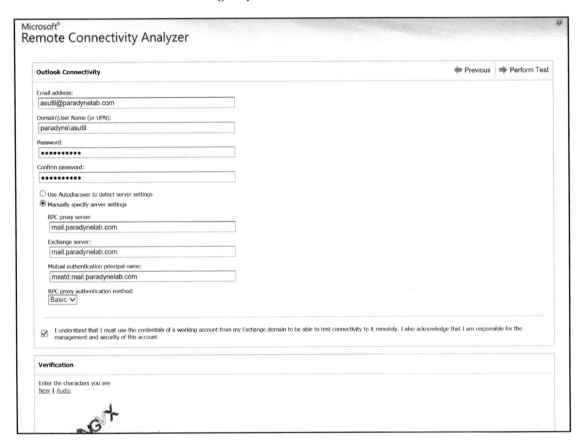

3. If your environment is correctly configured, the tests will complete successfully (with or without warnings).

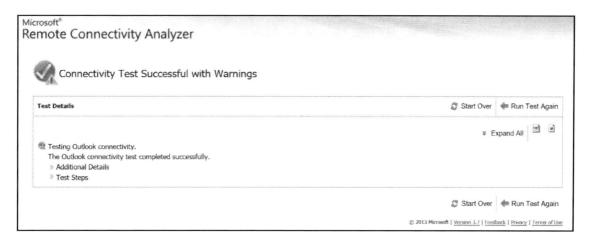

If the test failed, you will need to work through the issues listed to remedy them before attempting to run the analyzer again.

It is imperative that you achieve a successful test before attempting to perform a migration to Exchange Online.

Requirements for staged versus cutover migration

If you plan to perform a cutover migration of your Exchange Server to Exchange Online, there is no additional requirement for the implementation of the **Azure Active Directory Connect** (**AAD Connect**).

Conversely, however, a staged migration cannot be performed *without* the prior implementation of DirSync.

Previously the DirSync appliance could not be installed on a domain controller, which is no longer the case. Even though this is now possible, it must be approached with considerable thought due to the fact that the DirSync appliance requires a SQL Lite database to be installed. As such, the best practice is that it should be installed on a separate server, which is not always possible in SBS-based deployments.

Summary

In this chapter, we have walked you through some of the common scenarios seen when performing a simple migration to Exchange Online.

By now, your environment should be ready, and both you and your users ready to take the final step and begin migrating your emails to the cloud.

In the next chapter, we'll cover the steps required to perform the actual migration so that you can leave your existing mail platform in the dust!

6
Performing a Simple Migration

So far in this book, we have guided you in getting your Office 365 environment up and running, as well as acquainted you with the options available for your organization.

In the previous chapter, we walked you through the steps for preparing your environment for a simple migration to Exchange Online, as well as provided you with an overview of migration options.

In this chapter, we will walk you through the various options to get you migrated to Exchange Online successfully. We'll cover the following topics:

- Migrating from non-Exchange Server systems
- Migrating from Exchange Server

Let's take a look at the steps involved, in each of the migration processes in the following diagram. Looking at the steps involved we can see that if you are migrating from an Exchange Server it is much easier to perform using Outlook Anywhere. If you don't have an Exchange Server, then there are a few more steps involved when using IMAP, but we will cover all the steps in detail to ensure success:

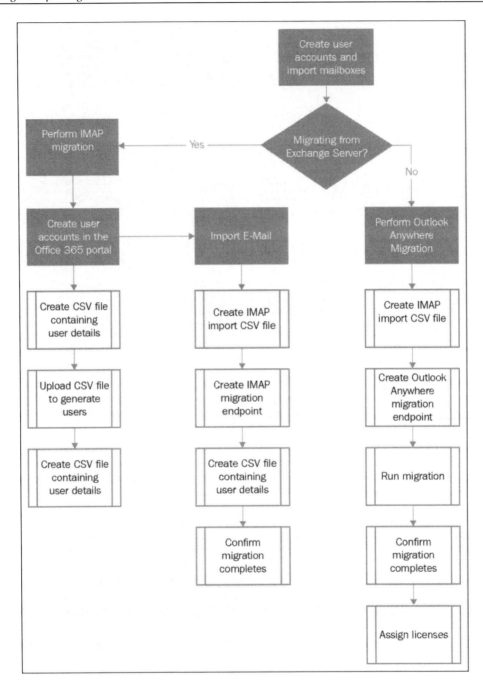

Migration from non-Exchange Server systems

If you are currently using an e-mail system that is not based on Exchange Server 2003, 2007, 2010, 2013, or 2016, the migration is not as seamless as moving directly from Exchange. However, it is still almost as quick and easy.

The two main steps involved in performing a simple migration from a non-Exchange system are creating the user accounts in Office 365 and then performing a mailbox content migration using one of several methods.

Creating user accounts

If you are creating more than a handful of users, it is recommended that you create the accounts using the bulk account creation method, as this will save a considerable amount of time.

This involves populating a **comma-separated values** (**CSV**) file with information about your users and uploading it to the Office 365 admin console.

While the CSV file allows you to populate many fields with user information, the two key fields required to create any user account are described in the following table:

Field	Description
User Name	The maximum total length of the username is 79 characters (including the @ symbol). It must be in the `name@domain.<extension>` format. The user's alias cannot exceed 30 characters and the domain name cannot exceed 48 characters.
Display Name	The display name can be up to 256 characters long. Usually it's the full name of the person.

It is also recommended that you fill out the **First Name** and **Last Name** fieldsâ⊚⊚each of which is limited to 64 characters.

CSV files must follow the same format every time, so if you choose to leave any fields blank, you must use a comma before moving on to the next field.

An example of using the **User Name**, **First Name**, **Last Name**, and **Display Name** fields looks as follows:

```
ian@office365lab.co.uk,Ian,Waters,Ian Waters,,,,,,,,,,
```

If we choose to use just the required fields, **User Name** and **Display Name**, the result would look as follows:

```
ian@office365lab.co.uk,,,Ian Waters,,,,,,,,,,
```

Despite the fact that we have not used the **First Name** or **Last Name** fields, we had to still put a comma to allow the CSV reader in Office 365 to treat the field as blank. The additional commas shown after the full name in the preceding example refer to the other fields; for example, **Department**, **Phone number**, **Country**, and many others that are commonly left blank.

You do not need to necessarily generate a CSV file yourself as a sample CSV file can be obtained from the **Users** section of the Office 365 administration portal. To obtain this sample CSV file or to begin importing your created CSV file, go to **Active Users** and then **Import multiple users**, as shown in the following screenshot:

You can select to download a blank CSV file that you can start using straight away, or download a sample to see some examples. Click on **Download a CSV file with headers only** or the sample file and edit the entries, then open it up using Notepad or another text editor:

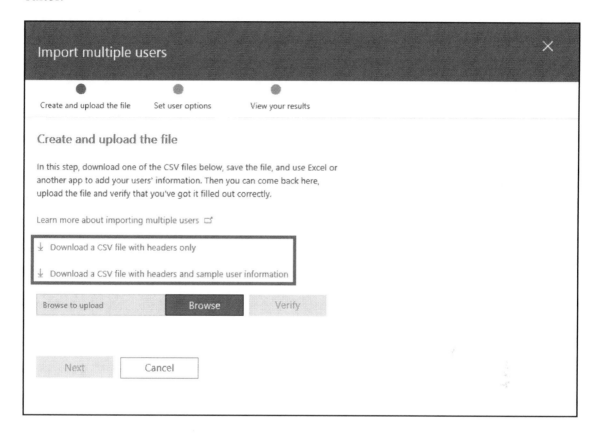

In this example, let's create seven users using a few basic fields. We can let the users update their profiles in their own time by logging into the Office 365 portal later. Here we create a CSV file containing the user account details, using the sample CSV file as a template. Save the file ready for the next step:

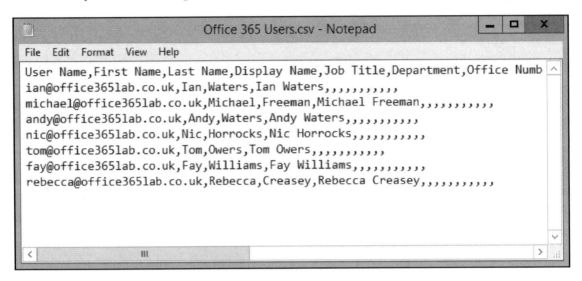

On the **Import** page, click on the **Browse** button and select our `Office 365 Users.csv` file. Then press the **Open** button:

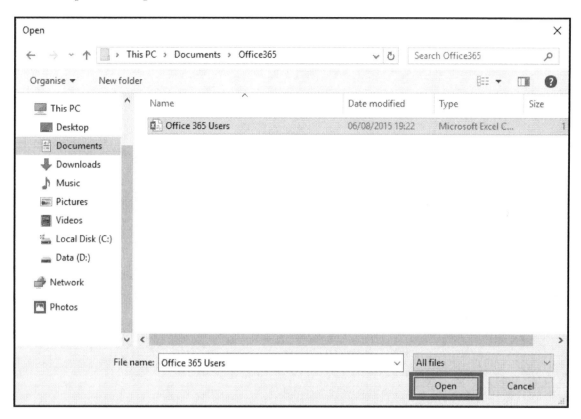

Press the **Verify** button to begin verification of our CSV file:

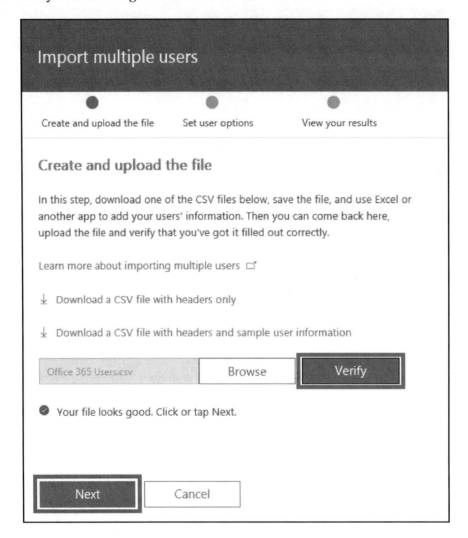

If the file passes validation, press **Next** to select the sign-in status and to assign licenses.

Step three lets you select whether the users can log in after the import has completed. During the start of your migration, you may want to stop the users from signing in until everything is ready, but in this example let's allow the users to log in so we can log in as them during the migration to check that things look correct along the way.

Next we select which licenses are going to be assigned to each user. If you don't want your users to have access to Skype for Business, then you can untick the box and continue. Here we want to make the most of the Office 365 features, so everything gets selected and we press **Next** to continue:

 In Chapter 11, *Performing a Hybrid Migration,* we demonstrate how to assign licenses to users using PowerShell.

In step three we can view the results, and in our case we see that all seven user accounts have been created. If you receive any errors here, you can click on **Download results** to view the errors. Here we will tick the box to e-mail the results to our admin account which includes all the usernames and passwords for the accounts. Press **Send and close**:

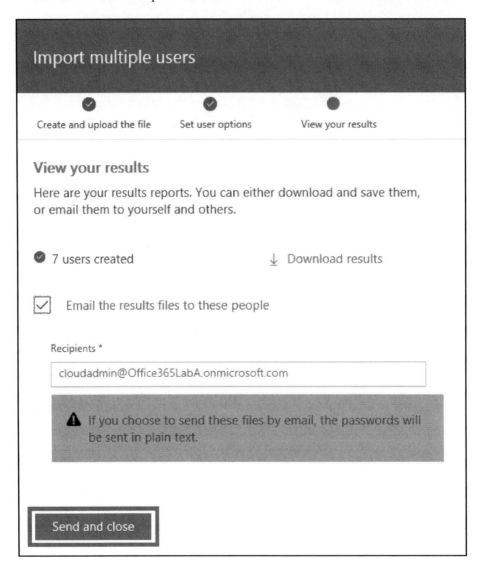

At this stage, we need to wait a few minutes while the system prepares a mailbox for each user. Typically, it only takes one to two minutes per user, so wait a few minutes and click on a user account to confirm each mailbox is ready. You can see if this process is still in progress because it will then say **We are preparing a mailbox for this user** under the primary e-mail address, as shown here:

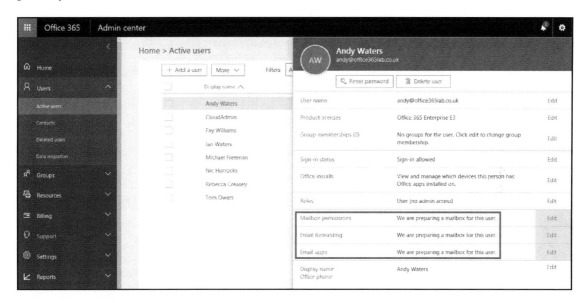

Importing mailbox content

At this point, you will need to determine which approach you should take to import mailbox content.

The following table will provide you with some guidance on selecting the best option:

Current mail setup	Recommended migration method.	Requirements
A few users with POP3 mailboxes using Outlook	Import PST files to new mailboxes.	Outlook
Many users with POP3 mailboxes using Outlook	Use the Microsoft PST capture tool. Alternatively, third-party tools, available from organizations such as www.messageops.com, may be used.	Outlook (x64), which can be downloaded from
IMAP-based mail system	Exchange Online built-in migration tool. Many Office 365 customers and partners prefer www.migrationwiz.com to perform migrations from hosted mailbox systems to Exchange Online.	CSV files
Google apps	MigrationWiz	CSV files Access to all mailboxes
Other hosted mail systems	MigrationWiz	CSV files Access to all mailboxes

As third-party mail solutions are not supported by Microsoft, it is recommended that you engage the supplier directly or a Microsoft Office 365 partner.

IMAP migration

IMAP migrations are a great way to get e-mail into Office 365 from other e-mail service providers, including Google mail. However, it does have a few drawbacks because the following items don't automatically get moved during the migration process:

- Contacts
- Tasks
- Calendars
- E-mail aliases
- Distribution groups

You have to manually export these items to a PST file and import them into the user's new e-mail profile which points to Office 365. That being said, the most time consuming part of the migration is getting e-mail migrated so this task can be run a few days before the planned changeover date. You are probably thinking *but what about new e-mail that comes in later, how will I migrate that?* Well don't worry, because as you will see later in this chapter, a migration batch will run incremental updates every 24 hours!

The key steps involved in performing an IMAP migration are as follows:

- Create an IMAP import CSV file
- Create an IMAP endpoint
- Run the migration to Exchange wizard

So now that we understand the manual processes involved in a successful IMAP migration, let's continue.

Create an IMAP import CSV file

When we start the migration wizard, it will ask for a CSV file containing the e-mail addresses, usernames, and passwords for the users we wish to migrate from the source e-mail system.

The CSV file you create should be in the following format:

```
EmailAddress,UserName,Password
```

These fields are explained as follows:

- `EmailAddress`: It specifies the user ID for the user's cloud-based mailbox
- `UserName`: It specifies the user log on name for the user's mailbox on the IMAP server
- `Password`: It is the password for the user's account in the IMAP messaging system

Here is what the CSV file looks like for our live migration:

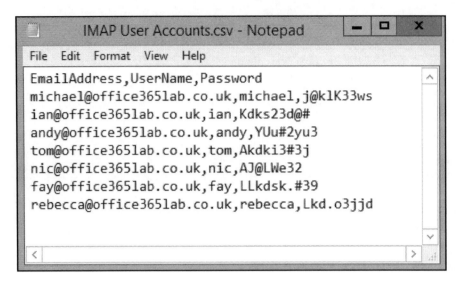

We can see our seven user accounts displaying their Office 365 e-mail addresses and their corresponding IMAP usernames and passwords. Save this file somewhere handy, ready for the next stage—creating an IMAP endpoint.

Creating an IMAP endpoint

As with the other endpoints we saw in the previous chapters, an IMAP endpoint specifies the server connection details required to connect to the source e-mail server. Let's start by going into the Exchange Admin console by clicking on **Admin centers** and then **Exchange** from the main portal:

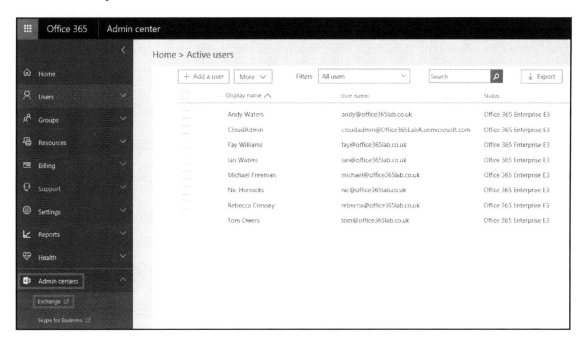

From the **Exchange admin center** dashboard, click on **Migration**:

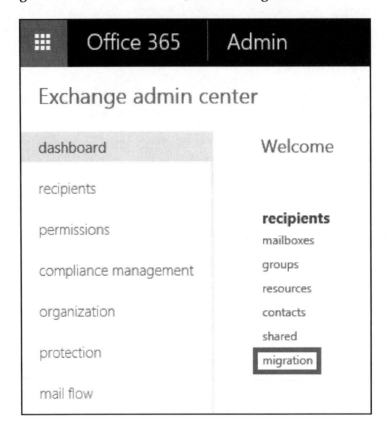

You should be directed straight into the migration page, but if not, click on the **migration** button along the top of the page. Next, click on the three dots followed by the **Migration endpoints** button to begin creating the actual endpoint we will use for this migration:

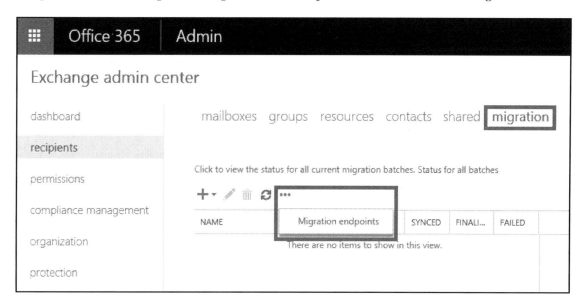

On the migration endpoints page, click on the add button highlighted in the following screenshot:

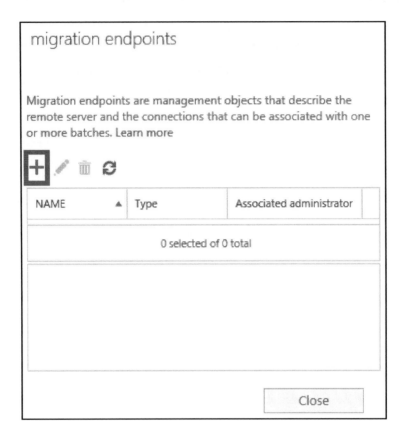

Next, we select the type of endpoint we want to use. We will be looking at the other options on this page later on in this chapter, so for now select **IMAP** and press **Next**:

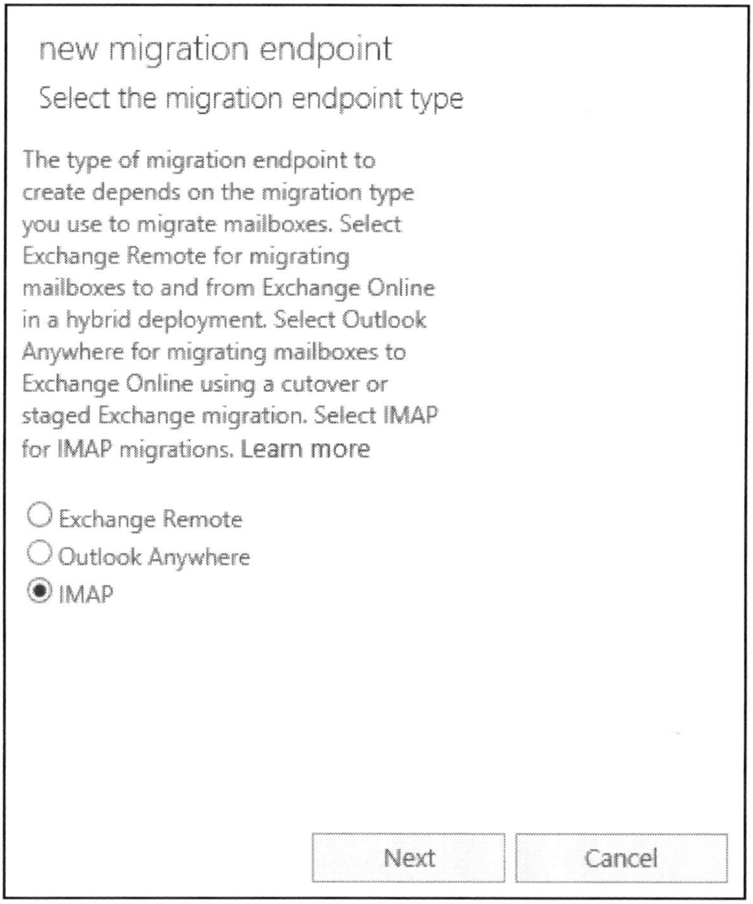

new migration endpoint

Select the migration endpoint type

The type of migration endpoint to create depends on the migration type you use to migrate mailboxes. Select Exchange Remote for migrating mailboxes to and from Exchange Online in a hybrid deployment. Select Outlook Anywhere for migrating mailboxes to Exchange Online using a cutover or staged Exchange migration. Select IMAP for IMAP migrations. Learn more

○ Exchange Remote
○ Outlook Anywhere
◉ IMAP

Next   Cancel

Here we specify the FQDN of the IMAP server we are connecting to, along with the authentication, encryption type, and port number. Enter the required details for your server and click **Next**:

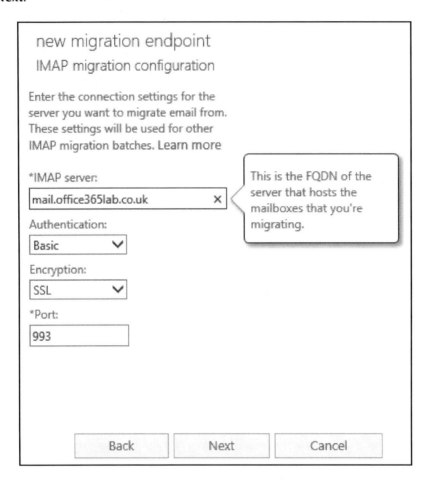

Now we give the new migration batch a name, which can be any short name to identify your migration on the system. We also need to specify the maximum number of concurrent migrations and incremental sync jobs. There is a limit of 100 concurrent migrations for each type of migration endpoint, so if we have no other migrations in progress we can select a value of 100 so the maximum number is spread over all the batches.

When selecting a value, we need to consider our bandwidth requirements, the size of mailboxes, and the possible load it could put on our Exchange Servers. I recommend limiting the number of concurrent migrations to ten so as to not slow down our network for users. Since migration batches will incrementally sync every 24 hours, there should be no need to try and rush the migration. If we do, then the batch can pause due to slow response from the Exchange Server or due to connection timeouts on our internet connection.

We will be going into the bandwidth considerations in more detail in `Chapter 7`, *Preparing for a Hybrid Deployment and Migration*, in the section named *Bandwidth evaluations*. Be sure to take note and apply them to your environment during the migration planning phase.

Here we have a handful of users with small mailboxes so a value of ten is acceptable. Press the **new** button to finish creating the endpoint:

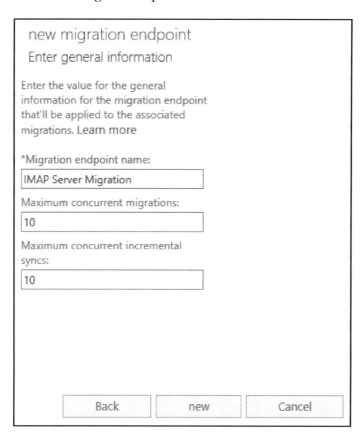

If everything is okay with the endpoint it will show up in the endpoint list as shown in the following screenshot. So let's move on to setup a migration task:

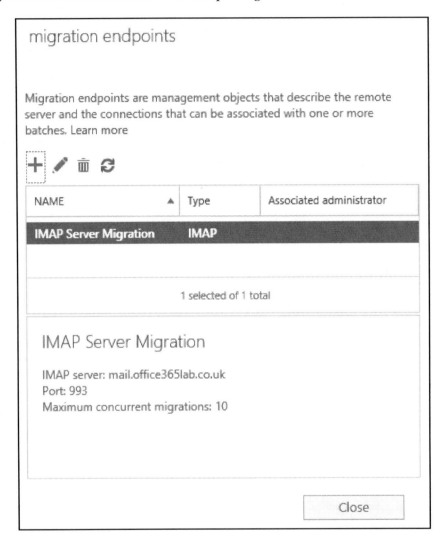

Running the migrate to Exchange Online wizard

To start the migrate to Exchange wizard, click on the plus symbol and select **Migrate to Exchange Online**:

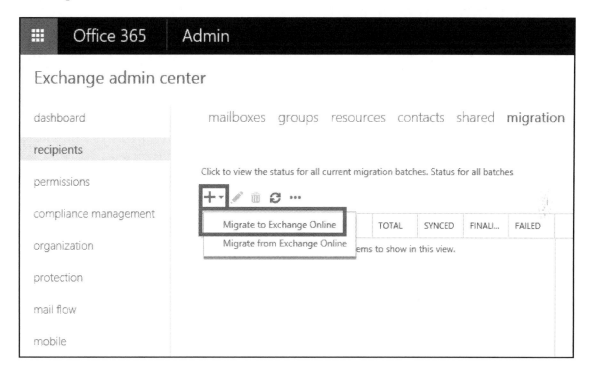

Select **IMAP migration** and press **Next** to continue. We have already looked at a few of the other options shown here in previous chapters in the book and we will be covering the cutover migration method later in this chapter:

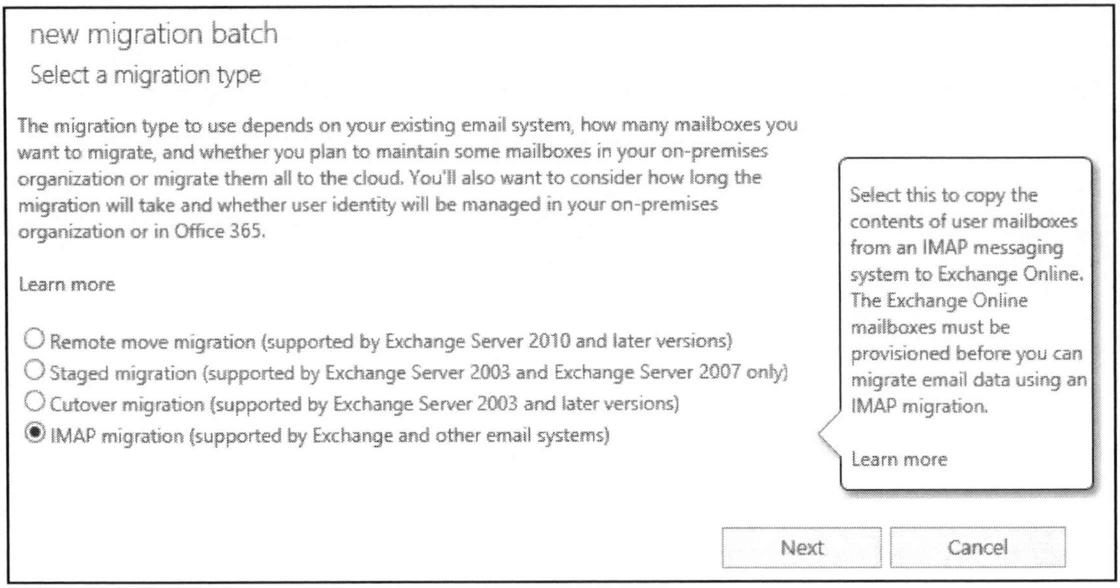

new migration batch

Select a migration type

The migration type to use depends on your existing email system, how many mailboxes you want to migrate, and whether you plan to maintain some mailboxes in your on-premises organization or migrate them all to the cloud. You'll also want to consider how long the migration will take and whether user identity will be managed in your on-premises organization or in Office 365.

Learn more

○ Remote move migration (supported by Exchange Server 2010 and later versions)
○ Staged migration (supported by Exchange Server 2003 and Exchange Server 2007 only)
○ Cutover migration (supported by Exchange Server 2003 and later versions)
⦿ IMAP migration (supported by Exchange and other email systems)

Select this to copy the contents of user mailboxes from an IMAP messaging system to Exchange Online. The Exchange Online mailboxes must be provisioned before you can migrate email data using an IMAP migration.

Learn more

Next   Cancel

We now need to select the `IMAP User Accounts.csv` file we created earlier by clicking on **Browse** and selecting the file. Hopefully, you kept it in a safe place! Once selected, press **Next** to continue:

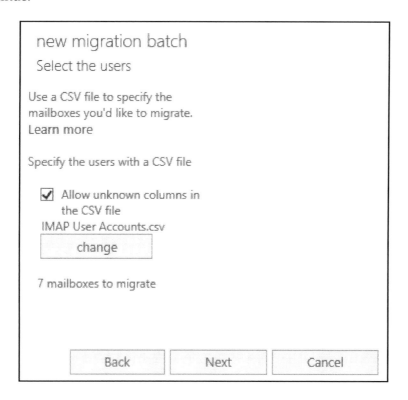

new migration batch

Select the users

Use a CSV file to specify the mailboxes you'd like to migrate.
Learn more

Specify the users with a CSV file

☑ Allow unknown columns in the CSV file
IMAP User Accounts.csv

change

7 mailboxes to migrate

Back Next Cancel

The wizard will check connectivity to your IMAP server using your settings before proceeding to the next screen. Press **Next** to continue:

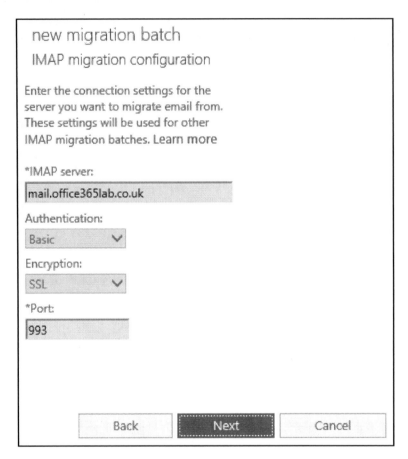

We are now given the chance to specify any folders we want to exclude from the migration. During our migration preparation phase, we want to work with the users to reduce the size of their mailboxes. This gives us the best chance for a swift and successful migration.

It is recommended to exclude the trash folders or deleted items to minimize the mailboxcontent and the time required to migrate. At the time of writing, only up to 50,000 items can be migrated (including calendar and contacts):

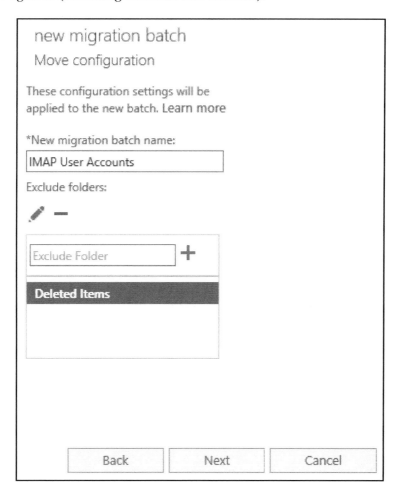

Next, we can select an e-mail address which will be sent the migration report when it completes. Here we select our **CloudAdmin** account. We also need to specify if the migration process will start automatically or if it will need manual starting. It may be convenient for us to configure the migration during business hours and resolve any errors so we can easily and quickly start it in the evening when there are less users on the network. We want it to start now, so we select **Automatically start the batch** and press **new** to continue:

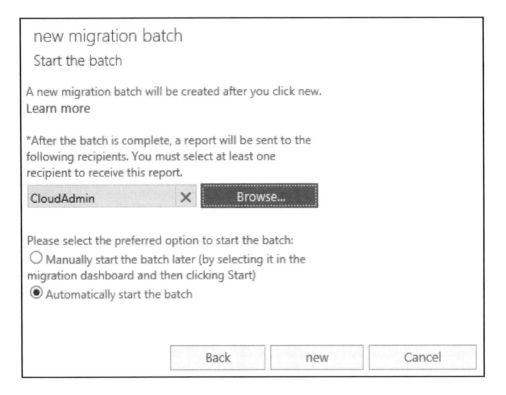

Once the wizard window closes, we are shown the status of the current batch. It will take a few minutes to initialize but you can check the status of each user's mailbox by clicking on **Status for all batches**:

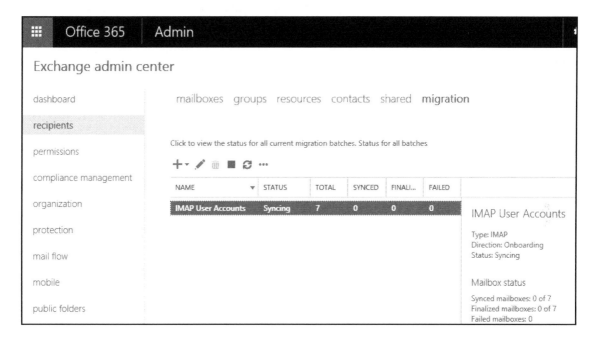

A few minutes later, we can see in our environment that the users' mailboxes have already synchronized. You can see the number of items in each mailbox in the **ITEMS SYNCED** column. I did say our users had small mailboxes! You can also see the number of skipped items. It is quite normal to see a number of failed items, especially on older, larger mailboxes, but having a high number may warrant making a note of so you can have the user check over the mailbox to ensure nothing major is missing:

IMAP User Accounts

🗑 ⟳

IDENTITY ▲	STATUS	ITEMS SYNCED	ITEMS SKIPPED
andy@office365lab.co.uk	Synced	2	0
fay@office365lab.co.uk	Synced	2	0
ian@office365lab.co.uk	Synced	7	0
michael@office365lab.co.uk	Synced	2	0
nic@office365lab.co.uk	Synced	3	0
rebecca@office365lab.co.uk	Synced	7	0
tom@office365lab.co.uk	Synced	3	0

1 selected of 7 total

Using our bulk import report e-mail that we received earlier while creating our users, we can log in as a few users to check whether things look good. Here we log in as Rebecca and everything looks great. She can log in to the Office 365 portal and all her e-mails are ready:

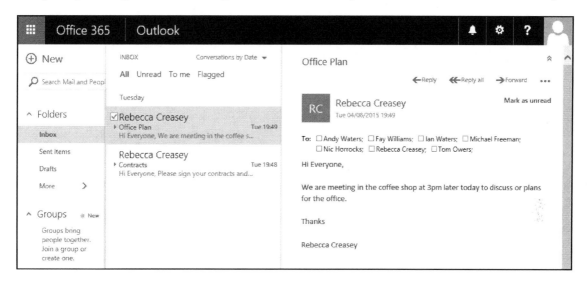

You may remember me saying earlier that the migration job will run an incremental sync. This is a great feature of migration batches because so long as the migration job is left running on the system, it will perform an incremental sync of all the mailboxes in the batch every 24 hours. Knowing this, you can start your live migration days or even weeks before the final migration takes place. Getting the e-mail into Office 365 is usually the longest part of the migration process, so incremental syncs make the process a lot easier.

In our migration we wait 24 hours and log Rebecca in to the Office 365 portal and open up her e-mail. Voila! All new e-mail has been automatically synced from the on-premises Exchange Server:

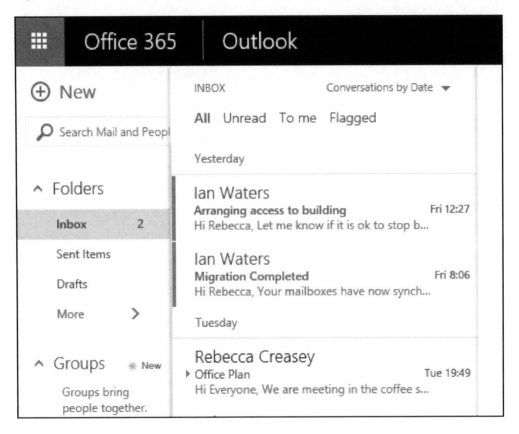

Migrating from Exchange Server

If you are migrating from an existing Exchange Server environment, the steps are relatively similar to the IMAP migration method. Office 365 Business Essentials and Office 365 Business premium plans allow Directory Synchronization, but we need to decide whether we are going to utilize it in our environment. If you are migrating to Office 365 to decommission your office server and remove Active Directory, then you won't be able to make use of it. However, if you are keeping a server with Active Directory for user and computer management, you will need to perform a hybrid or staged migration. In this example, we are migrating to Office 365 to remove the need for an onsite server, so we will perform a cutover migration, which gives us lots of benefits over a simple IMAP migration. As well as migrating each mailbox, like we did using IMAP, we get the following benefits:

- Users are automatically created or matched to the existing users in Office 365
- E-mail aliases assigned to users in the on-premises Exchange are copied to the 365 account
- User calendars are migrated
- Tasks are migrated
- Distribution groups are automatically generated along with aliases
- Contacts are migrated

The key steps involved in performing a migration from an on-premise, Exchange Server are:

1. Ensure that remote connectivity is possible using RPC over HTTP (as discussed in Chapter 5, *Preparing for a Simple Migration*).
2. Grant the migration user full access to the mailboxes or mailbox store.
3. Create an Outlook Anywhere migration endpoint.
4. Run through the migrate to Exchange Online wizard.
5. Assign Office 365 licenses to the user accounts.
6. Reset all user passwords.

Granting access to all mailboxes in Exchange Server

Assuming that you have successfully prepared your Exchange Server environment to allow RPC over HTTP, and tested it using the Exchange Remote Connectivity Analyzer, we can now move towards the steps involved in migrating the mailboxes.

The first task required is to provide the migration administrator permissions to access all the mailboxes in order to migrate the contents to Exchange Online.

Assigning permissions in Exchange Server 2003

The process for this is relatively straightforward. Follow these steps:

1. Start **Active Directory Users and Computers**.
2. On the **View** menu, ensure that the **Advanced Features** checkbox is checked.
3. Select all the users you want to migrate, right-click on the selection, and click on **Properties**.
4. In the **Exchange Advanced** tab, click **Mailbox Rights**.
5. Click **Add**, select the migration administration account you are using, and click **OK**.
6. Make sure that the user is selected in the **Name** box. In the **Permissions** list, click **Allow** next to **Full Access**, and click **OK**.

Assigning permissions in Exchange Server 2007, 2010, 2013, and 2016

Using the Exchange PowerShell console, we can assign full access permissions to all the mailboxes with one simple script:

```
Get-Mailbox | Add-MailboxPermission -User '<Migration Administration
Account>' -AccessRights 'FullAccess'
```

So in our migration, we run the script specifying the domain administrator account, but you can use any account you wish:

Create a new Outlook Anywhere migration endpoint

An Outlook Anywhere endpoint allows the Office365 system to connect to the on-premises Exchange Server in the same way that Outlook uses when connecting remotely. This allows it to access the full mailbox, contacts, calendars, and tasks.

Select **Outlook Anywhere** and press **Next** to continue:

Now enter the e-mail address, username, and password of our migration user who we granted full access to all mailboxes earlier. Press the **Next** button to continue:

new migration endpoint
Enter on-premises account credentials

Enter the email address of one of the users whose on-premises mailbox will be migrated using this endpoint. Also enter the name and password for an on-premises user account that has administrative privileges to perform the migration. This information will be used to detect the migration endpoint and test the connectivity to the user mailbox. Learn more

Email address:

administrator@office365lab.co.uk

Account with privileges
(domain\user name):

office365lab\administrator

Password of account with privileges:

●●●●●●●●●

| Back | Next | Cancel |

If the system fails to connect to the on-premises server, you will be asked to manually enter the connection details. In our case, we enter the FQDN we use to connect to the exchange outside our network for both the Exchange Server and **Remote Procedure Call (RPC)** server. Set your authentication type and specify whether you are using a domain administrator account to connect to Exchange. If you are not using a domain administrator account, then set the **Mailbox Permission** drop-down box to **Full Access**. Press the **Next** button to continue:

Choose an appropriate name to identify the endpoint on the system later and select the maximum number of concurrent migrations the system will attempt. The advice is the same as before when we looked at how to perform an IMAP migration; select a low number so we don't overload the onsite Exchange Server and the internet connection. Press **New** to finish creating the endpoint:

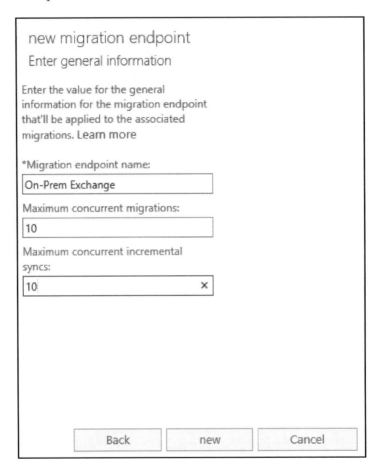

Migrate to Exchange Online wizard

Log in to the Exchange Control Panel in Office 365, click on **migration**, click the plus symbol, and then click **Migrate to Exchange Online**, as we did to start the migration wizard earlier. The only option we will select differently is on the **Select a migration type** screen. Here we select a **Cutover migration**.

A cutover migration is used to create identical mailboxes in Office 365 so we can simply stop using the local on-premises Exchange Server and decommission it later. As with the IMAP migration, this is a big bang approach because all our Exchange mailboxes will be switched over at the same time. I use this method in organizations where they have 50 users or less because we can easily upgrade and reconfigure the Outlook e-mail client as well as the decommissioned exchange in a weekend's work. If you intend on your users exclusively using the Office 365 portal to access e-mail, then you can easily use this method to migrate more users since you won't need to reconfigure anything but merely remove the users e-mail profiles from their PCs. For larger networks, it's recommended you use a staged or remote move migration because they allow you to use both the on-premises, Exchange and Office 365 at the same time.

We are only migrating a handful of users here and will be decommissioning all our onsite servers, so let's continue by selecting **Cutover migration** and press the **Next** button:

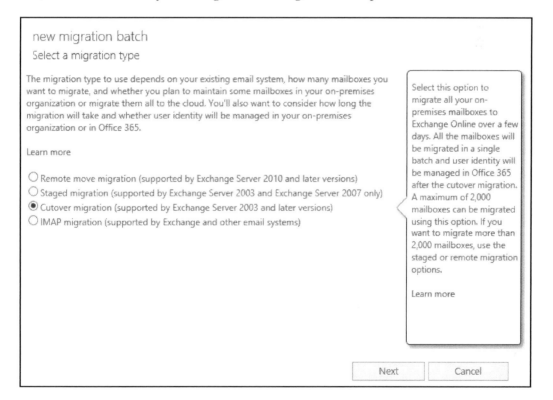

Once you have completed the migration wizard, you can view its progress by clicking on **View details**, which is available by highlighting the migration.

You may have noticed we haven't needed to create any user accounts in our Exchange cutover migration. Well, that is another time saver and benefit of migrating from an on-premises Exchange Serverâ◎◎the migration task automatically generates all user accounts for us! In the following screenshot, we can see this in action as it is showing a status of **Provisioning** for each mailbox hosted on our local Exchange Server:

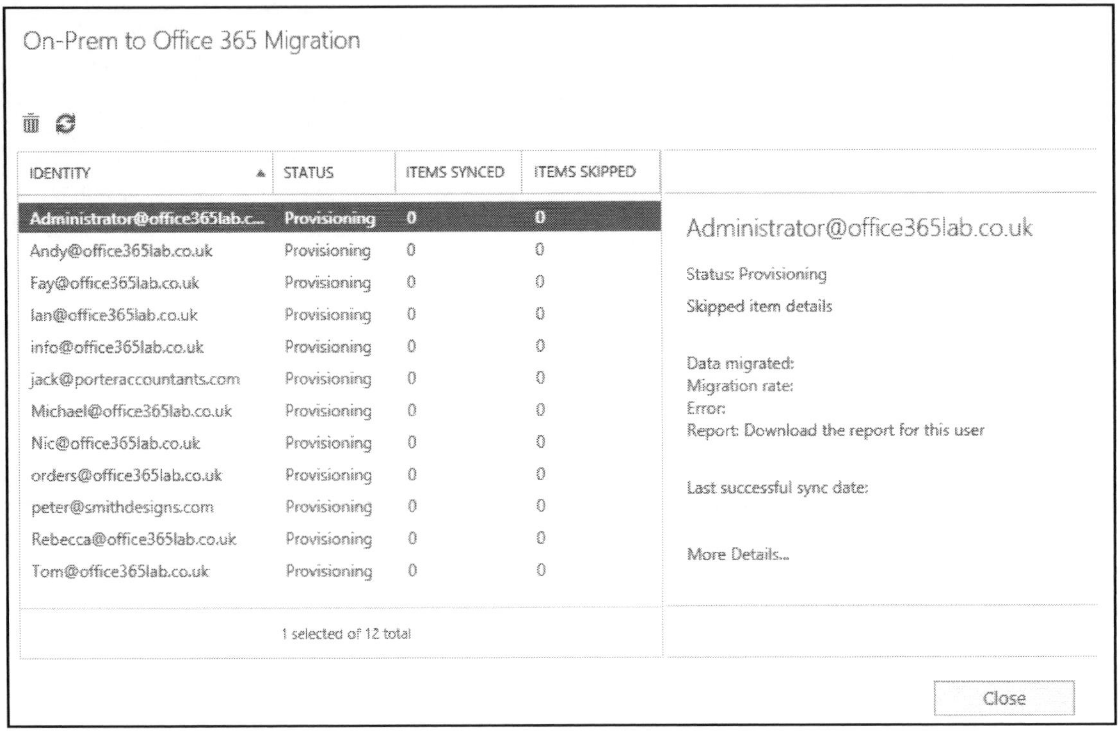

After a few minutes or hours, depending on the number and size of your users' mailboxes, you will receive the migration report. You can see that at the bottom of this report, it tells you that licenses still need applying to each of the new user accounts, so let's continue and do that now:

Assign licenses to new user accounts

As shown in the earlier chapters, we can bulk edit all our new user accounts by entering the **Users** menu and then clicking on **Active users**. Tick each user and select **Edit product licenses** from the right-hand menu:

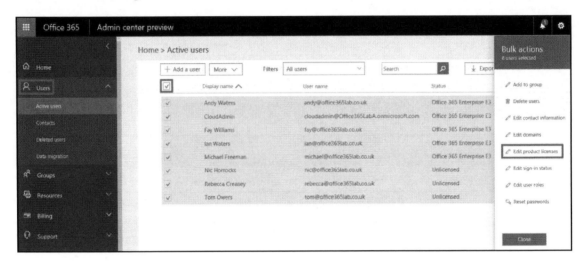

Run through and accept all defaults until you get to the **Select product licenses** page. At this point you only need to select Exchange Online plan 1, which gives the user the rights to use e-mail. In our migration, we are going to assign all features available in our E3 subscription to our users and press the **Replace** button to apply the licenses. On the next screen it will let you know if the licenses were applied successfully. So click **Close** to complete assigning the licenses:

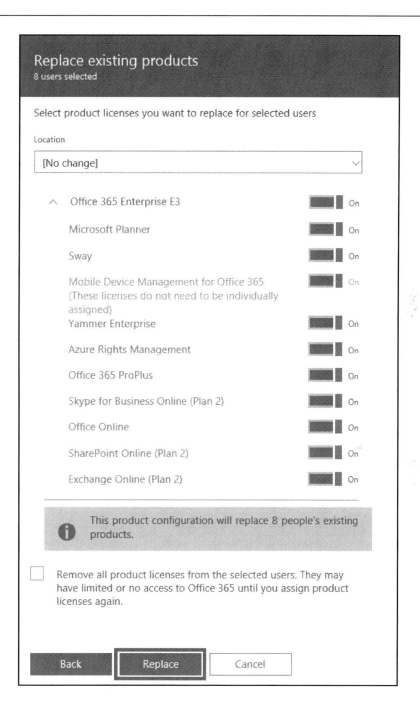

Reset all user passwords

Because the migration task created the users for us and it doesn't send us a list of passwords, we need to manually reset the password of each user. To do this, log in to the **Admin center** portal, select **Users**, then **Active users**, then select all our users, and finally select **Reset passwords** from the right-hand menu. This will reset all the passwords in bulk and we can send the results to an e-mail address for future reference:

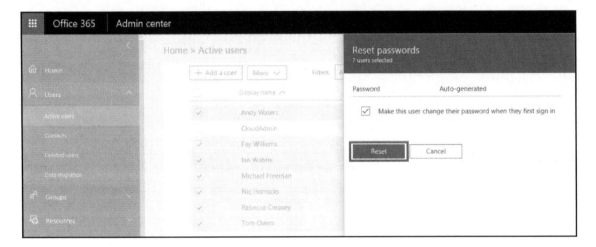

Summary

In this chapter, we saw how to perform the two methods available for performing migrations from a variety of systems to Exchange Online.

By now, your migration should be well on its way and there are several post-migration considerations for you to review, which are covered in Chapter 10, *Deploying a Hybrid Infrastructure – Exchange Hybrid*.

7
Preparing for a Hybrid Deployment and Migration

By now, you should have a relatively defined plan on what integration services you plan to leverage from Microsoft Office 365, along with how you plan to scale out these services. Our next objective is to start preparing our environment for the integration services. In this chapter, we will focus on working through the various core services available to Office 365 and their integration requirements for your environment. We will assume you have an existing Exchange Organization within your environment, consisting of Exchange 2013, or you are planning to add Exchange 2013 for this effort. To prepare, we will focus on the following areas:

- Preparing your Office 365 subscription
- Active Directory preparation and readiness check
- Basic infrastructure preparation
- Defining the migration process
- Bandwidth requirements

Preparing your Office 365 subscription

As you prepare for integration with Office 365, one of the first and most important steps is to ensure you have registered all your **User Principal Names** (**UPNs**) and e-mail domains you plan to use with the service. This also includes any e-mail domains you plan to coexist with but will leave on-premises. Let's recap on why both UPNs and e-mail domains are important to register.

A UPN is an individual's log on to Active Directory. In many cases, you are likely to use `domain\%username%` as the user log on. We need to change this to their UPN, which is also likely `%username%@domain` (in some cases it may be `domain.local` or a `public domain.com`). We need to ensure your UPN is a public domain. Ideally, we should have the public domain match the user's primary e-mail address.

E-mail domains are also important to register within Office 365. First off, you cannot assign a primary or secondary e-mail address to a mailbox if the e-mail domain is not registered with the service. Also, if you choose to enable Exchange Hybrid, you will not be able to see free/busy for on-premises users if those e-mail domains (set as their primary e-mail address) are also not registered within the service. If you do not plan to use that e-mail domain or no longer need it, remove it from your user's `email/proxyAddresses` attributes.

To register e-mail domains, you simply need to go to the Office 365 admin portal at `https:/ /portal.office.com/AdminPortal` and log on as a global administrator or the account you signed up to the service with. Click on **Domains**.

Now, add and verify all the domains by repeating the following process:

1. Click **Add domain**, as shown in the following screenshot:

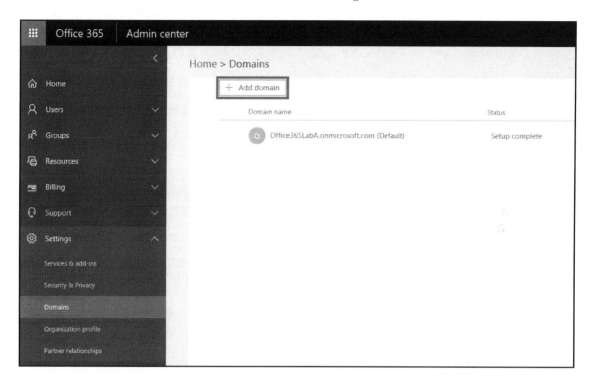

2. The **Add a domain** wizard should have now opened.

3. Now type the domain name you plan to add to your subscription and click **Next** as shown in the following screenshot:

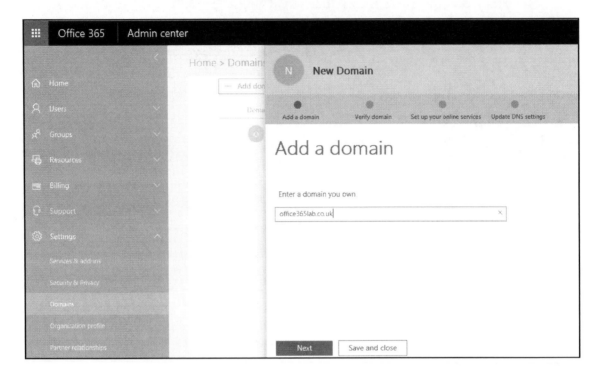

4. You must now create a record within your DNS provider to validate your domain. To do so, select either **TXT record** or **MX Record**. In this example, we will select **TXT record**. Keep the page open to reference this information in the next step.

5. Most DNS providers allow you to create a **TXT record** within your service. If you do not see this option in your DNS admin console, contact your DNS provider to have one added manually. Create the required **TXT record** in your domain's DNS. As an example, the following is what the entry would look like within your DNS service:

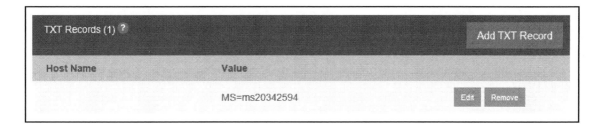

6. Once you have added your TXT record to your DNS provider, click **Verify**. If your domain does not verify, you may see the following message. If you do wait a few minutes until DNS propagates, but you can come back and verify your domain at any time:

> ⚠ We didn't find the record you added for office365lab.co.uk. If you just added this record please allow 5 to 10 minutes for the change to be replicated through the system, sometime it can take significantly longer depending on your registrar.

7. Once you click **Verify**, you enter **Set up your online services** page, as shown in the following screenshot:

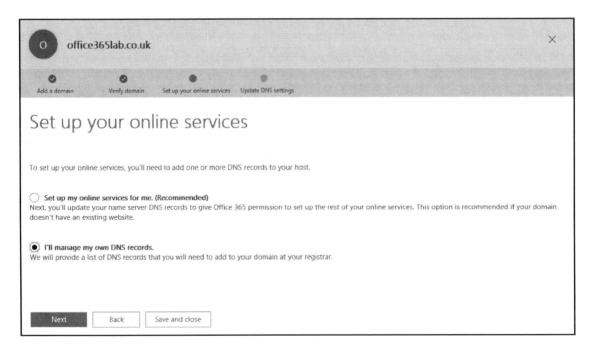

In the **Setup your online services** section, you will need to decide whether you want Office 365 to manage your DNS or if you want to do it yourself. If you choose **Set up my online services for me** then Office 365 will take over DNS management of your domain. If you want to keep DNS management with your current provider, then select **I'll manage my own DNS records**. Here, we select to manage our own DNS records and press **Next**.

Now we are presented with a list of all the DNS records we need to set for the domain. Ensure all the entries are added so that all Office 365 features work as expected. Once you have added the records you will again have to wait for DNS to propagate before the changes can be verified.

Be very careful when changing these DNS records because updating existing records in DNS can break your on-premises configuration. For example, editing the MX records will make e-mail flow directly into Office 365, which you may not want at this stage. Also, changing the Autodiscover record may prevent the users from accessing their mailboxes on-premises correctly. You can update these at any time when you are ready to migrate these services fully over to Office 365.

Once you have added the records, click **Verify** as shown in the following screenshot to continue. If verification fails, wait for a few minutes and try again. But remember, sometimes DNS takes 24 hours or more to propagate completely:

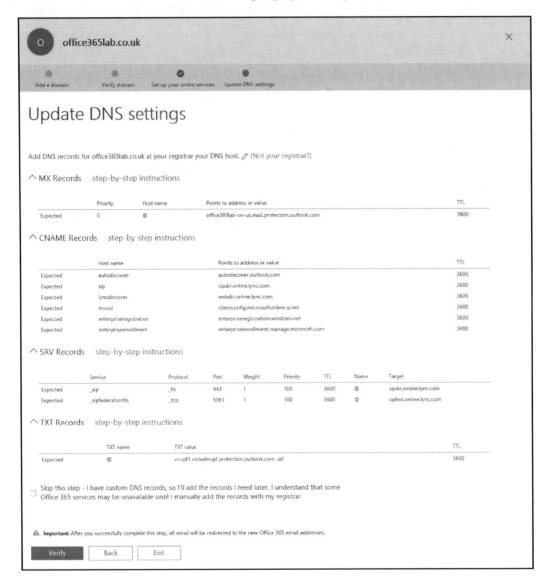

Once the DNS has propagated and verification completes, you will see the following screen indicating that you have been successful in adding the domain to your tenant:

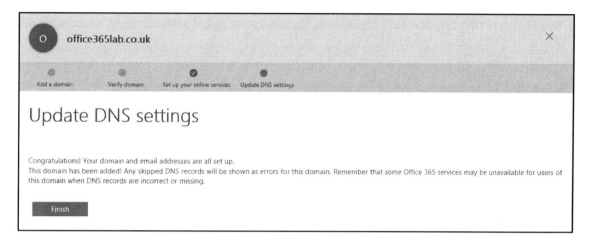

Click **Finish** to complete the wizard, and you will see the domain listed in the **Domain name** list, as shown in the following screenshot:

Repeat these steps to add the remaining UPNs and e-mail domains.

Active Directory preparation and readiness check

Our next focus is to ensure **Active Directory** (**AD**) is ready for Office 365. The purpose of this section is your readiness to synchronize AD with Office 365, leverage AD FS, and enable Exchange Federation.

To easily identify the necessary changes, run the Office 365 health, readiness, and connectivity checks tool at `https://portal.office.com/tools`. Be sure to run this tool from a Windows-based workstation, while connected to the same Active Directory forest and Exchange Organization that you will be connecting to Office 365.

Launch the tool and select both the **Quick** and **Advanced** check boxes, and then click on **Next** to run the checks as shown in the following screenshot. Also, you may have to install some desktop components for Office 365. These components may include the Azure Active Directory Sign-in Assistant and the Azure Active Directory Module for Windows PowerShell:

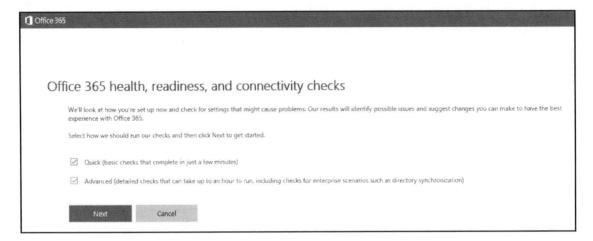

By running this tool, we will uncover key changes that may be necessary to leverage the service. Once you run this tool, you will be able to identify potential issues or changes required for the following:

- Mail/e-mail domains
- Forest/domain structure
- Active Directory users, contacts, and, group objects, and single sign-on
- User software

Mail/e-mail domains

As mentioned in the previous section, *Preparing Your Subscription*, add all your e-mail domains to the Office 365 Admin center. This tool will highlight all the e-mail domains discovered from users within your messaging system. If you are unaware of it, this tool will help you uncover those e-mail users. To easily find users with an e-mail domain attached to them, open **Active Directory Users and Computers** from a domain controller within your Exchange Organization. From there, do a custom search and choose your domain. Now go to the **Advanced** tab and type `proxyAddresses=smtp:*@domain.com` (`domain.com` being the domain that you are searching for users bound to).

The following is an example of the query:

Forest/domain structure

Directory synchronization using Azure AD Connect and Active Directory Federation services supports single and multi-forest configurations, including all sub-domains under those forests. Verify that all the accounts you plan to synchronize will be accounts you plan to directly log on with. In addition, it's assumed you have already deployed Exchange 2013 service pack 1. The only catch to the multi-forest support is that Public Folder migration or hybrid configuration is only supported in single forest configurations. If you only have small Public Folders, using export/import migration methods may suffice, or you may have to look into using third-party tools to migrate your Public Folders.

 Source: `https://technet.microsoft.com/en-GB/library/jj873754(v=exchg.15).aspx`

Active Directory users, contacts, and, group objects and single sign-on

Now we review the domains, users, and groups, and sections for attribute updates that may be necessary.

The key items to address are mostly user, contacts, and group objects when you integrate with Office 365. It's likely you will not have to change many of your user objects, unless you have steered far away from AD best practices. The item that comes up frequently is unsupported characters applied to objects that will synchronize. The following are the attributes you should review as you prepare for synchronization.

Users

Quite often, the following attributes cause conflict with directory synchronization, so review objects with invalid characters and check for additional constraints, such as:

- `sAMAccountName`:
    - Invalid character examples: !, #, $, %, ^, &, {, },|, \, /, {, `, ~, ",[,], :, @, <, >, +, =, ;, ?, *
    - Maximum number of 20 characters
- `displayName`:
    - Invalid character examples: ?, @, +

- `mail:`
  - Invalid character examples: [, !, #, $, %, &, *, +,\, /, =, ?, ^, `, {, },]
- `mailNickname:`
  - Invalid character examples: \, !, #, $, %, &, *, +, /, =, ?, ^, `, {, }, |, ~, <, >, (,), ', ;, :, „ [,], ", @ and no spaces
  - Maximum of 64 characters
  - Must not begin or end with a period
  - No duplicates allowed
- `proxyAddresses:`
  - Invalid character examples: [, !, #, $, %, &, *, +, \, /, =, ?, ^, `, {, },]
  - Maximum of 265 characters per address
  - No duplicates allowed
- `userPrincipalName:`
  - Invalid character examples: }, {, #, ', *, +,), (, >, <, \, /, =, ?, `
  - Maximum of 64 characters can be used in front of the @ sign
  - Maximum of 256 characters preceding the @ sign
  - No duplicates allowed

Groups

In order for a group to be mail enabled, it requires a display name and an e-mail address. The same invalid characters for a user object apply here.

Contacts

Contacts require a `displayName`, `proxyAddress`, and `targetAddress`. The same invalid characters for user objects apply here.

Directory Synchronization checking tools

Not too long ago, Microsoft started releasing tools to help administrators resolve common Directory Synchronization issues. First they released the IdFix tool application, and have now started to implement the same checks in a new online scanning tool. Both these tools check all the issues we have been reviewing in this chapter. Although it's a good idea to know what the common causes of synchronization failures are, these tools help you quickly identify any minor mistakes and major issues that need to be resolved.

IdFix

The IdFixtool should be downloaded to a domain joined workstation and run from a domain administrator account in the domain. Download the tool from `https://www.microsoft.com/en-gb/download/details.aspx?id=36832`.

Follow these steps to check for any potential synchronization issues caused by configuration issues within your Active Directory objects:

1. Launch the IdFix tool and press the cog icon in the top right of the window:

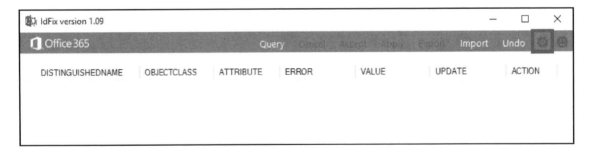

2. Update the settings to include all domains you intend to synchronize and change the rules to **Dedicated**, which will perform checks on additional objects in your domains. Click **OK** to return to the main window:

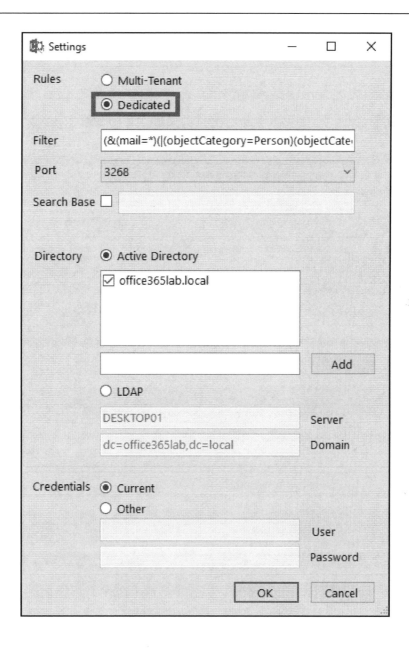

3. Press **Query** from the main window, which will trigger the software to run its checks on the Active Directory objects in your domains:

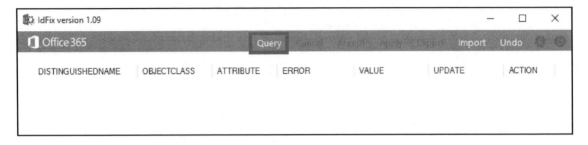

4. You will now need to resolve any issues found by the tool. Here we can see that several objects are missing their **displayName** and **targetAddress** attributes. Also, note here that the **Marketing** group has a typo in the domain. This tool will also identify missing domains in your environment that may need adding to the Office 365 portal before they can be successfully synchronized. Since there are few errors here and the updates are easy, we can specify an action for each error. Here we select **EDIT** so the program changes the incorrect values for those shown in the **UPDATE** column. Press **Apply** to have the values updated for you:

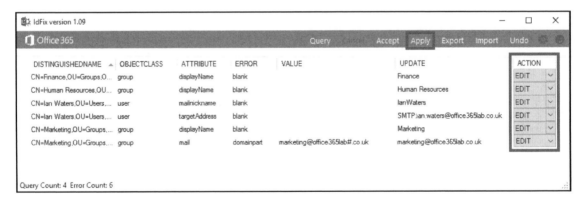

If you have several errors, then it's a good idea to export the data and resolve issues on a one-to-one basis. This will stop the program from making changes you may not want if you incorrectly chose the action type on any of them.

Once you have used the IdFixtool to identify and resolve potential synchronization issues, move on to the Directory Synchronization readiness wizard to check for any other issues that may be present.

Directory Synchronization readiness wizard

To perform a check on your Active Directory using the **Directory Synchronization** readiness wizard, follow these steps:

1. Log in to **Admin center** from a domain joined workstation logged in using a domain administrator account, and click **Settings**, s**ervices & add-ins** and then **Directory Synchronization**:

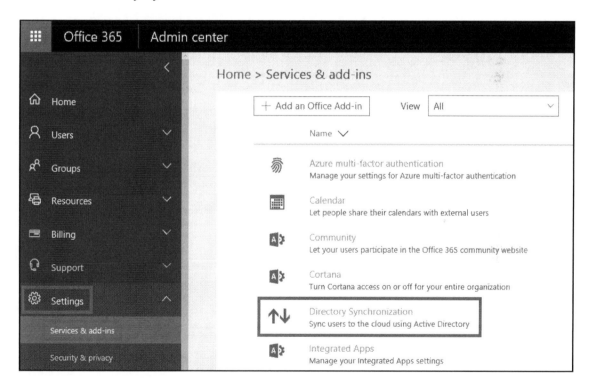

2. Launch the readiness wizard by clicking on **Go to the DirSync readiness wizard**:

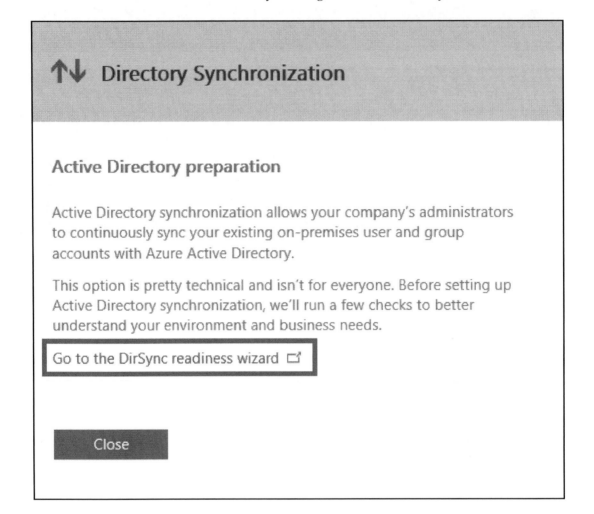

3. Launch a scan by clicking on **Start scan**:

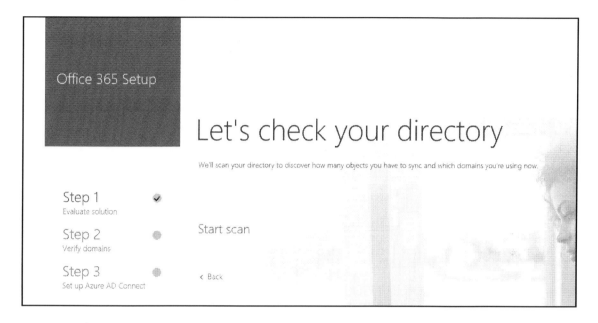

4. Click on **Run checks** and install any components requested by the system. Once the additional components have been installed, a scan of the system will begin:

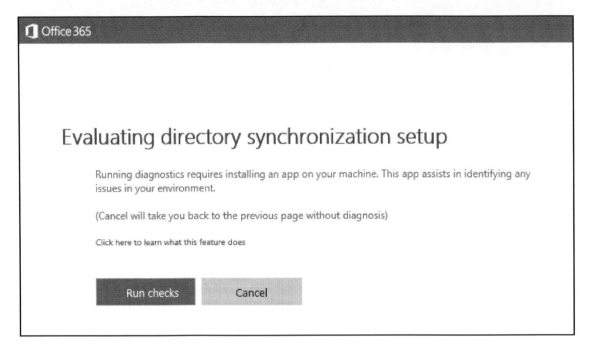

5. When the checks complete, the results are displayed. Your goal is to resolve any issues found and rerun the checks until no issues are found:

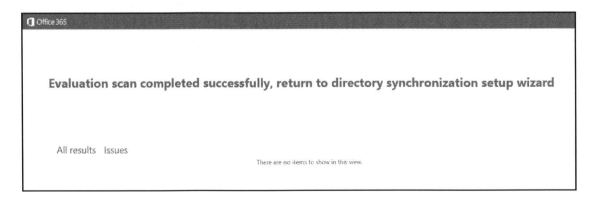

User software

If you plan to run Office 365 on a workstation that has Office 365 Pro Plus and a modern operating system, then likely you will not require any other client-side installs. You will only require the planning/deployment of the Office 365 Pro Plus install.

The reason why Office 365 has desktop requirements is primarily due to older versions of Office, which require the Office 365 Service Sign-In Assistant. In this section, the readiness check tool will identify operating systems that are not supported. You may have some computers that will show up in this report; however, those computers may also not exist. Since this report pulls from Active Directory, it is possible you may have some old objects that have not been removed. Verify that your computers meet the minimum requirements for the Office 365 Service Sign-In Assistant, as well as the version of Office you plan to leverage.

Basic infrastructure preparation

To simplify our approach, let's start with a basic source Exchange 2013 environment. The following is a diagram of the scope of the requirements:

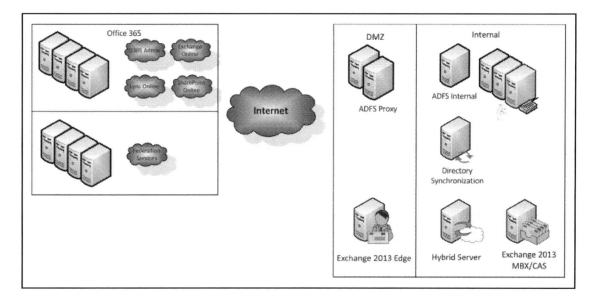

Let's focus on the necessary requirements for the following components:

- Directory Synchronization server
- Active Directory Federation services
- Exchange Hybrid server

Directory Synchronization server

Only one Directory Synchronization server can be actively used within a single Office 365 subscription. The following are the base requirements for this server:

- 64-bit deployment
  - Windows Server 2008 SP1+,Windows Server 2008 R2 SP1+, Windows Server 2012, or Windows Server 2012 R2
- AD domain joined within the forest that you plan to synchronize with Office 365
- Microsoft .NET Framework version 3.5 SP1 and 4.0 installed
- Windows PowerShell version 3.0 or later installed
- 6 GHz+ processor
- 4 GB RAM (16 GB for 50-100 K objects and 32 GB for 100 K+ objects)
- 100 MB or 1 GB Nic
- 100 GB+ free disk space, for an object count fewer than 100K (if you plan to synchronize over 50 K objects, you will need to consider deploying Directory Synchronization on a SQL server)

You need to provide the Directory Synchronization software with an enterprise admin account during install. Beyond the install, the enterprise admin privileges are no longer needed and are not saved. You also need to provide an Office 365 global admin account. Create a dedicated account for the synchronization service and set its password to never expire. If you are unable to set the account password to never expire, you will eventually have to rerun the setup to set those new credentials on this server.

Active Directory Federation Services (AD FS)

As we discussed in the `Chapter 4`, *Integration Options for Midsize and Enterprise Organsizations*, you have many deployment scenarios in which you can pursue your AD FS farm(s). To keep things simple, we are going to focus on deploying a single AD FS internal and proxy server. Unless you plan to deploy more than five AD FS internal servers in a single farm, plan to span servers across slow WAN links, or you have more than 60,000 users leveraging AD FS, proceed with these steps. If any of the previous items apply, you may need to consider deploying AD FS on a SQL environment. If you are a candidate for a larger farm or a more complex deployment, you can still follow these requirements, but you need to consider adding a SQL deployment to the mix.

To get started, let's cover the minimum server specifications as we prepare for Office 365. These servers can be physical or virtual machines:

- AD FS 3.0 Federation server requirements:
    - Windows Server 2012 R2
    - AD domain joined (member only)
    - 4 GB RAM
    - Quad core 2 GHz
    - 100 MB free disk space
    - Microsoft .NET framework version 4.5 installed
    - Windows PowerShell version 3.0 installed
- AD FS proxy Server requirements:
    - Windows Server 2012 R2
    - Non-domain joined (recommended)
    - 4 GB RAM
    - Quad core 2 GHz
    - 100 MB free disk space
    - Microsoft .NET Framework version 4.5
    - Windows PowerShell version 3.0 installed

One major key item to note on deploying both AD FS servers is their operating systems. Microsoft has packaged different installs for Windows Server 2008, 2008 R2, 2012, and 2012 R2. It is highly recommended that you keep both the internal and proxy servers at the same base operating system level.

Next, we will need to create service accounts to manage all AD FS services. Here are some example service accounts:

Service account	Service account purpose
ADFS-admin	Domain user account used for AD FS service log on for internal AD FS server farm. Domain user account with user access to the AD FS.
ADFS-service	Local computer account used for AD FS service log on for AD FS proxy servers.
ADFS-auth	Used for authentication between AD FS server farm and AD FS proxy server.

Now let's prepare for DNS entries that will be required for AD FS. For every domain, create an internal and external DNS record. Your internal DNS record will point to your internal AD FS server, while your external DNS record will point to your AD FS proxy server. If you are using a load balancer or plan to deploy multiple AD FS servers, point these records to the virtual IP address of this load balancer. Here is an example of the records you may create:

ADFS			
Type	**Host**	**Points to address**	**Where**
A	`sts.DOMAIN.com`	AD FS VIP address	Internal DNS
A	`sts.DOMAIN.com`	AD FS proxy VIP address	External DNS

Let's review the firewall rules you will need to enable:

- Create a firewall rule internal to your network to NAT, the virtual IP of the ADFS proxy server
- TCP 443 to and from Internet to proxy servers
- TCP 443 to and from ADFS proxy servers and internal ADFS server farm
- TCP 80 outbound for Certificate Revocation List (**CRL**) checks

Finally, let's review what you should expect for certificate requirements:

- Third-party SSL certificates are required to maintain a high level of security for Office 365 services. (subject name = `STS.Domain.com`)
- Standard X.509 certificate will be used for securely signing all tokens that the federation server issues and that Office 365 will accept and validate.
- It is recommended to use the token-signing certificate generated by the AD FS server, as the AD FS server will auto-generate a new certificate prior to expiring.

You will be required to manually update the federation trust properties by running the following PowerShell command from the AD FS server:

```
Update-MSOLFederatedDomain -DomainName <domain name>
```

Use the following table to check that your third-party certificates are compatible for use with AD FS services:

Certificate guidelines
Certificate's key length should be at least 2048 bits
Signing algorithm should be either SHA-1 or SHA-256
Should be valid for a long term (since this will be managing your authentication)
Key usage must be both server authentication (1.3.6.1.5.5.7.3.1) and client authentication (EKU = 1.3.6.1.5.5.7.3.2)
There should be no dotless subject names (for example, servername)
Must be from a well-known CA provider, such as Verisign, Entrust, and so on
The private key must be exportable
Root certificate authority is shared between the internal and proxy server
SAN certificates can be used for the Exchange Hybrid implementation, but is not recommended for the ADFS implementation

Exchange Hybrid server

Our last integration component is an Exchange Hybrid server. Let's assume you have Exchange 2013 in your environment today. Let's assume we do not want to impact the existing Exchange 2013 server and we are going to add a single Exchange 2013 server to manage the Hybrid or integrate with Office 365. To start out, let's identify some initial server requirements. The following are the base requirements for this server:

- Windows Server 2008 R2 (non-Windows core)
- Windows Server 2012 or Windows Server 2012 R2 (non-Windows core)
- Windows management framework 3.0 or 4.0
- Exchange 2013 will identify any missing features and install them on Windows Server 2012
- Exchange 2013 SP1 including all the latest updates

Physical server recommendations:

- x 64 bit architecture/processor, 64-bit AMD
- 8 GB RAM minimum
- Disk space
    - OS partition 30 GB+
    - Exchange installation and working directory 30 GB+
- 1 GB **Network Interface Card (NIC)**

In order to apply changes to the ExchangeOrganization, we need permissions to the Exchange Organization, as well as global administrator rights within Office 365.

We will need to create DNS records to help route mail to Office 365, as well as support the migration of Outlook clients. The following are example DNS settings we will set up when we are ready to change the mail flow so e-mails are delivered directly into Office 365. If you are configuring a hybrid configuration, we will update these records once all the mailboxes have been migrated to the cloud and we are ready to decommission the on-premises Exchange servers if that is your ultimate goal. If not, then these records will remain unchanged and should still point to your on-premises servers.

Exchange Online				
Type	Priority	Host	Points to address	TTL
MX	0	@	Domain-`com.mail.protection.outlook.com`	1 hour
CNAME	–	`autodiscover.DOMAIN.com`	`autodiscover.outlook.com`	1 hour
TXT	–	@	`v=spf1` `include:spf.protection.outlook.com -all`	1 hour

The preceding entries are used for the following:

- Domain.com
    - Mail routing to Office 365 for migrated users
    - Autodiscover lookups
    - Text records used to validate your domain, to be sent from the service

Let's review the Firewall rules you will need to enable:

Firewall rules
Create firewall rule to NAT (Exchange Hybrid) server IP Allow port 443 to and from the Internet to the Exchange Hybrid server (AutoDiscover, Exchange Web Services, and so on) Allow port 25 to and from the Internet to the Exchange Hybrid server (an Exchange Edge 2013 server can also be used) TCP 80 outbound for **Certificate Revocation List (CRL)** checks
SMTP relay (if required) TCP 587 and required TLS
Mail routing (if required) TCP 25

Often, organizations will ask what specific IPs the service connects to. These questions come up primarily so that the firewall administrators can restrict traffic routing out of the organization. Microsoft provides a list, but recommends that you create exclusions by the names of the connecting service rather than the IPs. To find the names and IPs for Exchange, follow `http://technet.microsoft.com/library/hh373144.aspx`.

If you decide to track by IP, you may want to follow this RSS feed to ensure you are proactive in your changes: `http://go.microsoft.com/fwlink/?linkid=236301`.

Finally, let's review the certificate requirements for the Exchange Hybrid role. A public certificate is required to setup Exchange Federation. A public certificate will essentially address both the Exchange web services and Autodiscover. In addition, the Exchange Federation trust is recommended by Microsoft to be self-signed with an internal CA or a public facing certificate. Exchange will automatically create a self-signed certificate, if one does not exist.

Defining the migration process

Now that we have started the process of provisioning your servers, we also need to start thinking about the migration process and areas you need to consider. At a high level, there are a few areas we should prioritize. These areas include:

- Bandwidth evaluations (user connectivity and migration traffic)
- Public Folder use
- Communicating and training

Bandwidth evaluations

While planning your migration to Office 365, bandwidth is one area that cannot be overlooked. Most organizations planning to move to Office 365 likely host their messaging infrastructure internally. This means that you have not prepared your primary egress points for the traffic you are going to send over it. Much of your traffic may be internal or traversing over separate WAN links. When you move your users to Office 365, those users will then leverage the egress points you have in place for internet traffic.

There are two areas that you need to be preparing your bandwidth for. These two areas are the bandwidth you will use while migrating to Office 365 and your day-to-day bandwidth.

Migration bandwidth

Let's review the migration bandwidth needed to migrate to Office 365. There are many considerations when planning for bandwidth. These include:

- Total size of data to migrate
- Average mailbox size
- Number of users to migrate and the logical breakdown of these users (such as business units, facilities, and so on)
- How many Exchange Hybrid (client access) servers you have
- How much existing bandwidth you have
- Go-live helpdesk support capacity

Let's first start with how to estimate what you can currently achieve and if you need to expand further. First, let's start with a baseline of example information. Let's say we have an organization with the following information:

- 200 MB average mailbox size
- 500 GB of mailbox data
- 2,300 users, 200 shared resources
- 45 mbps internet connection

We can start by calculating what's possible. To do this, let's grab a simple calculator found at `http://www.dslreports.com/calculator`. Let's start by putting in our total mailbox data and our line speed, and then calculating the time:

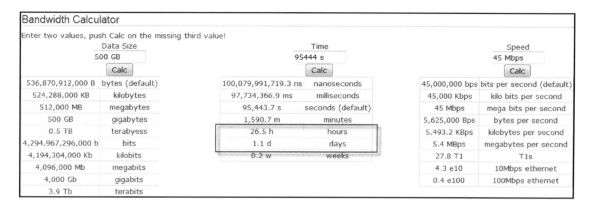

As you can see, it will take approximately 26.5 hours on a maxed-out 45 mbps internet connection to migrate 500 GB of data. Realistically, you are likely using some of that 45 mbps connection, not to mention there is always bandwidth overhead. To be safe, you need to evaluate what's truly available during your migration. In addition, you should add a buffer so you are not planning for that full 45 mbps connection.

Let's say you had minimal applications leveraging that 45 mbps connection. It may be more realistic to plan for 30-35 mbps of bandwidth, when planning your migration. That would look more like this:

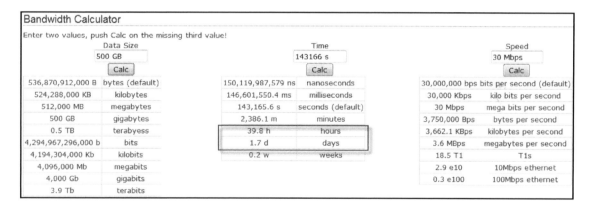

Now, I know what you're probably thinkingâ⊚⊚how can we spend 40 hours doing a migration? Well, I probably would not. Most often, if you are planning to migrate as many users as possible, you are likely doing it over a weekend. When planning for a migration, I would consider only calculating bandwidth for half the weekend. (This gives you a nice buffer in the event you have migration issues.) Let's assume the weekend is only 48 hours, which means you would only have 24 hours to migrate the data. Let's now focus on data size in our calculations and set the time to 24 hours. That would look like this:

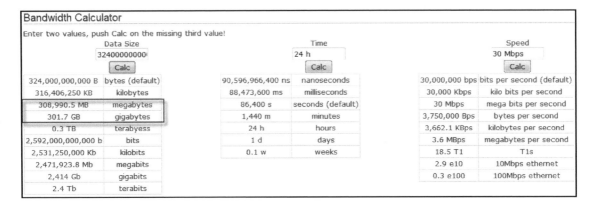

Based on the calculations, it looks like the results are about 300 GB of data or 1,500 mailboxes, based on our average mailbox size. You now have some decisions to make. These decisions may include the following:

- Do you plan to migrate in two or more weekends or a variety of non-business hour weeknights?
- Do you enforce cleanup on the source side, resulting in a smaller amount of data to be migrated?
- Can your helpdesk support the number of users you migrate over a single weekend? (Calculate this based on iterations of pilot users testing.)

Whichever path you take, you will need to be able to support that path. As an example, do you have enough Exchange Servers to support 30 mbps of traffic? You may have to build two or more servers to support that. The best way to evaluate this is to build your first one or two CAS servers in an array. Test mailbox moves by creating a sampling of migrations in concurrency. Migrating one or two users at a time will not provide you with a sampling of what's realistic. Start with 50 mailboxes and evaluate the size of data migrated, along with the time it took to migrate a majority of those mailboxes when they were running concurrently. From there you can determine if you have enough migration consoles or you need more.

A recommended approach when using Exchange 2013 is to utilize its ability to suspend migrations. What this means is, you can migrate about 95 percent of the mailbox and suspend the migration before it completes the move to Exchange Online. This won't impact the user as the last 5 percent is used for the reconfiguration and delta migration of what the mailbox collected during the migration process. As an example, you could migrate a larger number of mailboxes during some of the week and weekend and suspend all of the moves before they are completed. This will allow you to ensure all of the mailboxes you selected are ready for the migration go-live you planned.

User bandwidth

The amount of bandwidth a user needs is significantly different than the amount of bandwidth you need for a migration. Migration bandwidth is point-in-time bandwidth, while user bandwidth is something that you need to support day to day. To calculate this, we need to understand where and how your users work.

First, we need to divide your users into their egress points (collection of users going out over a specific internet connection). Let's say you have three sites, which look like the following:

- Site 1 – 1,000 users, 100 mbps internet connection (40 percent utilized)
- Site 2 – 700 users, 45 mbps internet connection (60 percent utilized)
- Site 3 – 500 users, 10 mbps internet connection (50 percent utilized)

Now, let's figure out how these users use Outlook today. Refer to this table, provided by Microsoft to categorize their usage (https://blogs.technet.microsoft.com/oscarmh/29/5/18/ancho-de-banda-en-bpos-company-network-requirements/#comments):

Activity	Light	Medium	Heavy	Very heavy
Messages sent per day	5	10	20	30
Messages received per day	20	40	80	120
Average message size	50 KB	50 KB	50 KB	50 KB
Messages read per day	20	40	80	120
Messages deleted per day	10	20	40	60
OWA log on and log off per day	2	2	2	2

Now let's determine which e-mail client they will be using:

E-mail client	Light	Medium	Heavy	Very heavy
Office Outlook	1,300 KB/day/user	2,600 KB/day/user	5,200 KB/day/user	7,800 KB/day/user
OWA	6,190 KB/day/user	12,220 KB/day/user	24,270 KB/day/user	36,330 KB/day/user

Let's say site 1 users fall into the following categories:

E-mail client	Light	Medium	Heavy	Very heavy
Office Outlook	100	500	200	100
OWA	50	40	10	0

Now let's calculate what site 1 would look like. To start, we need to know what the formulas are. Microsoft provides the following examples:

- If your company has 100 heavy Office Outlook users, here's how to calculate the average network traffic, measured in bytes per second: *Network bytes/sec = (100 heavy users Ã⤠(5,200 KB/user Ã· day)) Ã· (8 hr/day Ã⤠3600 sec/hr) = 18.5 KB/sec.* Assuming a daily peak of twice the average usage, your network connection would need to support approximately 37 KB/sec.

- If your company has 100 medium OWA users, here's how to calculate the average network traffic, measured in bytes per second: *Network bytes/sec = (100 medium users Ã⤠(12,220 KB/user Ã· day)) Ã· (8 hr/day Ã⤠3600 sec/hr) = 42.4 KB/sec* Assuming a daily peak of twice the average usage, your network connection would need to support approximately 84.9 KB/sec.

Let's assume all site 1 users work during the same business hours:

Bandwidth (KB/sec.)					
E-mail client	Light	Medium	Heavy	Very heavy	Total
Office Outlook	10	91	73	55	229
OWA	22	34	17	0	73
Total	32	125	90	55	302

Based on these calculations, site 1 would need 302 KB/sec of bandwidth or 2.5 mbps during normal business hours. Since site 1 has a 100 MB connection and is only 40 percent utilized, Site 1 should have enough bandwidth to support users connecting to Office 365.

Take this calculation example and apply it to all the sites that have direct internet bandwidth. To do so, consider the following:

- Total bandwidth available
- What the utilization is during normal business hours
- Calculate how your users will use the bandwidth, based on the preceding calculations
- Determine if there is enough available bandwidth, based on the calculated bandwidth required

If your internet connection is also your WAN link to your data center and you will continue to use the same internet connection, you may be trading bandwidth for bandwidth. What I mean is, if you are removing Outlook/Exchange bandwidth over the same internet connection, but adding at back for Exchange Online over the same WAN link, then you likely have a site you will not have to calculate (unless you are changing the Outlook connectivity method).

Public Folder use

Public Folders have been widely used by many organizations back in the early Exchange days. Those Public Folders have likely been migrated during every Exchange upgrade to your current one. Modern Public Folders are now supported in Exchange Online, but the continued use of Public Folders is not something I typically recommend (that is, if you have the time to remediate the use of them). Public Folders can be difficult to govern and often become an unknown in how they are used.

The challenge with Public Folders usually comes up when a large quantity is deployed and a regular clean-up does not occur. If you do not have many public folders then your job is somewhat easy. If you have many, you may need to take a closer look at what's in use. In general, most organizations convert Public Folders to shared mailboxes or SharePoint lists/libraries. You can setup Public Folder Hybrid and eventually migrate those Public Folders to Exchange Online, in certain scenarios. There are Public Folder limits, but those limits have changed over the past few updates in Exchange Online. Check `http://technet .microsoft.com/en-us/library/dn249373(v=exchg.15).aspx` for the most recent supported Public Folder scenarios.

If you are using Exchange 2007 or later, Microsoft has provided some useful migration PowerShell scripts. These scripts make importing public folders into Office 365 much easier (`https://www.microsoft.com/en-gb/download/details.aspx?id=3847`).

You can leverage third-party tools, such as the Public Folder migrator for SharePoint. Refer to `http://www.quest.com/public-folder-migrator-for-sharepoint`. If you plan to migrate Public Folders to shared mailboxes, you can simply do so by adding a shared mailbox and opening it with Outlook 2010. From there, find your Public Folder and drag the contents from the Public Folder to the shared mailbox. You may have to perform additional steps, such as assigning permissions or moving email addresses to this new shared mailbox.

If you have a large quantity of Public Folders then you may need to evaluate what's in use today. To do this, you can grab a free Exchange tool.

- Exchange 2003/2007
    - Tool name: `PFDavAdmin`
    - Download: `http://www.microsoft.com/download/en/details.aspx?displaylang=en&id=22427`
- Exchange 2010 and later
    - Tool name: `ExFolders`
    - Download: `https://gallery.technet.microsoft.com/Exchange-21-SP1-ExFolders-e6bfd45`

With these tools you can evaluate who owns a Public Folder, when it was last used, and so on. This should help you survey your Public Folder use and make some easy decision on what to Archive off and what to migrate.

Communications and training

Communications and training are two of the most important components of any migration plan of a major user service. When you plan to migrate users from one service to another, what they experience is how well communications were and what their go-live experience will be like.

Communicating with users on what to expect and what their experience will be like on day one is very important. Some of the communications you should consider are:

- Business announcement of the change from someone in the leadership team, such as a director or executive

- Migration date for the user being migrated
- Migration expectations (examples)
    - How to log on to Outlook
    - How to communicate with non-migrated users
    - Reconfiguration of their mobile device
    - New service available
    - Where to go for help (FAQ site, different helpdesk numbers, who to find if helpers are walking the floors, and so on)
    - Migration schedule (if migrations are performed in waves)
- Post migration surveys (especially when doing pilot migrations or waves of migrations)
- Building the hype (people will embrace change if there is excitement in the air for it; distribute information, have stand up kiosks for users to see what the experience is like, hang up posters or banners, create an Office 365 FAQ site, and so on)

Training is also an important focus area when performing a migration. This is less necessary for users moving from Exchange to Exchange Online. Training will likely be required when users change Outlook clients or are moving to use only **Outlook Web Apps** (**OWA**). If an organization is moving from a non-Exchange messaging system, then training is critical. Some areas you should consider for non-Exchange to Exchange Online training are:

- Distribution of Outlook cheat sheets (quick reference guides)
- In class or virtual introduction training
- Sign up for in class or virtual power user training
- Video training, posted on an Office 365 internal site
- Training of power users or pilot users and having them walk the floors on go-live

There are certainly quite a bit of technical and business tasks to perform in order to prepare and execute a migration; often the users do not see these tasks occurring. What the users do see is how aware and ready they are for the shift to a new platform. The more time you spend on communications and training, the more likely you will have a successful migration. Spend some time reviewing the Office 365 adoption guide and other great documentation at http://success.office.com/.

Summary

By now we should have a good understanding of how to prepare Office 365 for the integration servers, are starting to prepare our internal infrastructure for integration, and are thinking about how to prepare for the process. This preparation should guide us to start the initial integration and ready our pilot users to measure their experience with Office 365.

In the next chapter, we will build the necessary integration components to prepare for our first migrations to Office 365.

8
Deploying a Hybrid Infrastructure – AD FS

Now that we have learned about the preparation requirements for integration, let's start to build the initial foundation that will enable us to prepare for integrated use and a migration to Office 365. By now, we should have the necessary physical or virtual servers, firewall, and DNS ready or in place. We will now focus on building three core services, enabled by Office 365. These core services are:

- Deploying **Active Directory Federation Services** (**AD FS**)
- Office 365 Directory Synchronization
- Exchange Hybrid

It's critical that we deploy these services in the order they are listed. If you choose to install these items out of order, some alternative configuration changes will be required and they are not described. Currently, they are listed in order suggested by Microsoft best practices. In this chapter, we will focus on the build out of AD FS with a **Windows Internal Database** (**WID**) as our database source (you may want to consider SQL for deployments requiring a larger scale).

In this chapter, we will look at the deploying AD FS topic.

Deploying Active Directory Federation Services

We are going to start by building the minimum requirements for AD FS. To do so, we need one AD FS internal server and one AD FS proxy server. The AD FS internal server will be the primary AD FS server that manages the AD FS database on WID. The AD FS proxy server will refer to the AD FS internal server when passing authentication. The servers should be prepared and placed according to the preparation requirements found in `Chapter 7`, *Preparing for a Hybrid Deployment and Migration*. Let's start by building the servers in the following order:

- Active Directory Federation Services internal server
- Active Directory Federation Services Web Application proxy server
- Basic testing of Active Directory Federation Services

Installing Active Directory Federation Services internal server

The following high-level steps will be performed when installing the AD FS internal server:

1. Installing AD FS
2. Installing the Microsoft Online Services Sign-In Assistant
3. Installing the Azure Active Directory module for Windows PowerShell
4. Configuring the AD FS internal server
5. Converting the domain to a federated domain in Office 365

Installing AD FS

To start installing AD FS, let us look at an example. We are going to build the AD FS internal server with the following specifications:

- Windows Server 2012 R2
- 4 GB of memory
- Quad core 2Ghz
- Active Directory joined
- All the latest Windows updates applied
- Computer name: `DGADFSINT1` (you will want to name this server based on your standard AD object naming scheme)

To start, let's make sure we have the proper software and certificate located on the server.

Make sure you have the proper certificate loaded into the personal certificate store on the local computer. In my example, I'm using a wildcard certificate. You may use a wildcard certificate or one named specifically for the AD FS service (for example, `adfs.yourdomain.com` or `sts.yourdomain.com`). For more details on certificate requirements, refer to:

- URL: `http://technet.microsoft.com/en-us/library/dn554247.aspx#BKMK_1`
- Download the Microsoft Online Services Sign-In Assistant for IT professionals at `http://www.microsoft.com/en-us/download/details.aspx?id=4195`
- Download Azure Active Directory module for Windows PowerShell (64-bit version) at `http://technet.microsoft.com/library/jj151815.aspx#bkmk_installmodule`

Now that we have the necessary software ready to install on the server and the certificate imported, we are ready to install the AD FS role:

1. Start **Add Roles and Features Wizard** on your Windows Server 2012 R2 server being used for the AD FS internal role.

2. After launching the wizard, click **Next**, as shown in the following screenshot:

3. Ensure **Role-based or feature-based** installation is selected. Click **Next**, as shown in the following screenshot:

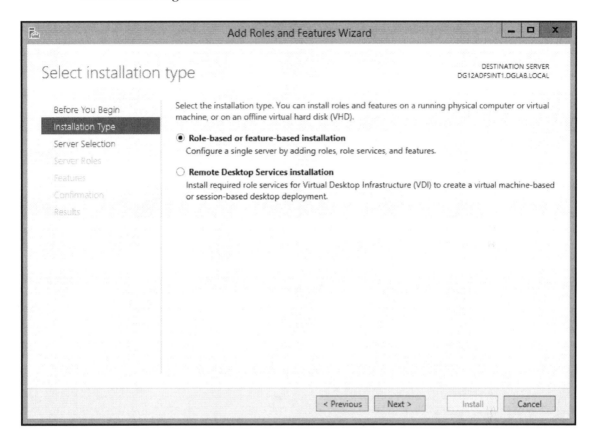

4. Select the server you are connected to and then click **Next**, as shown in the following screenshot:

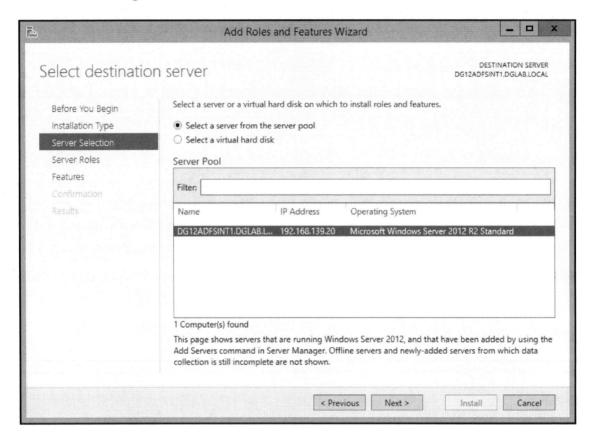

5. Now select **Active Directory Federation Services**. Then click **Next**, as shown in the following screenshot:

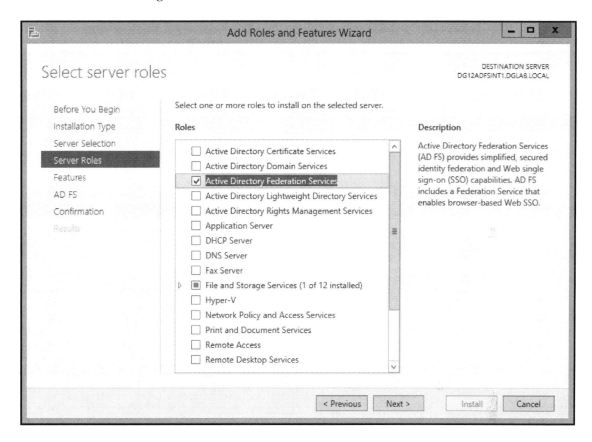

6. Click **Next** on the **Features** page, as shown in the following screenshot:

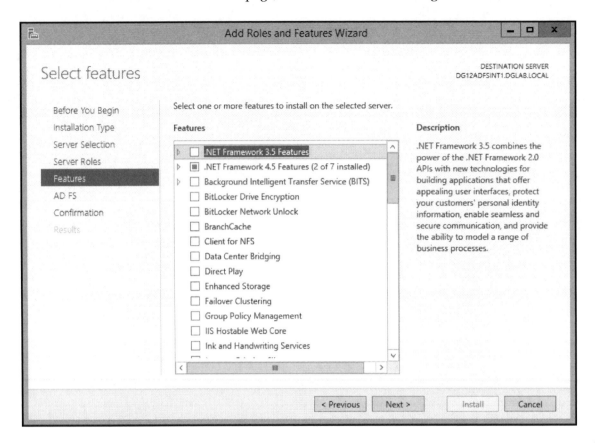

7. Click **Next** on the AD FS page, as shown in the following screenshot:

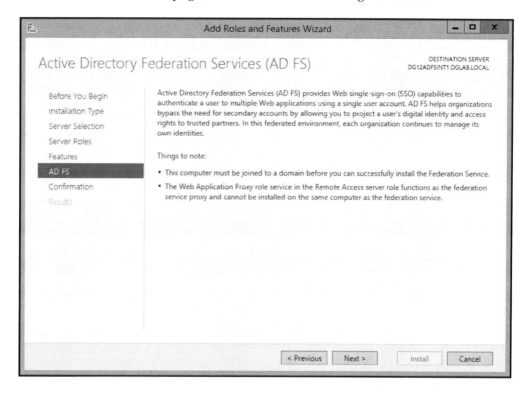

8. Check the **Restart the destination server automatically if required** option and then click **Install,** as shown in the following screenshot:

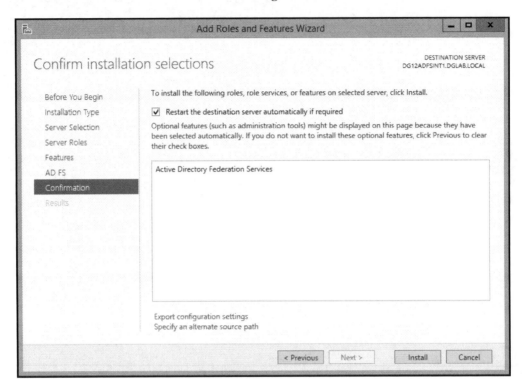

9. Once the install completes, you will be shown any errors that have occurred. However, if everything goes well, you will see an image similar to the following screenshot. Press **Close** to complete the installation:

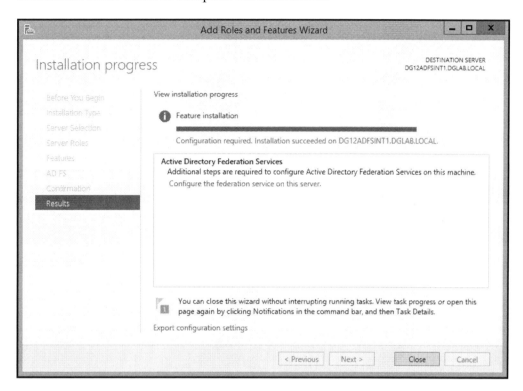

Installing the Microsoft Online Services Sign-In Assistant

To ensure we can communicate properly with the Office 365 service, we need to deploy the Sign-In Assistant software. Follow these steps to install the software:

1. Launch the `msoidcli_64` file after downloading it from
   `http://www.microsoft.com/en-us/download/details.aspx?id=41950`.

2. If you accept the terms, check the agreement and click **Install,** as shown in the following screenshot:

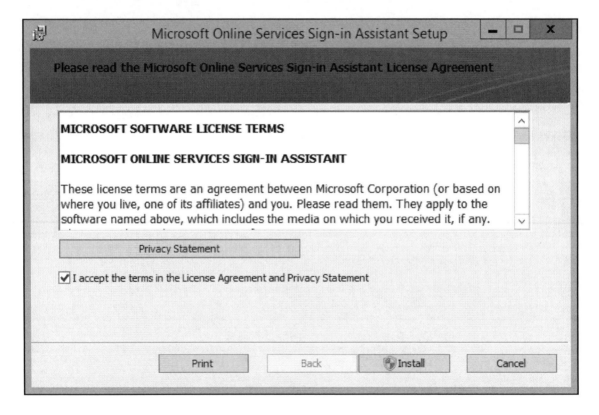

3. Once the install completes, click **Finish** as shown in the following screenshot:

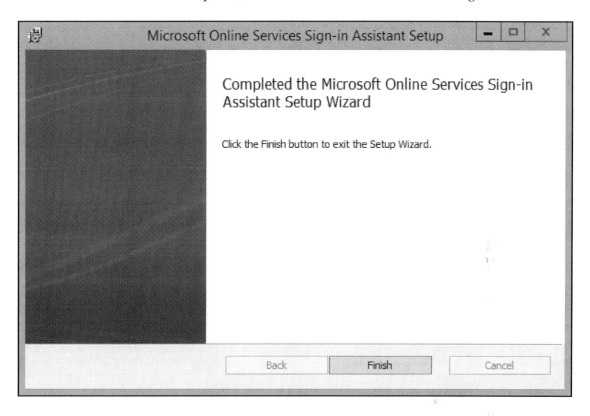

Installing the Windows Azure Active Directory module for Windows PowerShell

We need to run PowerShell commands to establish the trust. Follow these steps to simplify running these PowerShell commands:

1. Launch `AdministrationConfig-en`, after downloading the module found at (64-bit version). Click **Next**, as shown in the following screenshot:

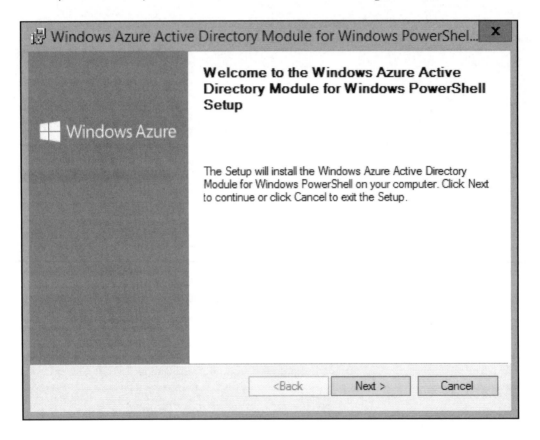

2. If you accept the agreement, click **Next** as shown in the following screenshot:

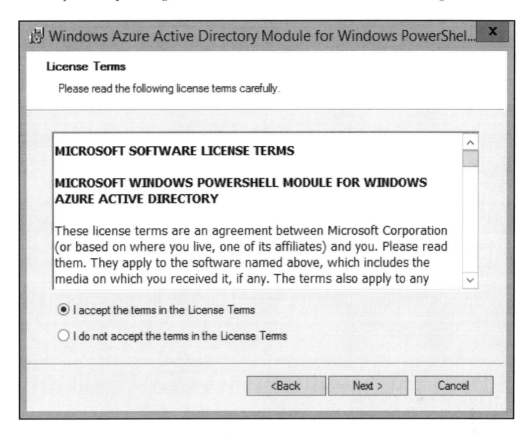

3. Accept the default path and click **Next**, as shown in the following screenshot:

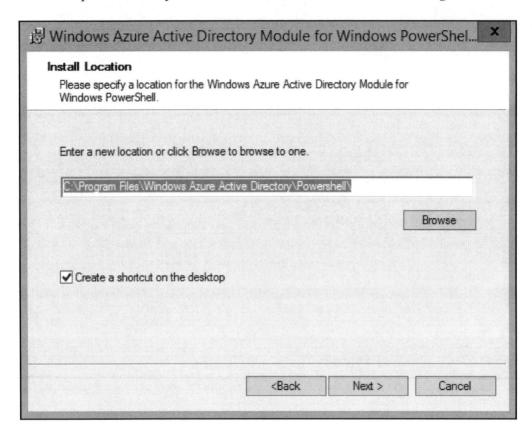

4. Now click **Install**, as shown in the following screenshot:

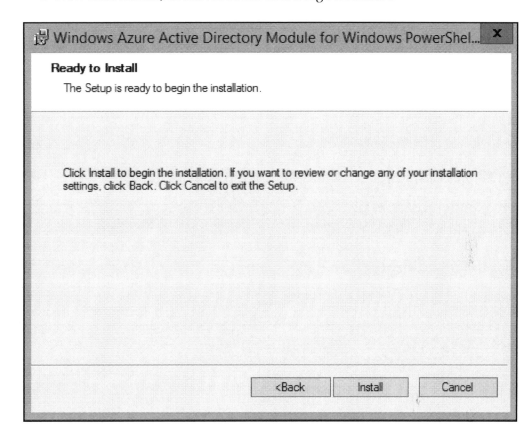

5. Finish the install by clicking **Finish.**

Configuring the AD FS internal server

Now that all our initial preparation steps are complete, let's start to configure the AD FS internal server by performing the following steps:

1. Open **Server Manager** from the **Start** menu.
2. Click on **Notifications,** which should be represented as a yellow triangle with an exclamation in the top-right corner of Server Manager.
3. Next, look for and click **Configure the federation service on this server**, as shown in the following screenshot:

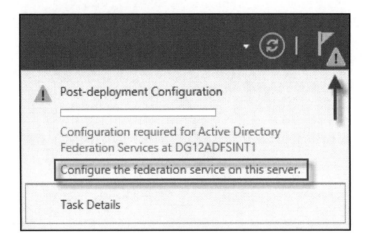

4. Select **Create the first federation server in a federation server farm**. Then click **Next** as shown in the following screenshot:

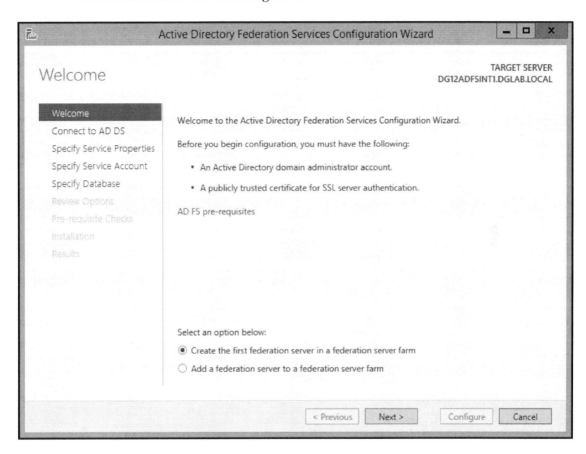

5. You will now need to specify a domain admin account to perform the install and configuration. Select that account and click **Next**, as shown in the following screenshot:

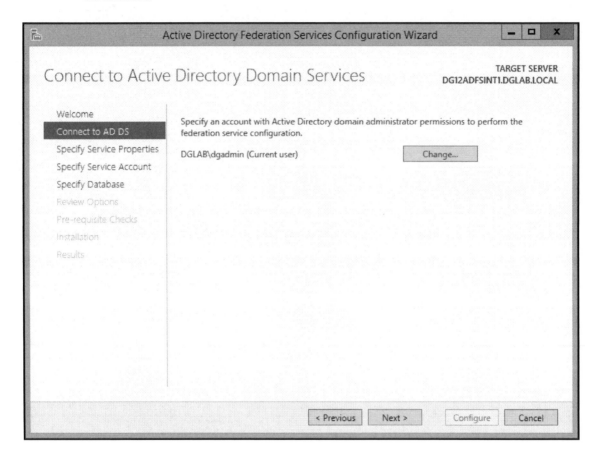

6. Verify that the public SSL certificate `adfs.yourdomain.com` is selected (this example will be `*.grevelab.com`—in this example, we are using a wildcard certificate), and the federation service matches the name of the certificate (in this case, I used the federation service name `adfs.grevelab.com`). After verifying these settings, type the name of the service. Users will see this display name. Then click **Next**, as shown in the following screenshot:

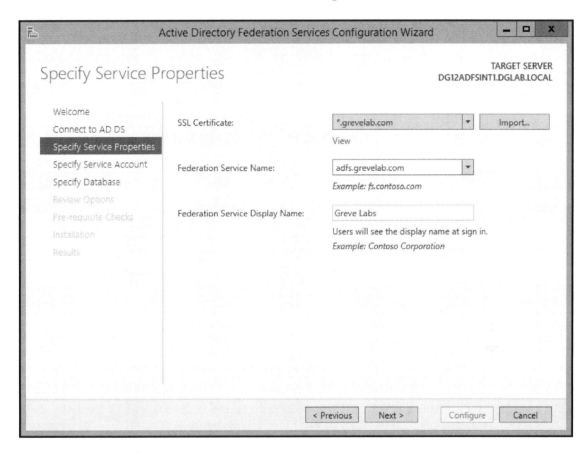

7. Browse to locate the ADFS-Admin service account and then provide the password for the service account. Click **Next** to continue, as shown in the following screenshot:

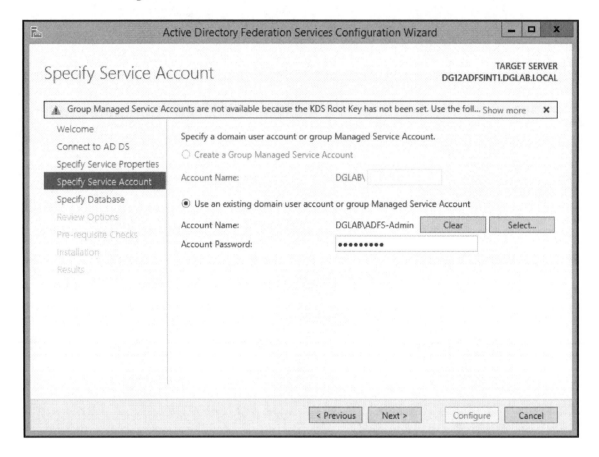

8. In our use case, we are only going to be using the Windows internal database. If you plan to have more than five AD FS internal servers, you may want to consider the use of a SQL Server database. Click **Next**, as shown in the following screenshot:

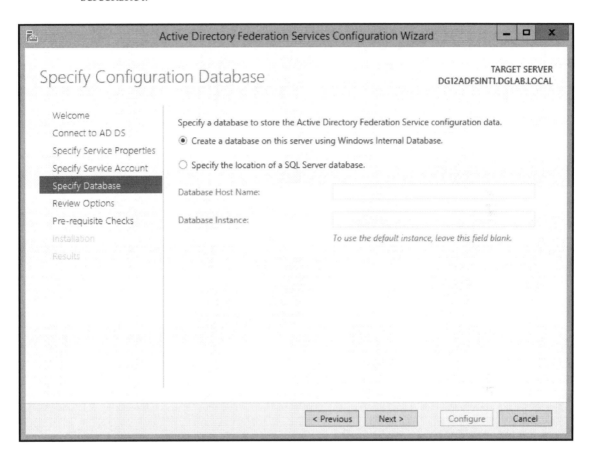

9. Review the summary and click **Next,** as shown in the following screenshot, when you are ready to start the **Pre-requisite Checks** and **Installation**:

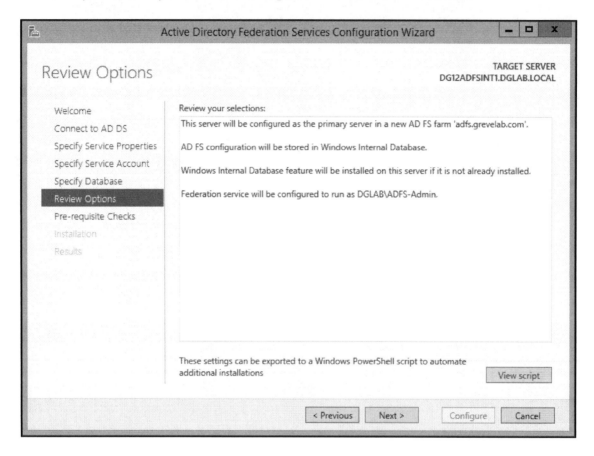

10. Once the **Pre-requisites Checks** are complete and pass successfully, click **Configure**, as shown in the following screenshot:

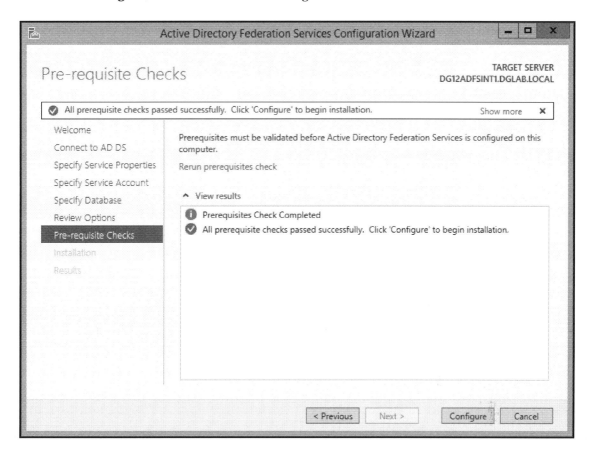

11. This will begin the installation of AD FS components on the server. The option to **Close** will become available when all components complete successfully, as shown in the following screenshot:

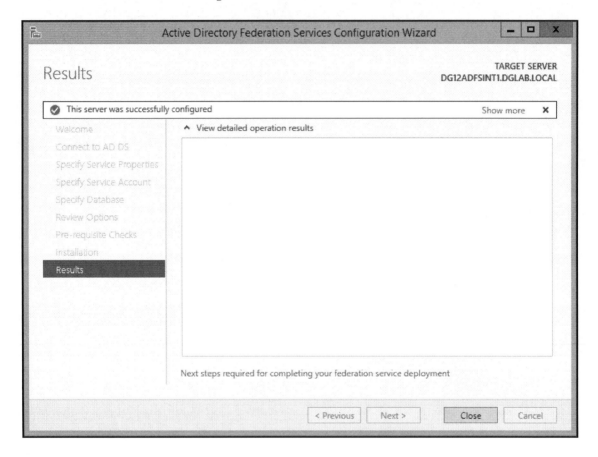

Converting the domain to a federated domain in Office 365

We will now federate the `grevelab.com` domian within the Office 365 service:

1. Open the Windows Azure Active Directory module for Windows PowerShell on the AD FS internal server, as an administrator. You will use your Office 365 admin credentials at the pop-up credentials prompt.

2. Type `set-ExecutionPolicy unrestricted`

   This allows you to run commands with elevated privileges.

3. Type `$cred=get-credential`

   Enter your Office 365 administration account credentials when prompted to log in.

4. Type `Connect-MsolService -Credential $cred`

   Connects to your Office 365 service.

5. Type `Set-MsolADFSContext -computer DG12ADFSINT1`

   Replace `DG12ADFSINT1` with your AD FS internal server name. This step is not necessary if running the commands from the AD FS server.

6. Type `Convert-MsolDomainToFederated â??DomainName grevelab.com`

   Replace `grevelab.com` with your domain.

7. Type `Update-MSOLFederatedDomain -domainname grevelab.com`

   This command updates Office 365 with your AD FS server info.

 If you need to add support for multiple domains, you will need to add the `SupportMultipleDomain` switch to `convert` and `update` cmdlts. `http:/ /community.office365.com/en-us/w/sso/support-for-multiple-top- level-domains.aspx`

The following is an example of what happens when we run the commands in our lab environment. The commands don't return much in the way of feedback; so long as they don't return any errors, the command should have run correctly:

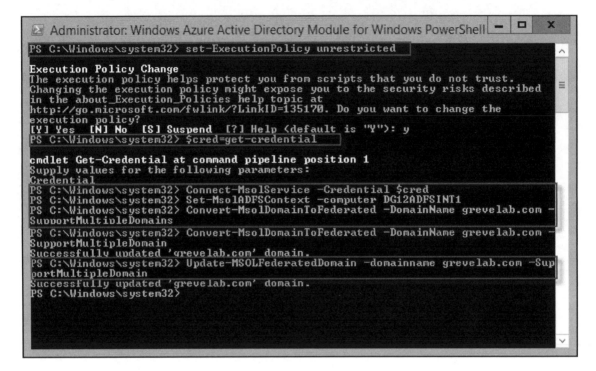

1. To determine whether federation has been enabled, type `Get-MSOLFederationProperty -DomainName grevelab.com`, where the output should show your `adfs.yourdomain.com` sign-in URLs.

2. Also, running the Get-MSOLDomain cmdlet will show the domain authentication property listed as Federated. Non-federated domains will have their authentication property set to Managed:

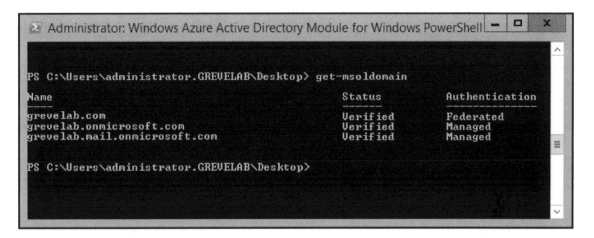

Installing Active Directory Federation Services Web Application proxy server

The following high-level steps will be performed when installing the AD FS proxy server:

1. Installing the Web Application proxy
2. Editing hosts files
3. Configuring the AD FS Web Application proxy server

Installing the Web Application proxy

Now we need to install the Web Application proxy, which is a replacement for the legacy AD FS proxy you may have used previously in other deployments. We are going to build the AD FS proxy server with the following specifications:

- Windows Server 2012 R2.
- 4 GB of memory.
- Quad core 2Ghz.
- Does not have to be joined to Active Directory.
- All the latest Windows updates applied.
- Computer name: DG12ADFSPXY1 (you will want to name this server based on your standard AD object naming scheme).
- Sits in DMZ – HTTPS (TCP 443) required to be open between proxy server and internal AD FS server, and also required from the Internet to AD FS proxy server. Port 80 outbound from the proxy server should also be allowed for CRL checking.
- Use the SSL certificate from the primary internal AD FS server, imported to the personal certificate store on the local computer.
- Make sure you have the proper certificate loaded into the personal certificate store on the proxy server. In this example, we are using a wildcard certificate. You may use a wildcard certificate, or one named specifically for the AD FS service (for example, adfs.yourdomain.com or sts.yourdomain.com). For more details on certificate requirements, refer to http://technet.microsoft.com/en-us/library/dn554247.aspx#BKMK_1.

Let's start with the AD FS install:

1. If this computer is not domain-joined, which is recommended, you need to create a local user account with administrative privileges and then log on with that account for all installs.
2. Start the **Add Roles and Features Wizard** on your Windows Server 2012 R2 server that is being used for the AD FS proxy role.

3. After launching the wizard, click **Next**, as shown in the following screenshot:

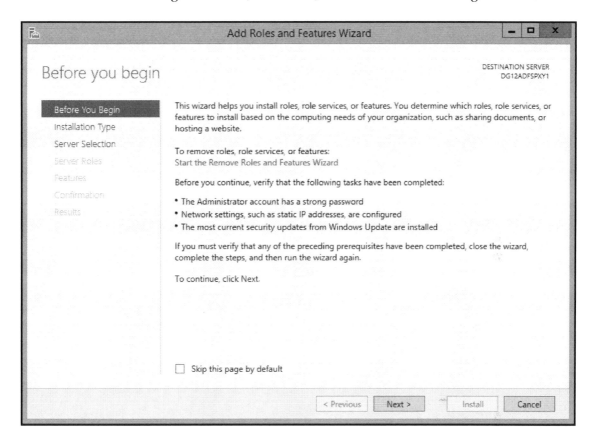

4. **Ensure** `Role-based or feature-based installation` **is selected. Then click Next**, as shown in the following screenshot:

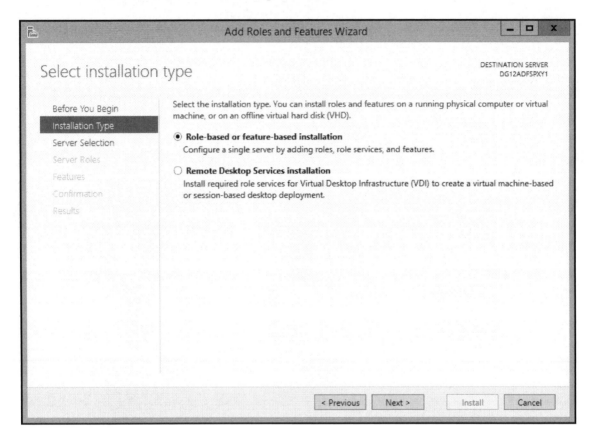

5. Select the server you are connected to and then click **Next** as shown in the following screenshot:

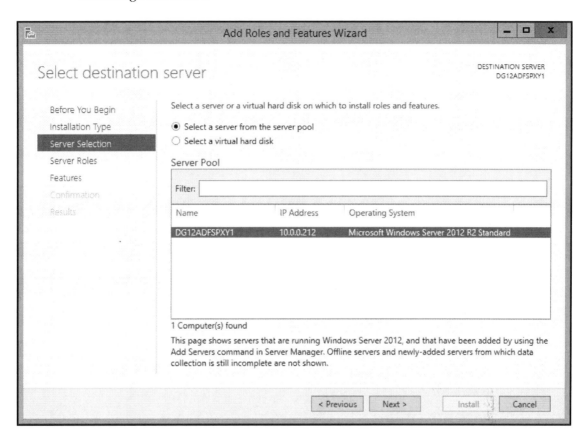

6. Now check **Remote Access** to add the Web Application proxy capability. Then click **Next** as shown in the following screenshot:

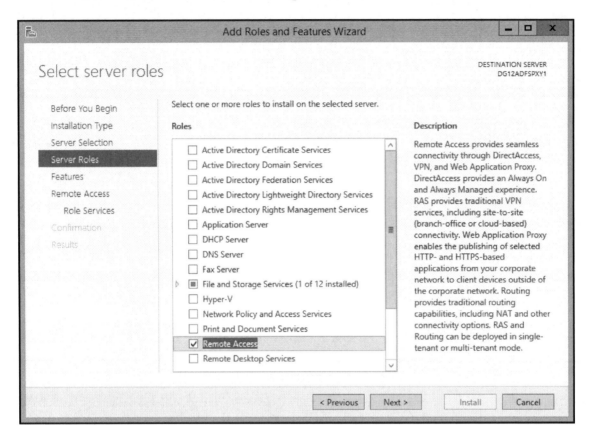

7. On the **Features** screen, click **Next** as shown in the following screenshot:

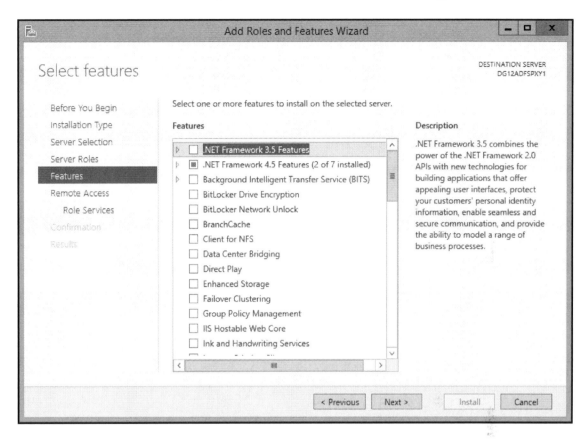

8. On the **Remote Access** screen, click **Next** as shown in the following screenshot:

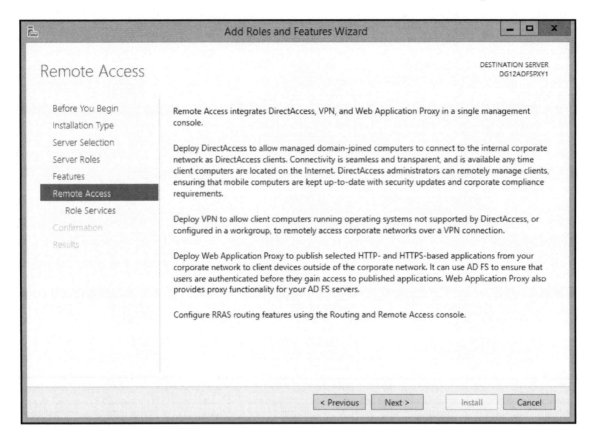

9. Now select **Web Application Proxy**, as shown in the following screenshot:

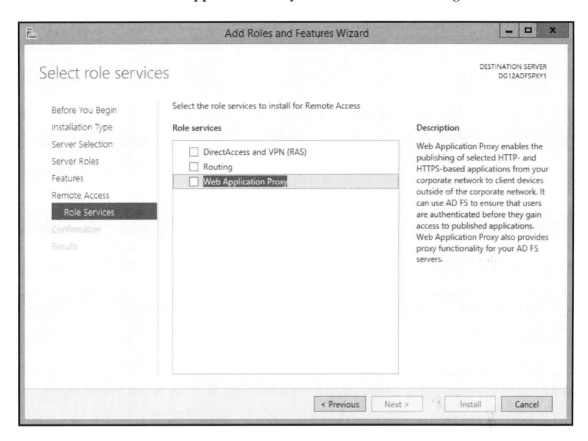

10. A popup for additional roles will appear. Click **Add Features,** as shown in the following screenshot, and then click **Next:**

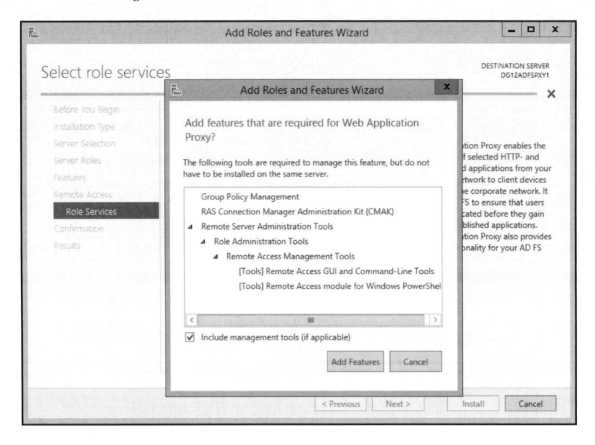

11. The wizard will install all the necessary roles and features. Check **Restart the destination server automatically if required** and then click **Install,** as shown in the following screenshot:

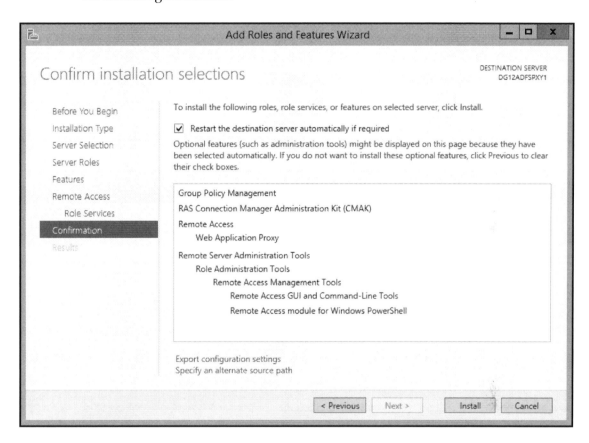

12. At this point, continue to monitor the install until all the roles and features are installed, as shown in the following screenshot:

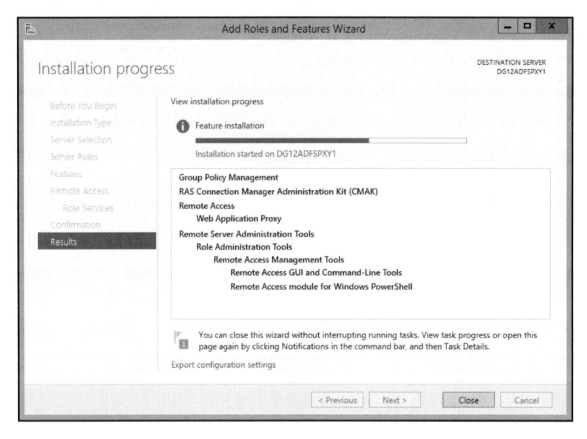

13. When the installation is complete, click **Close** as shown in the next screenshot:

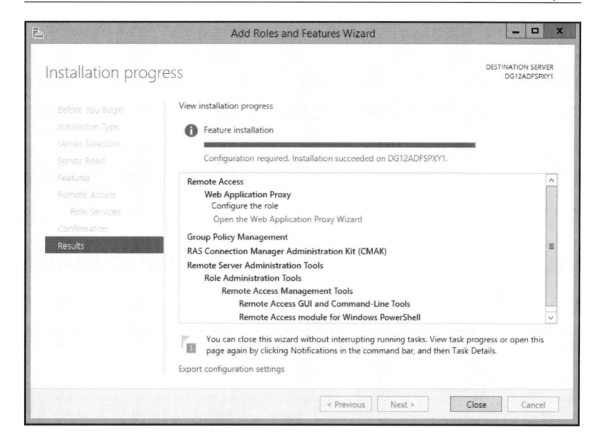

Editing the hosts file

We need to edit the hosts file on this machine to ensure the AD FS proxy can communicate with the AD FS internal and not rely on external DNS entries.

1. Edit the hosts file and add an entry to resolve the federation server's URL to the internal IP address.

External users should be directed to your AD FS proxy when reaching `adfs.yourdomain.com`.

2. To edit the hosts file, open Notepad as an administrator and find the hosts file under C:\Windows\System32\drivers\etc, as shown in the following screenshot:

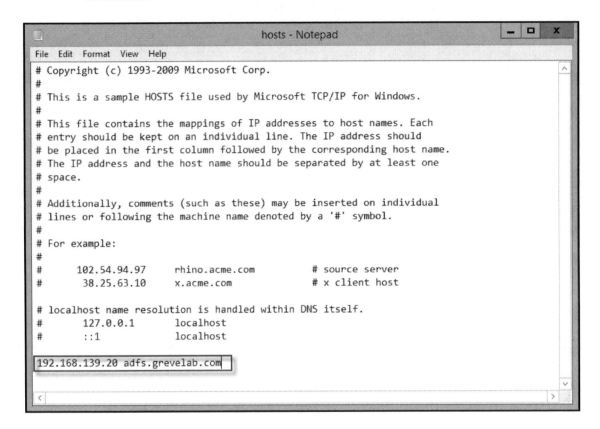

Configuring the AD FS Web Application proxy server

Now that we have completed all our preparation requirements, let's begin the AD FS proxy configuration. You need to perform the following steps:

1. Open **Server Manager** from the **Start** menu.
2. Click on **Notifications,** which should be represented as a yellow triangle with an exclamation in the top-right corner of **Server Manager**.
3. Next, look for and click **Open the Web Application Proxy Wizard,** as shown in the following screenshot:

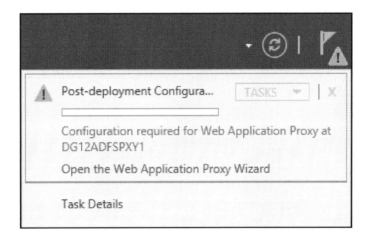

4. Click **Next**, as shown in the following screenshot:

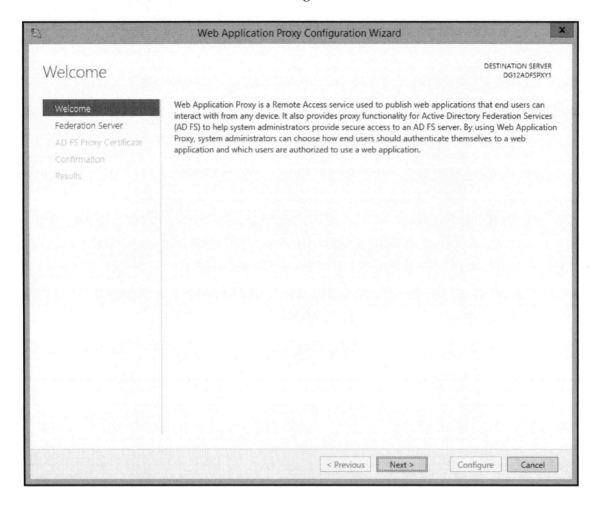

5. Type the name of the AD FS service (for example, `adfs.yourdomain.com`). As mentioned in `Chapter 7`, *Preparing for a Hybrid Deployment and Migration*, you will need to have a local administrator account on the AD FS internal server. In this example, we will use the account suggested in `Chapter 7`, *Preparing for a Hybrid Deployment and Migration* identified as `adfs-auth`. Click **Next**.

> If you receive an error, double-check and ensure the AD FS-Auth account is a local admin on the AD FS internal server.

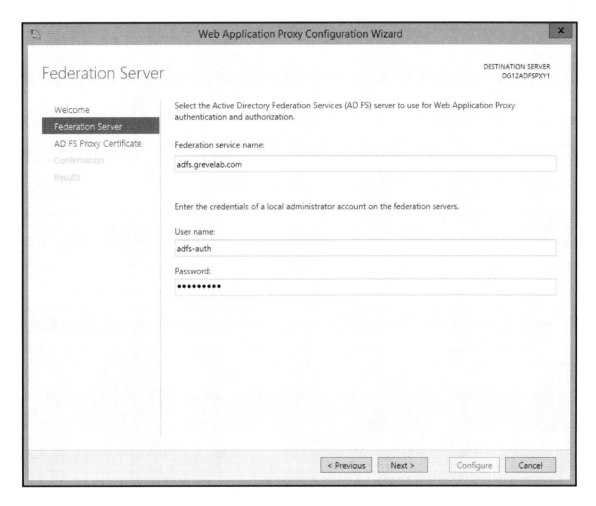

6. Now select the certificate you used on the AD FS internal server, which should be in the local personal store of the AD FS proxy server. Then click **Next**, as shown in the following screenshot:

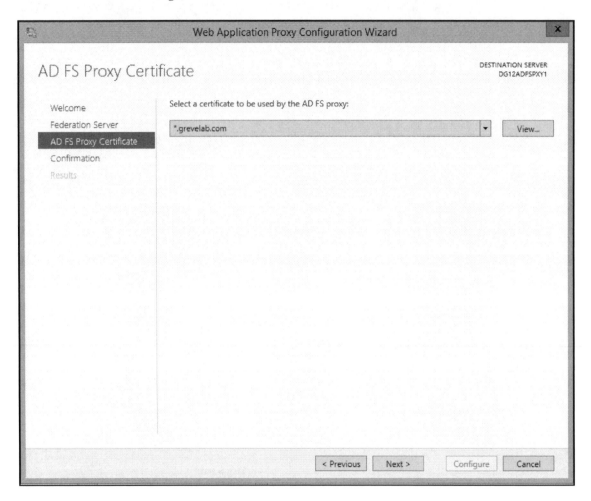

7. Confirm the configuration settings and then click **Configure**, as shown in the following screenshot:

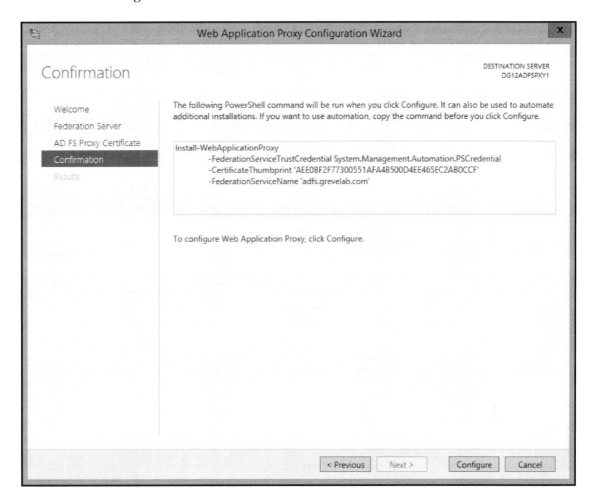

8. Confirm the **Web Application Proxy Configuration Wizard** finishes successfully and then click **Close,** as shown in the following screenshot:

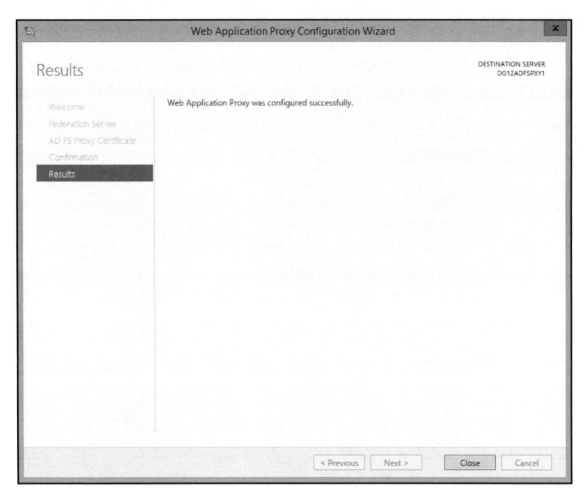

9. The **Remote Access Management Console** will now open. Click **Publish** in the **Tasks** column on the right, as shown in the following screenshot:

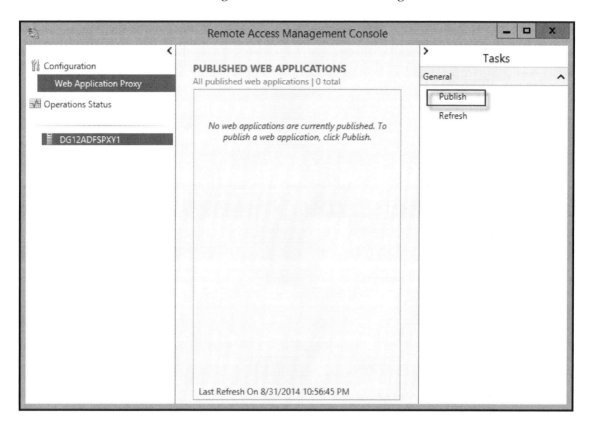

10. Click **Next**, as shown in the following screenshot:

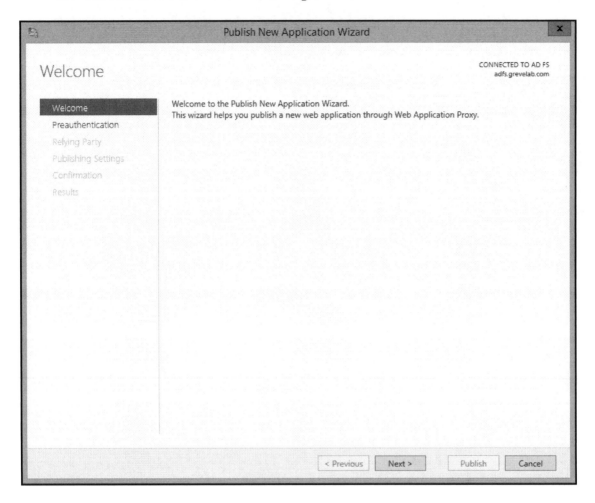

11. Select **Pass-through** and then click **Next**, as shown in the following screenshot:

12. Name the published service. Add the external URL, which should automatically update the backend server URL. In our example, the external URL would be `https://adfs.grevelab.com`. Now choose the same certificate you selected for the AD FS internal server. Then click **Next**, as shown in the following screenshot:

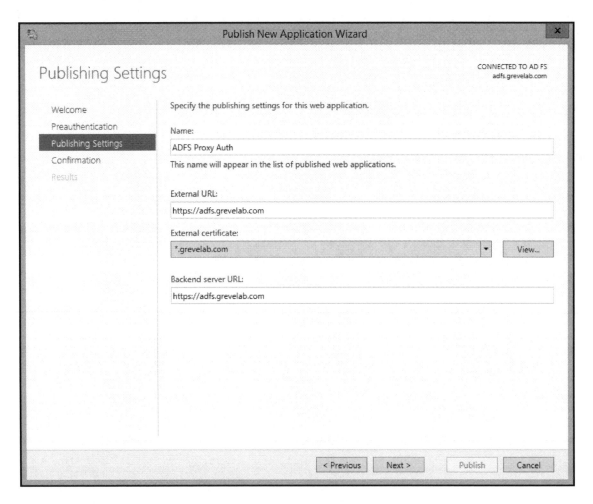

13. Click **Publish**, as shown in the following screenshot:

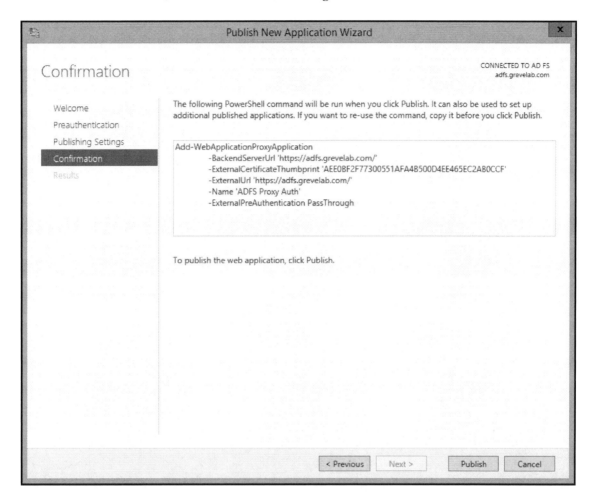

14. Once the configuration completes successfully, click **Close** as shown in the next screenshot:

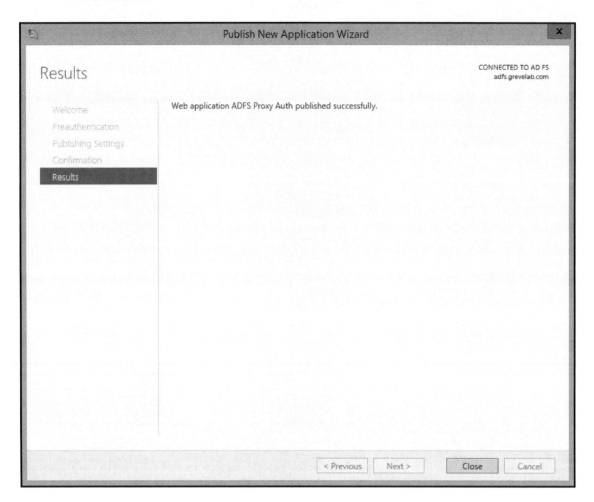

15. Once complete you should see a **PUBLISHED WEB APPLICATIONS** window, as shown in the following screenshot:

Basic testing of Active Directory Federation services

AD FS should now be functional, both internally and externally. To verify the functionality of AD FS, we can perform a quick test. To do so, follow these steps:

1. From a computer within the same network as your AD FS internal server, browse to `https://adfs.grevelab.com/adfs/ls/idpinitiatedsignon.aspx` (change `adfs.grevelab.com` to your AD FS FQDN).

2. Click **Sign in**, as shown in the following screenshot:

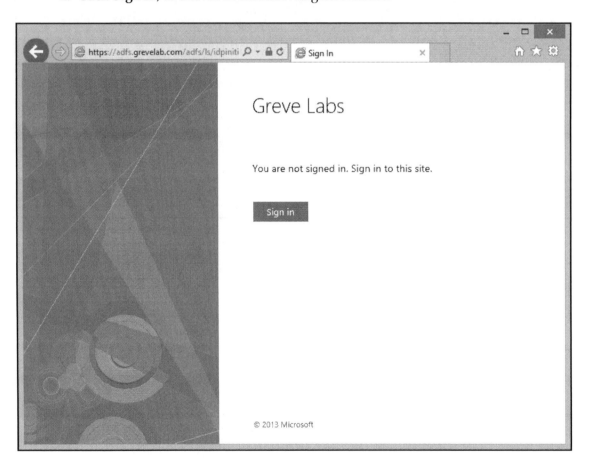

3. If you are prompted to authenticate, you may want to consider adding `adfs.yourdomain.com` or `*.yourdomain.com` to your intranet zone in Internet Explorer. If you are not prompted to authenticate and the service lets you in, you should see a **Sign Out** button. If you are prompted, you will see an authentication dialog popup requesting authentication. The following is an example:

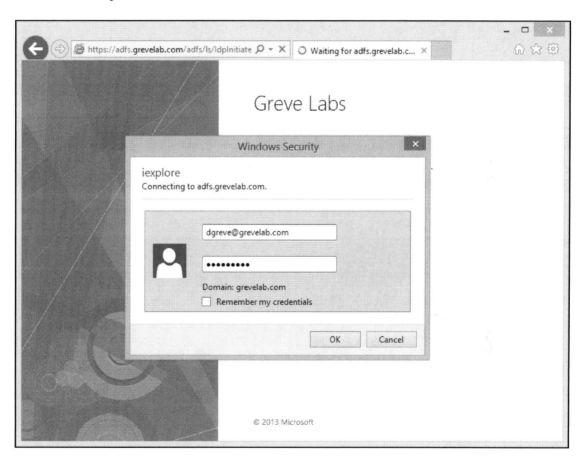

4. Now try to log on with the same address, but from an external machine from your organization (outside of your network and not connected to a VPN). Instead of a popup, you should see a forms-based logon from the AD FS proxy server, as shown in the following screenshot:

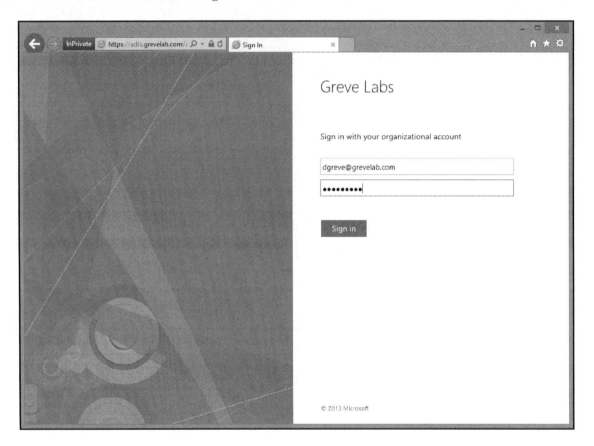

Summary

In this chapter, we learned how to build the first core integration point for AD FS to support authentication services with Office 365. We installed an internal AD FS server and configured a proxy server with the remote access role, and then configured the web application proxy service to improve security. Users can now authenticate to your on-premises network to gain access to the Office 365 portal and services. As your user base grows, you can build out your AD FS farm to improve redundancy and performance as required, by adding additional internal AD FS servers.

We now have our Office 365 tenant configured for single sign-on, improving the users' sign on experience. In our next chapter, we will focus on the build out of Directory Synchronization using **Azure Active Directory Connect (Azure AD Connect)**. Azure AD Connect is a critical component to the AD FS authentication. Directory Synchronization allows us to leverage the AD FS deployment by synchronizing and informing the service about who is federated and who is not.

9
Deploying a Hybrid Infrastructure – Directory Synchronization

Now that we have deployed **Active Directory Federation Services (AD FS)**, let's start to build our next core service, Directory Synchronization. By now you should have the necessary physical or virtual servers ready or in place. Directory Synchronization is the second service we need to build for our Office 365 integration. The core services and order of implementation are as follows:

1. AD FS
2. Office 365 Directory Synchronization
3. Exchange Hybrid

It's critical that we deploy these services in the order they are listed. If you choose to install these items out of order, some alternative configuration changes will be required and they are not described. Currently, they are listed in the order suggested by Microsoft best practices.

In this chapter, we will look at the deploying Directory Synchronization topic.

Deploying Directory Synchronization

After both AD FS internal and AD FS proxy are installed and configured, we need to start the installation of Directory Synchronization, before we can start testing whether AD FS was set up successfully for Office 365. The following high-level steps will be performed when installing the Directory Synchronization server.

1. Confirming preparation specifications
2. Running the DirSync readiness wizard
3. Installing AAD Connect
4. Verifying healthy Directory Synchronization

Confirming preparation specifications

Before deploying the AAD Connect tool, you must consider whether it is best for you to run the tool from an existing server, build a new one locally on your network, or provision a server within Azure. If you decide to run the tool on its own server then hosting it in Azure is definitely a good idea, especially if you don't have any virtualization resources on premises. Purchasing and building a new physical server is a costly exercise, but creating a new server in the cloud is relatively straight-forward. The downsides are that you have to maintain an Azure subscription and the necessary VPN infrastructure to support it.

If you wish to read up on how to deploy AAD Connect within Azure, visit the TechNet article at `https://technet.microsoft.com/en-us/library/dn63531(v=office.15).aspx`.

For this example, we are going to build the Directory Synchronization server locally with the following specifications:

- Windows Server 2012 R2
- 4 GB of memory
- Quad core 2Ghz
- Active Directory joined
- All the latest Windows updates applied
- .NET framework 4.5.1 installed

- Windows PowerShell 3.0 installed or later
- Computer name: `DG12DIRSYNC` (you will want to name this server based on your standard AD object naming scheme)
- SQL Server 2012 ExpressSP1+ (an external SQL server may be necessary, based on object sync requirements, which can be found at `http://technet.microsoft.com/en-us/library/jj151831.aspx#BKMK_ObjectLimits`)
- Installing the Directory Synchronization tool creates the `MSOL_{GUID}` account and three security groups:
    - ADSyncAdmins
    - ADSyncBrose
    - ADSyncPasswordSet
- This user and groups are located in the standard users organizational unit of the local Active Directory. This account is used by the Directory Synchronization tool to read the local Active Directory information. Do not move or remove this account. Moving or removing this account will cause synchronization failures.

The DirSync readiness wizard

The latest version of the Office 365 portal now includes a wizard to allow a smooth installation and configuration of the directory sync tool AAD Connect. The wizard will guide you through the process and also perform several checks, as we saw earlier in *Chapter 7, Preparing for a Hybrid Deployment and Migration*. Let's do a complete run through of the wizard to check, install, and configure Directory Synchronization.

From the Directory Synchronization server, log in to the Office 365 admin portal using an account with global admin credentials at `https://portal.office.com/admin`:

1. Expand the **Settings** menu, select **Services & add-ins**, and click on **Directory Synchronization**, as shown in the following screenshot:

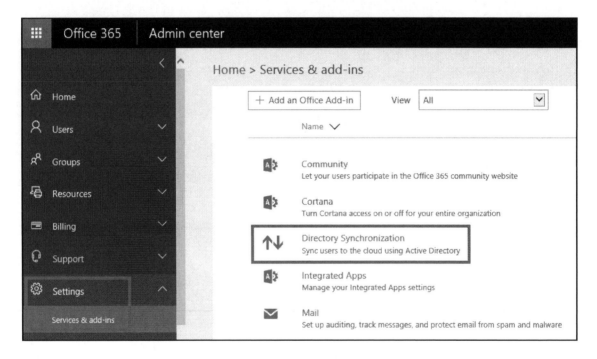

2. Click **Go to the DirSync readiness wizard**, as shown in the following screenshot:

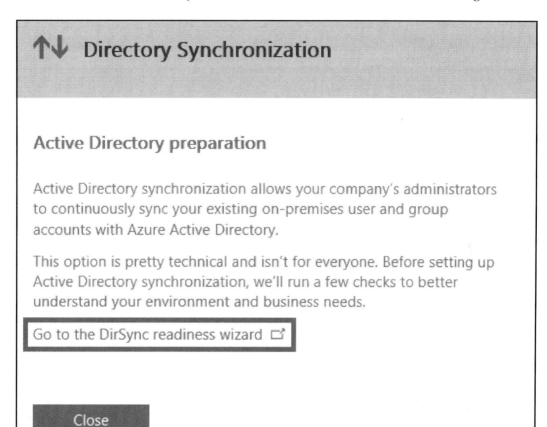

3. Click **Start Scan**, as shown in the following screenshot, and allow the wizard to install its scan tools and complete the required checks on your domain:

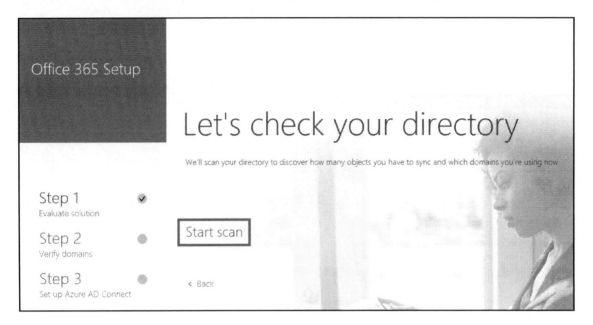

4. The wizard will now install its diagnostics tools and perform its checks. Click on **Run checks**, as shown in the following screenshot:

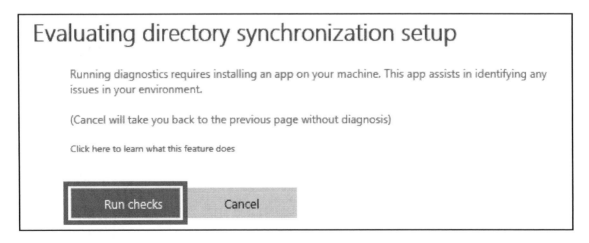

4. If all goes well, the scan will report no issues, as shown in the following screenshot:

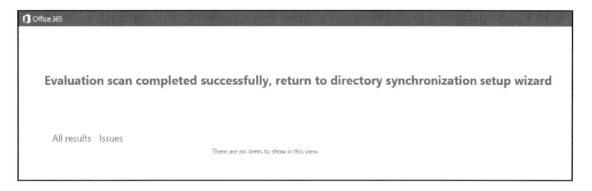

5. The wizard will now perform a scan on your Active Directory. Let it complete and click **Next**, as shown in the following screenshot, to view the results:

6. We can see all the objects the wizard found and verified. If the numbers don't look correct, you may have to perform some troubleshooting and run the checks again later. Assuming all looks okay, click on **Next** as shown in the following screenshot:

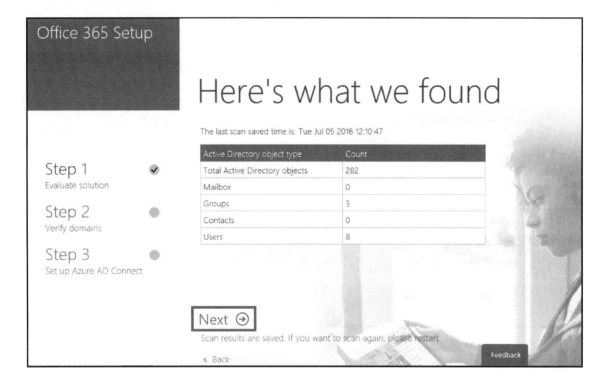

7. The wizard will now verify the domains registered in your Office 365 account and ensure that the domains listed in your Active Directory match. Click on **Next**, as shown in the following screenshot, to start the checking process:

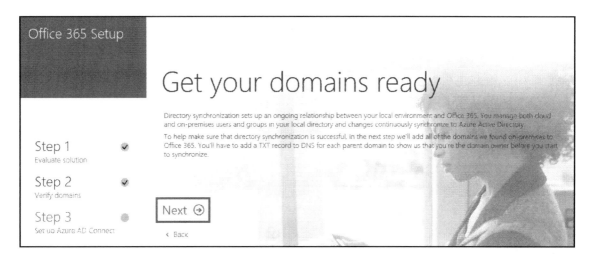

8. Here the wizard has verified that we are using two domains: our internal
   `office365lab.local` and our public `office365lab.co.uk` domains. Note
   that office `365lab.local` is not usable on the Internet so it won't be included.
   Click **Next** to continue:

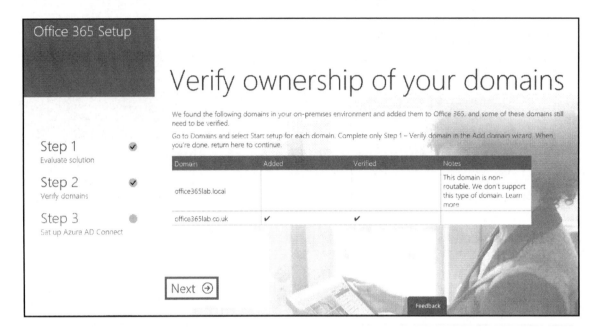

9. Now you are given the opportunity to download and run the IdFix tool, as we
   did in Chapter 7, *Preparing for a Hybrid Deployment and Migration*. If you haven't
   used this tool to check for inconsistencies in your Active Directory objects, then
   download it now and refer to the steps in Chapter 7, *Preparing for a Hybrid
   Deployment and Migration* for tips on correcting errors if found. Once you're ready,
   click **Next** as shown in the following screenshot to continue:

10. Use the **Download** link to download the latest version of the directory sync tool to the server ready for the next section, as shown in the following screenshot:

Installing Azure AD Connect

So far, the wizard has performed several checks for us and we have used the IdFix tool to correct any issues with our Active Directory objects. Now it's time to install and configure the directory sync tool, Azure AD Connect:

1. Launch the installer, accept the licensing terms, and click on **Continue** as shown in the following screenshot:

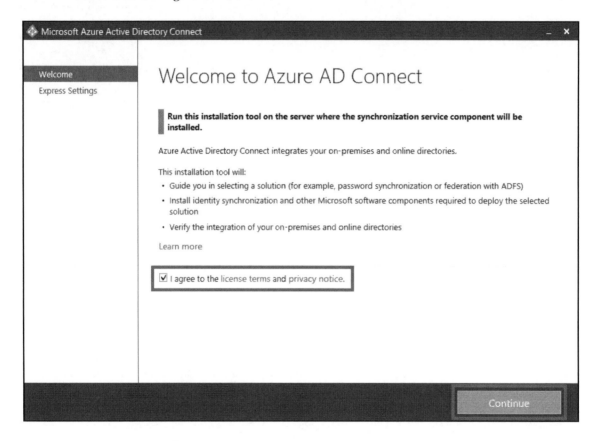

2. AAD Connect is constantly being developed so new features are being added all the time. In our environment, we are going to use the express settings, which will synchronize all the objects in our domain, including all their associated attributes. If you wish to use your own SQL server, or wish to explore many of the advanced options, then use the **Customize** button. We are going to be using the express setup, so click on **Use express settings** as shown in the following screenshot:

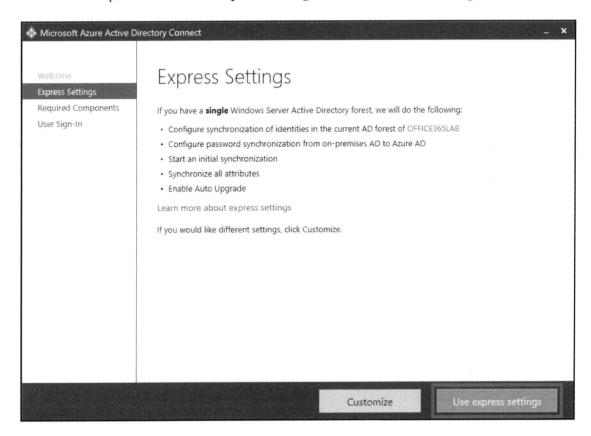

3. Now enter the credentials for your cloud administrator account and click on **Next**, as shown in the following screenshot:

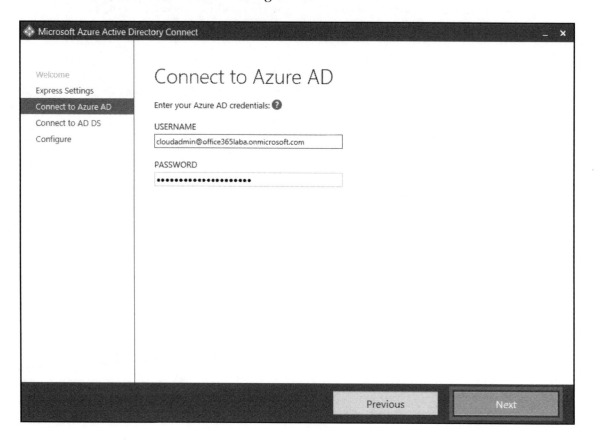

4. Enter the credentials of an enterprise administrator within your on-premises Active Directory and click on **Next**, as shown in the following screenshot:

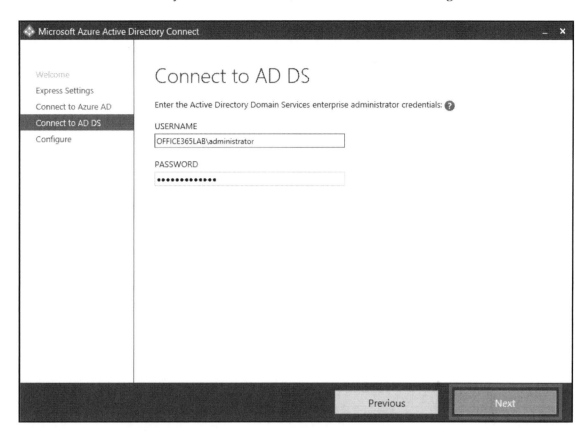

5. Here we are going to check the boxes to start the synchronization process after the installation completes, and because we are configuring an Exchange Hybrid, we must ensure the **Exchange hybrid deployment** option is selected.
6. Press **Install** to continue, as shown in the following screenshot:

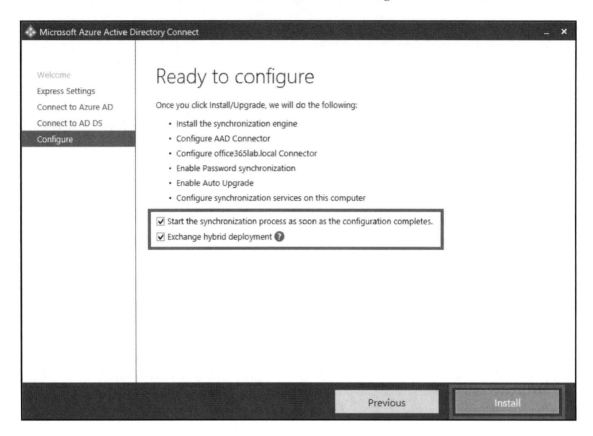

7. The installation will only take a few minutes to complete. Once it does, click on **Exit** as shown in the following screenshot to finish the installation:

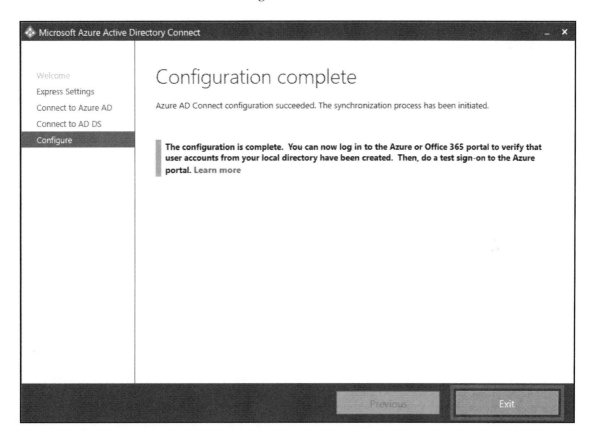

8. Now that we have completed the installation and configuration of AAD Connect, we return to the wizard on the portal and click **Next**, as shown in the following screenshot:

9. If all has gone well, the wizard will report **Directory synchronization is enabled** and will display the last sync time. Click on **Next** as shown in the following screenshot to continue:

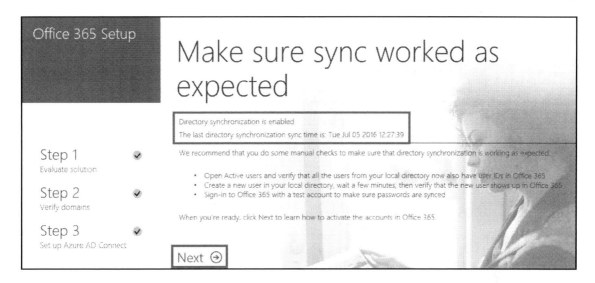

10. Now that the directory sync is enabled and active, the wizard will prompt you to check that all your users are listed and assign them licenses. Let's skip this step for now because we will check the health of our directory sync in the next section. Click on **Next** to continue, as shown in the following screenshot:

11. Congratulations, you're all ready to go! Click **Finish** as shown in the following screenshot to complete the wizard:

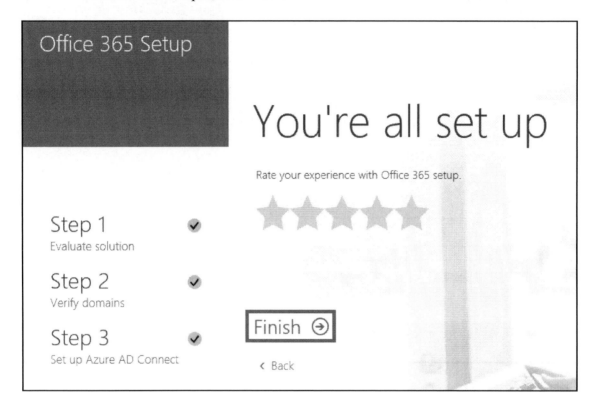

The Directory Synchronization should now be running. Based on your organization size, this could take a few minutes to a few hours. Check the Office 365 admin portal to see whether your accounts have synchronized. If after 24 hours you do not see synchronized accounts, you may have to troubleshoot for conflicts or restrictions in the environment.

Once you have confirmed that accounts have been synchronized to Office 365, you may want to take this time to validate that authentication works properly. To do so, just take one of your synchronized accounts in Office 365 and try to log on to `https://portal.office.com`. If everything is configured correctly, you should automatically be logged in. If logging on from a non-domain PC or if logging on externally to the network after you type in the user's UPN logon (`%username%@domain.com`), you should get either a logon dialog from your AD FS internal server or a forms-based logon from your AD FS proxy. After you logon as the user's Active Directory log on credentials (UPN), you should either receive a `You don't have a license to use Office 365 with the user ID assigned....` message or you will be provided with options that your account has been enabled with. Either way, if logging on from within your network and outside your network produce the same results, you should be in good shape to move forward.

If you do not receive a logon dialog from the internal AD FS server or a forms-based logon from your AD FS proxy, you may need to troubleshoot why authentication is not working. Most commonly, authentication does not work properly when either firewall rules are not specified properly, DNS records are not created properly, or the installation of AD FS and Directory Synchronization does not complete successfully.

Verify healthy Directory Synchronization

Now that we have AAD Connect installed and configured, you will need to verify that the users are listed correctly within the Office 365 portal. From **Admin center**, click on **Users** and then click on **Active users**. You should now see all your AD users listed and **Sync Type** should show **Synced with Active Directory**.

Perform a manual check of a few users to ensure all the properties have synchronized correctly and that each user has the correct user name. If you resolved all the errors and inconsistencies using IdFix, everything should be correct. Can you spot an error in the user list, as shown in the following screenshot? Note how Ian Waters has a user name of `ian.waters@office 365laba.onmicrosoft.com`. This has happened because the UPN was not set correctly to `@office365lab.co.uk` on the account in AD. However, this is not an issue because you can go back and make changes in AD as required, and the changes will be automatically synchronized every 30 minutes:

If you find that some users are missing or not working as expected, you can also view the **DirSync errors** section of **Admin center** in the **Settings** menu. If there are any objects that have invalid or conflicting attributes then they will be displayed, as shown in the following screenshot. Any issues will be highlighted for you so you can correct them from within your on-premises AD:

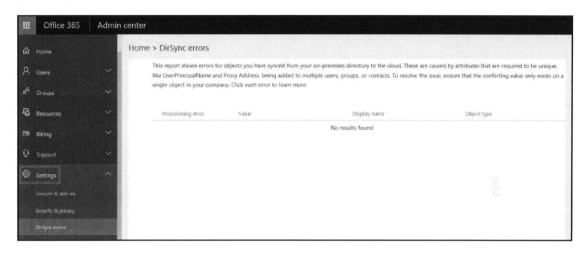

Within the **Admin center**, you can view information regarding the health of the directory synchronization by clicking on **Health** and then on **Service health** from the menu, as shown in the following screenshot. Here you can verify that the directory sync is enabled and check when the last sync occurred, which can be very useful when troubleshooting issues later:

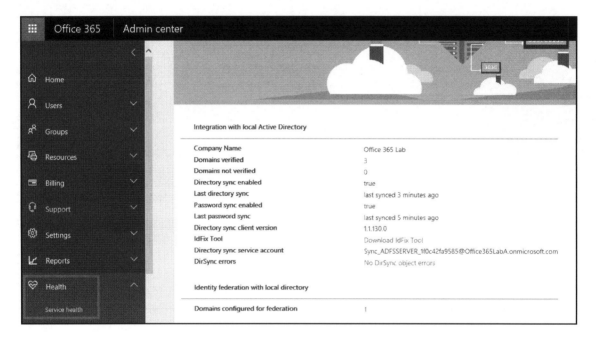

Once you are happy that all your AD objects have synchronized correctly, you can go ahead and assign them licenses as required, either in bulk or individually.

Advanced filtering options

When installing AAD Connect earlier in the chapter (see the *Installing Azure AD Connect* section), we used the express settings to set everything up. This is fine in most situations, but if you have a requirement to only synchronize specific objects within your AD then you will need to configure custom filtering options. To configure these options, follow these steps:

1. Open up **Azure AD Connect** from the start menu and click on **Customize synchronization options** as shown in the following screenshot. Then click on **Next**:

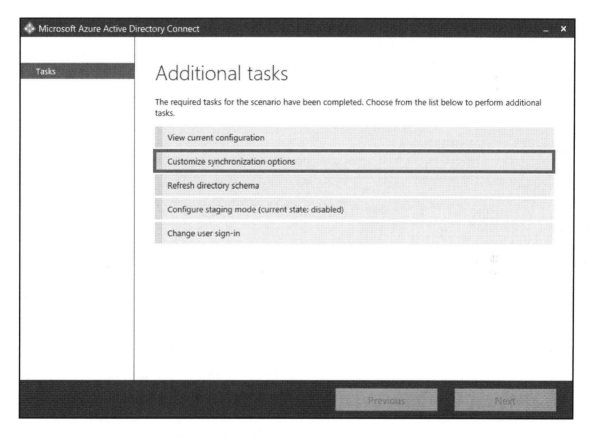

2. Enter your cloud admin credentials and press **Next**. Enter your local AD admin credentials and press **Next**.

3. Now you can configure which domains you wish to sync and even which **Organizational Unit (OU)**. Here we configure the **Head Office** OU in the `office365lab.local` domain and press **Next**.

What this will do is only synchronize objects within that OU and nothing else. You can use this type of filtering during the testing of AAD Connect. By moving users one by one into this OU, they will synchronize with Office 365, as shown in the following screenshot:

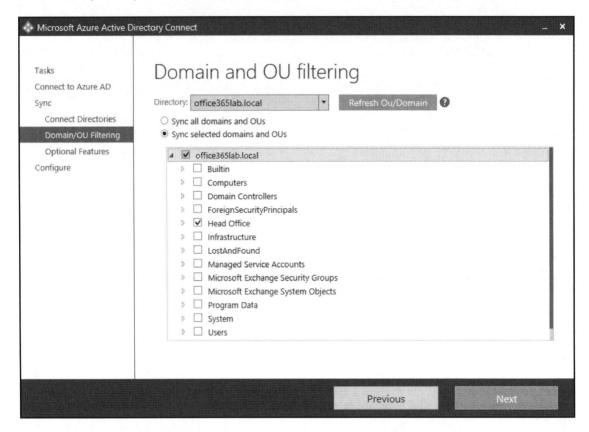

Now we can select some additional features. These are constantly being updated, improving the hybrid experience and blurring the lines between cloud and on-premises. We won't go through all the options here, but two additional ones that may be of interest are **Group** and **Password** write back. When these options are enabled, you can create groups and update passwords in the online portal and they will sync back to your on-premises AD. Without these options, all the changes need to be made in your on-premises AD and synchronized to the cloud.

Once you have made your selections, press **Next** as shown in the following screenshot and then press **Install** to complete the configuration changes:

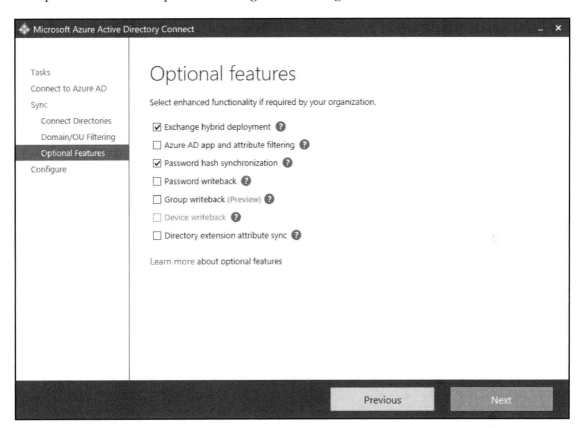

Synchronization schedule

By default, AAD Connect synchronizes the directories every 30 minutes. You can verify this by opening a PowerShell window on the Sync server and typing the following cmdlet: `Get-ADSyncScheduler`

This will return the current sync scheduler settings. Look for **CurrentlyEffectiveSyncCycleInterval**, which displays the current sync schedule, as shown in the following screenshot. 30 minutes is the minimum allowed sync schedule but you can increase this as you wish if you don't want to run the sync as often:

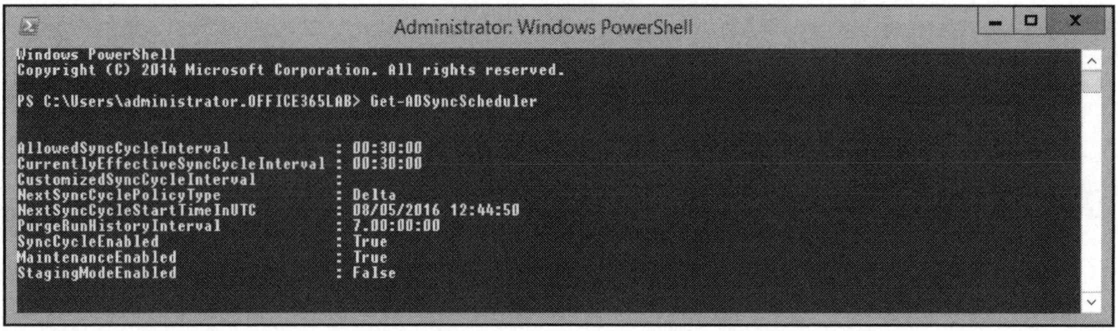

If you wish to make changes to the sync schedule, use the following cmdlet:

```
Set-ADSyncScheduler -CustomizedSyncCycleInterval 01:00:00
```

The preceding example will set the scheduler to run a sync every hour.

Manual syncing

Sometimes you will want to perform a sync manually rather than waiting 30 minutes or more for the schedule to kick in. This is often done after changing objects in AD that you want to sync to the cloud, a new user or a change of e-mail address. To perform a manual sync, open a PowerShell window on the sync server and run the following cmdlet:

```
Start-ADSyncSyncCycle -PolicyType Delta
```

The output will be as shown in the following screenshot:

As you can see in the preceding screenshot, there is no output to this cmdlet but it will start a sync and it can be verified by viewing the server's application log and checking for events with the source listed in Directory Synchronization.

Summary

In this chapter, we learned how to build the second core integration point, Directory Synchronization, to support authentication services, address book synchronization, and the future deployment of Exchange Hybrid with Office 365. We looked at how to filter objects so that only objects that are held in a specified OU get synchronized. Finally, we looked at the sync scheduler and how to change the frequency of the sync process, as well as how to manually start a sync.

In our next chapter, we will focus on the build out of Exchange Hybrid, which is a critical component of our migration to Exchange Online from Exchange on-premises.

10
Deploying a Hybrid Infrastructure – Exchange Hybrid

Now that we have deployed Directory Synchronization, let's start to configure our next core service, Exchange Hybrid. By now you should have the necessary physical or virtual servers, firewall, and DNS ready or in place. Exchange Hybrid is the third service we need to build for our Office 365 integration. The core services are:

1. AD FS
2. Office 365 Directory Synchronization
3. Exchange Hybrid

It's critical that we deploy these services in the order they are listed. If you choose to install these items out of order, some alternative configuration changes will be required that are not described in this book. Currently, they are listed in the order suggested by Microsoft best practices.

In this chapter, we will look at the deploying Exchange Hybrid topic.

Deploying Exchange Hybrid

By now, AD FS and Directory Synchronization should be deployed and tested. Do not proceed with Exchange Hybrid until Directory Synchronization has fully synchronized your environment. The following high-level steps will be performed when installing the Exchange Hybrid:

1. Confirming preparation specifications
2. Creating a hybrid configuration

We will gain a better understanding of these steps in the following sections.

Confirming preparation specifications

For this example, we are going to assume that you have already deployed an Exchange 2013 or 2016 server, with the latest rollup, within your environment. This should meet the following requirements:

- Exchange deployed on a Windows Server 2012 R2, with the Client Access Server and Mailbox Server roles deployed
- Existing Exchange versions within the same Exchange Organization can communicate properly with the Exchange Server deployed
- The Exchange server is externally accessible
- The Exchange server has a public certificate for Autodiscover and **Exchange Web Services** (**EWS**) installed

Creating a hybrid configuration

At this point, we should be prepared to create the hybrid configuration by enabling and running the hybrid configuration wizard.

1. In the **Exchange admin center**, click on the **hybrid** option in the left-hand navigation panel. Now click **enable** to start the hybrid configuration wizard, as shown in the following screenshot:

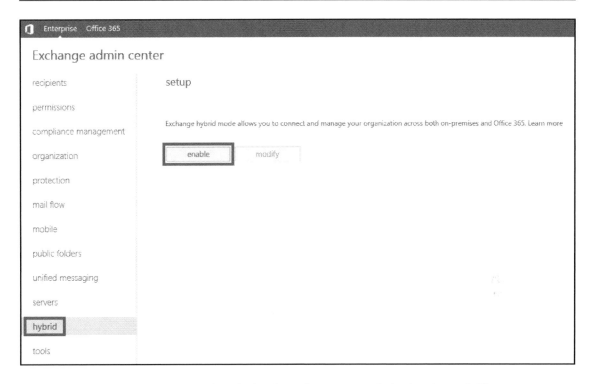

2. Since this will be the first hybrid configuration, click **sign in to Office 365** to attach your existing Office 365 tenant to the EAC, as shown in the following screenshot:

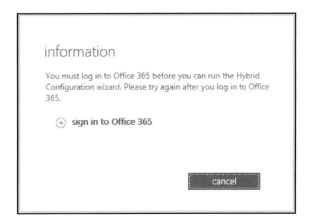

3. You will now be redirected to your Office 365 subscription. Log on to the Office 365 subscription with a global admin account, as shown in the following screenshot:

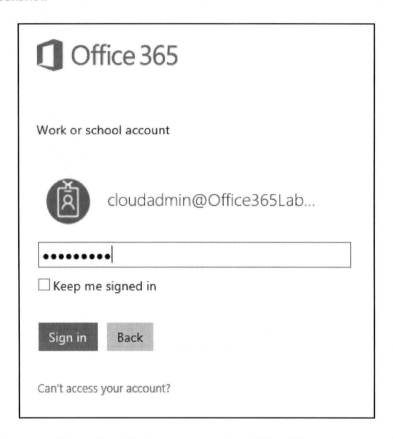

4. Exchange will now be able to connect to the Office 365 tenant and will activate the **Office 365** tab in the EAC.
5. In the EAC, while on the **Enterprise** tab, click on the **hybrid** option in the left-hand navigation panel. Now click **enable** again. This time you will be directed to start the **Hybrid Configuration Wizard**, as shown in the following screenshot.
6. Click click here to install the hybrid configuration wizard as shown in the following screenshot:

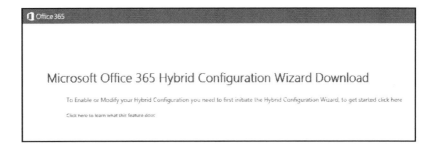

7. Once installed, the hybrid configuration wizard will start. Click **next** to continue, as shown in the following screenshot:

8. The wizard should detect the best Exchange Server to use to manage the hybrid configuration from. Here it has detected the exchange server we are running the wizard on. If your tenant is hosted in China, you will need to select **21Vianet** from the dropdown box. We shall leave this as **Microsoft Office 365**. Click **next** to continue, as shown in the following screenshot:

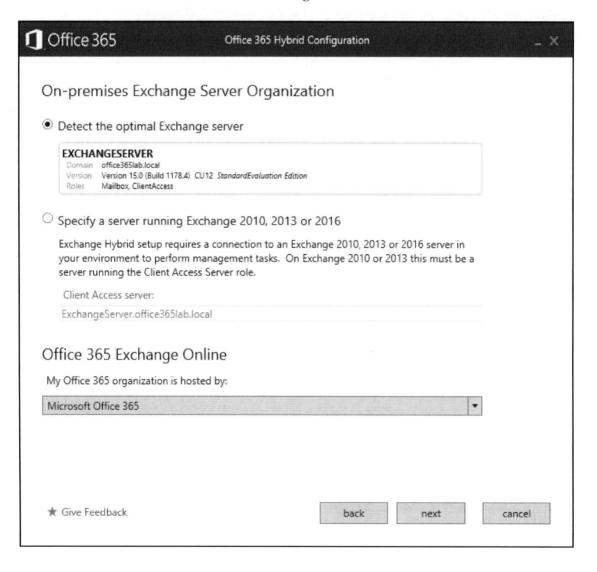

9. Now enter your AD and Office 365 admin credentials to allow the wizard to connect and configure both environments. Press **next** to continue, as shown in the following screenshot:

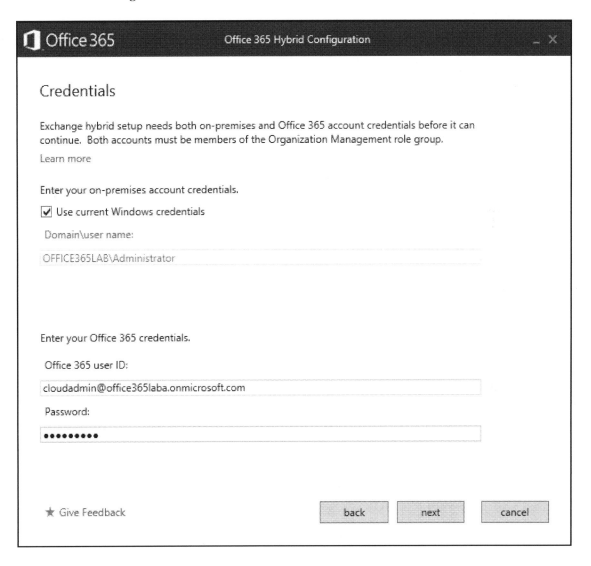

10. The credentials entered will be verified. If they fail, go back and check they have been entered correctly. Once they succeed, press **next** to continue, as shown in the following screenshot:

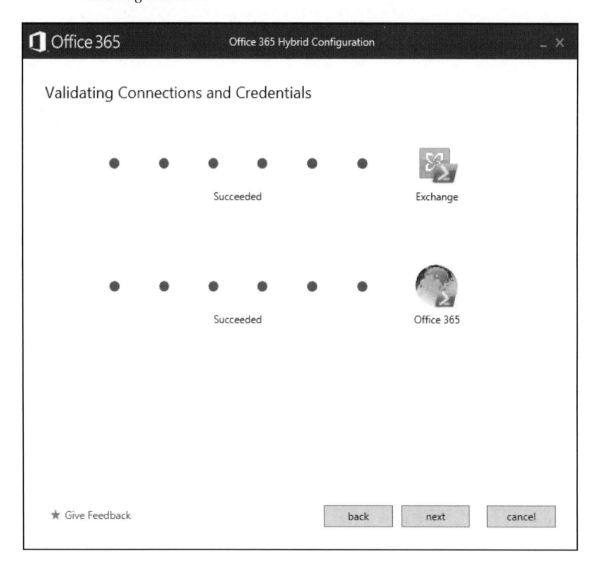

11. Next, we are prompted to create a new TXT record on the public DNS for the `office365lab.co.uk` domain. Copy the TXT token and create a new TXT record with this value, tick the check box, and press **verify domain ownership**. Once you have created the TXT record, it can take a few hours for your DNS host to make the changes live. If the verification fails, come back later and try again. Once the domain verifies, press **next** to continue, as shown in the following screenshot:

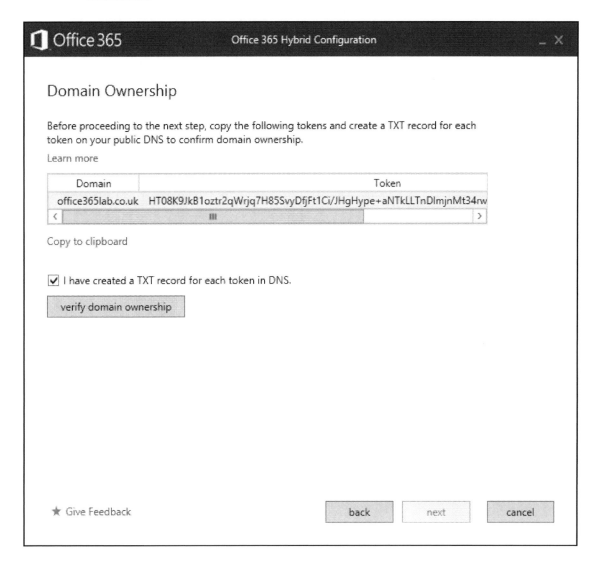

12. Depending on your mail routing configuration, you may be using a mixed role server or an Exchange edge server for mail routing. Click on the appropriate mail routing server (in our case, we will not be using an Exchange Edge server). Click on more options to show your mail routing options. If you plan to route all the e-mail sent from mailboxes hosted in Office 365 via your on-premises exchange deployment, check **Enable centralized mail transport** option. Most organizations that require a single point for journaling and delivery reports select this option. Then click **next**, as shown in the following screenshot.

You may want to route through your on-premises mail system for compliance reasons, to maintain existing banner messages, or to control on-premises routing rules – if you have not already pushed them to Office 365.

13. Now choose the Exchange Server that will receive the connector for Exchange Online. This server should have the appropriate certificate and external DNS names for name resolution. Click **next**, as shown in the following screenshot:

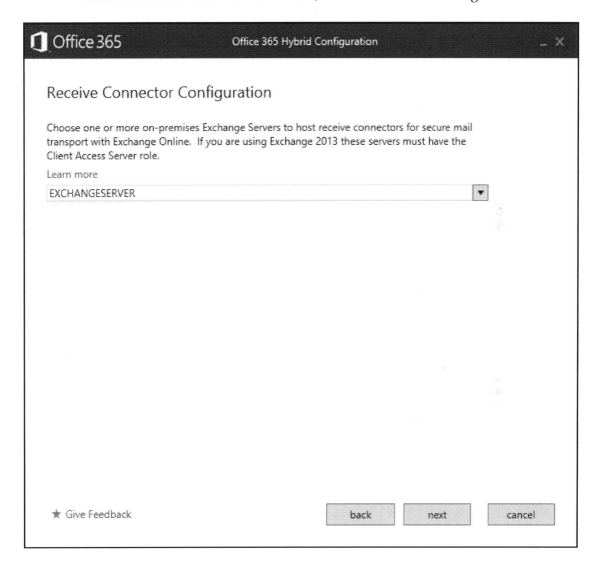

14. Now choose the Exchange Server that will send the connector for Exchange Online. This server should have the appropriate certificate and external DNS names for name resolution. Click **next**, as shown in the following screenshot.

 If you have not opened the firewall ports or assigned a record in DNS for your Hybrid server, be sure to do this now based on the guidance provided in Chapter 7, *Preparing for a Hybrid Deployment and Migration.*

15. At this point, if you installed your certificate properly, it should automatically be listed. If you have more than one certificate, make sure you select the proper one. Click **next**, as shown in the following screenshot:

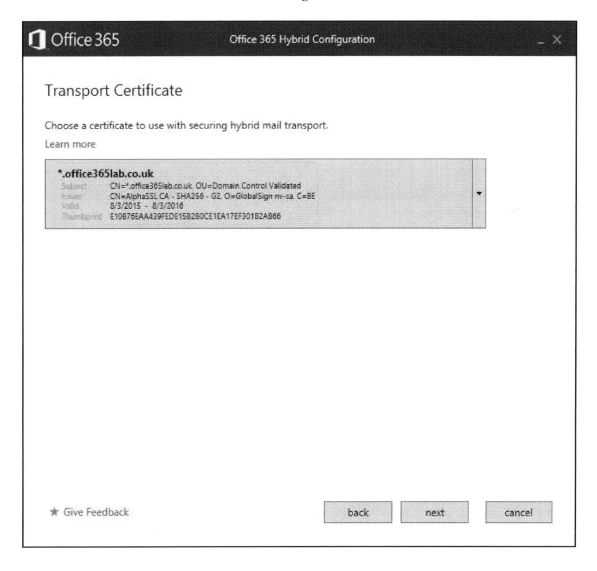

16. Now enter the name space you plan to use for mail routing, which is assigned to your on-premises server specified in the previous steps. Then click **next**, as shown in the following screenshot:

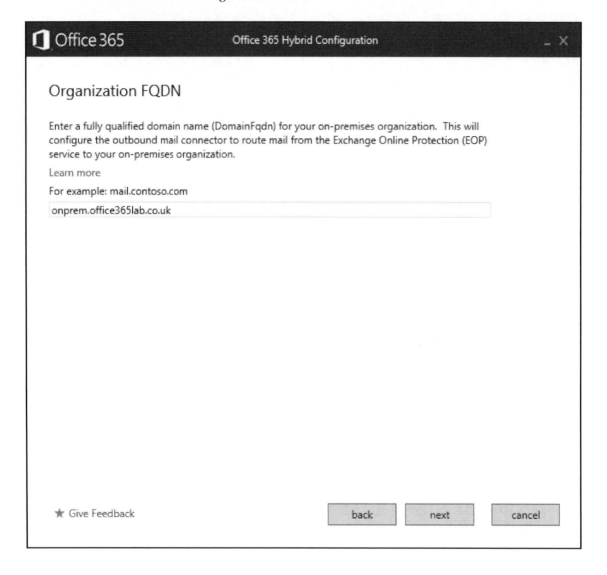

17. The wizard is now ready to configure the required settings to create a hybrid configuration. Click **update** to continue, as shown in the following screenshot:

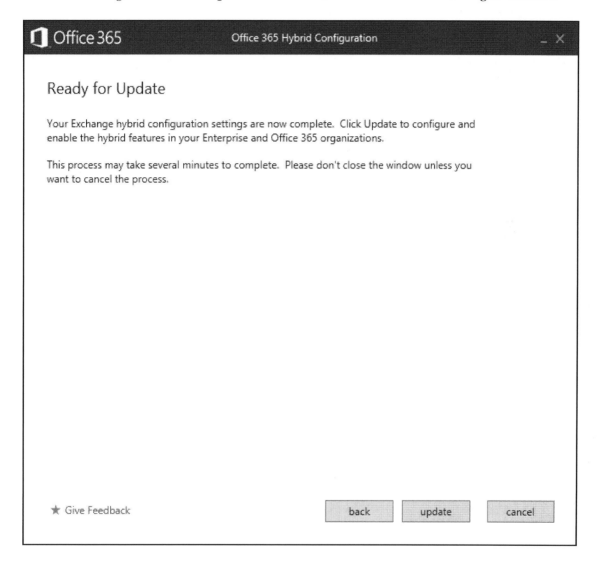

18. The wizard will run several PowerShell scripts in the background for a few minutes, as shown in the following screenshot:

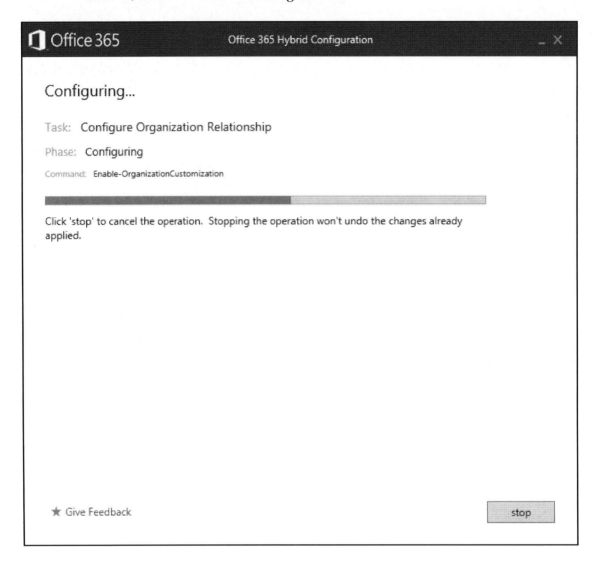

19. If everything is successful, the wizard will present a **Congratulations!** message on the screen, as shown in the following screenshot. If there were any errors, they will be listed here. You can correct any issues that are reported and rerun the wizard at any time without any concern. Click **close** to complete the wizard:

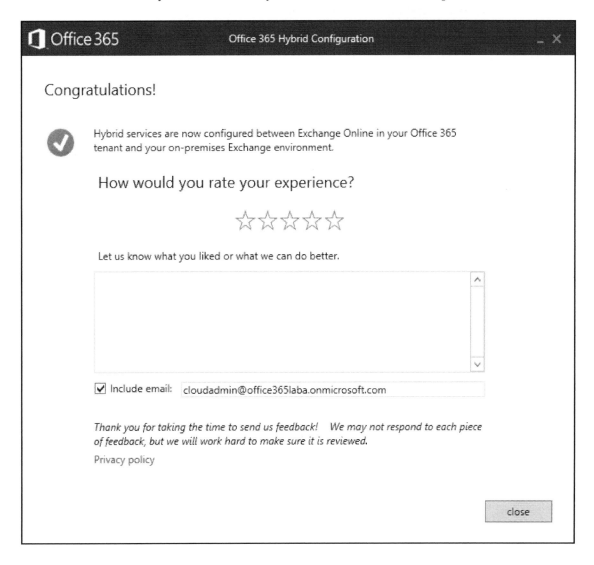

During the configuration, the following changes take place:

- Organization relationships between on-premises and Office 365 are created
- EOP inbound/outbound connectors are created
- MRSProxy is enabled (required for mailbox moves)
- E-mail proxy address of `<tenant name>.mail.onmicrosoft.com` is added to the default domain policy

> Earlier, in step 7, we were asked to create a TXT record for the domains we will be using. Ensure those TXT records are added to your external DNS and allow time for them to propagate over the Internet. If configuration errors occur, check to ensure Autodiscover is responding and your certificate is valid for Autodiscover. One way to check Autodiscover is to leverage an Exchange testing site provided by Microsoft: `https://www.testexchangeconnectivity.com`. In addition to certificates, check to ensure the two accounts you used have the proper permissions. Finally, validate Outlook Anywhere access is possible to this server, from the outside in.

Now verify that the organization relationship was created. In the on-premises Exchange Organization, click on **Organization** and then on **Sharing**. You should see an **On-premises to O365...** relationship, as shown in the following screenshot:

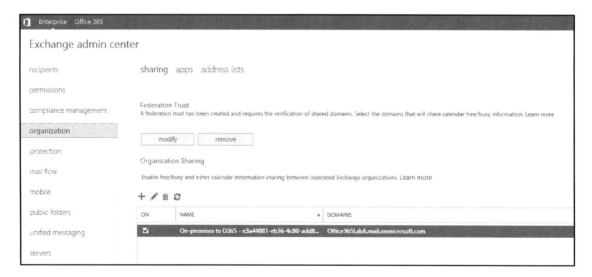

Now check the Office 365 organization configuration under your Office 365 subscription. Click on **Organization** and then on **Sharing**. You should see an **O365 to On-premises…** relationship, as shown in the following screenshot:

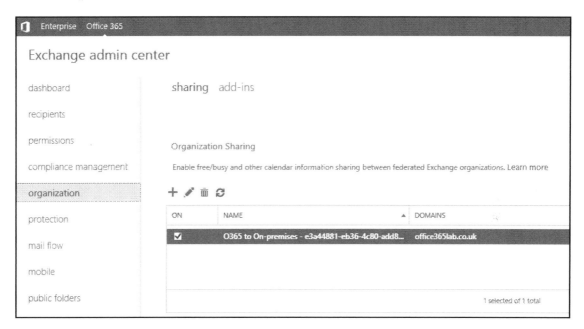

Verify **MRSProxy** is enabled by opening the **Exchange Management Shell** with an elevated prompt. Then type the following:

```
Get-WebServicesVirtualDirectory | fl Server, Name, MRSProxyEnabled
```

You will see the following output:

Verify the **Exchange Online Protection (EOP)** inbound/outbound connectors were automatically created. Click on Office 365 in the EAC, then click on **Mail Flow** on the left navigation, and then on **connectors,** as shown in the following screenshot. You should now see two hybrid connectors, one inbound and one outbound, if you enabled centralized transport:

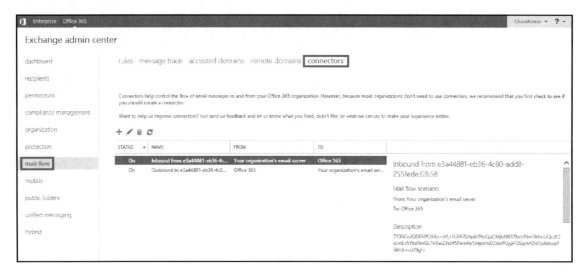

This completes our Exchange Hybrid configuration. If you were able to validate all settings, no additional steps are required for the hybrid configuration.

Summary

In this chapter, we learned how to build our third core integration point, Exchange Hybrid, to enable rich coexistence and simplify the migration process to Office 365. This key integration point allows us to leverage Office 365, as if it were an extension of our on-premises Exchange Organization.

In the next chapter, we will learn how to leverage all the integration points to start migrating mailboxes from on-premises to Office 365.

11
Performing a Hybrid Migration

Now that we have implemented all the core integration components for Office 365, it's time to start testing and performing the migrations of mailboxes. There are many ways to perform migrations, or even account provisioning. Our focus will be to perform migrations from the Exchange Admin Center. Before we get started, let's make sure your end users are ready for the migration. Once we validate end user readiness, we will perform both types of migrations. Specifically, we will focus on the following points:

- Preparing the end user for Office 365
- Performing a migration from the Exchange Admin Center

Preparing the end user for Office 365

There are two primary ways to deploy updates to the end users in preparation for Office 365. These two ways include:

- End user self-deployment
- Distribution from a software deployment service

End user self-deployment

This method consists of the end user navigating to the Office 365 portal and running the Office 365 desktop setup:

1. To simplify the process, you can provide your users with the URL that takes them directly to the downloads page. This URL is `https://portal.office.com/OLS/M ySoftware.aspx`. The users will have to log on with their Active Directory account, since the portal will now be using AD FS for all user accounts that were synchronized to Office 365.

2. Once the users are on this page, they will be able to see what is available for installation. If you have not altered the user's licenses, prior to navigating to this link, the portal will notify them that they do not yet have a license, as shown in the following screenshot:

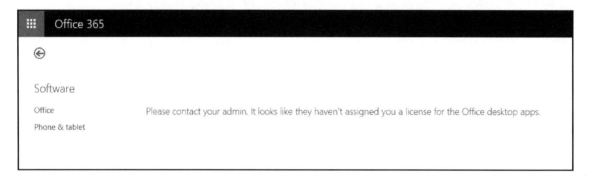

3. If you plan to deploy the Office suite from Office 365 and Lync, then you may want to license the users you are migrating for those services. By doing so, the users will have more install options as they prepare for Office 365. To assign licenses, let's log on as an admin to `https://portal.office.com`, then navigate to **Users** | **Active users**, as shown in the following screenshot:

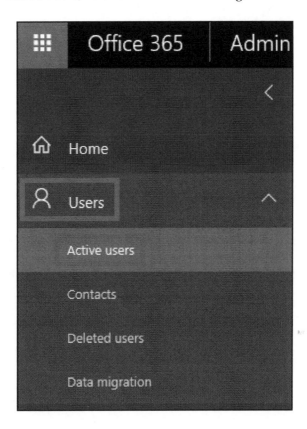

4. Click on the user you wish to add a license to and then click **Edit** next to **Product licenses** and enable all the licenses you plan to assign to this user, as shown in the following screenshot:

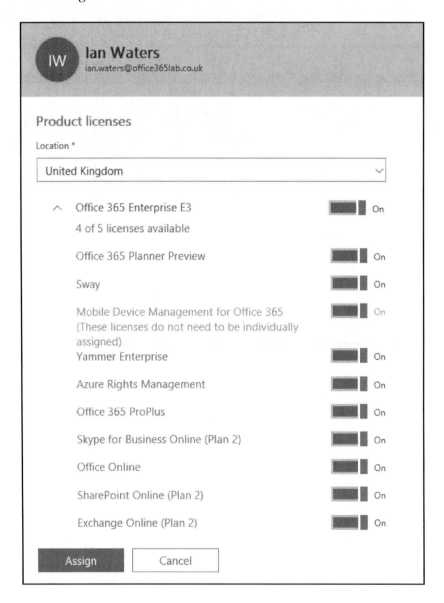

5. Be sure to also set the user's location correctly, before saving. Not setting the location correctly can result in certain features, such as hosted voicemail and Skype audio and video, to stop working due to Microsoft usage restrictions. Once you have completed these steps, click **Save**.

The user you enabled can now navigate to `https://portal.office.com/OLS/MySoftware.aspx`. In this example, we enabled a user with all the licenses in the E3 plan. When the user navigates to this page now, they will see more install options, as shown in the following screenshot:

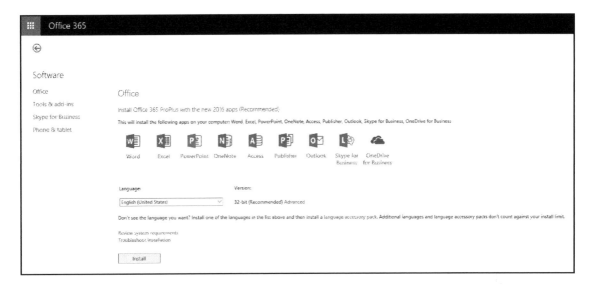

At this point, the user can install Office 365 Pro Plus, Skype for Business standalone, or Office apps for their mobile device. To simplify the transition of an on-premises Exchange mailbox to Exchange Online, we recommend you deploy Office 365 Pro Plus to the end-user's workstations/devices.

Distribution from a software deployment service

Larger organizations typically do not allow local administrative access to workstations. Because of this, Microsoft has provided a list of requirements for the end user's workstations. These requirements can be found at `http://technet.microsoft.com/en-us /library/office-365-system-requirements.aspx`. Specifically for Exchange Online, it's important that Office/Outlook has the most recent updates/service pack applied. Some methods to deploy the latest Office software can be deployed through:

- **Group Policy Object (GPO)**
- **System Center Configuration Manager (SCCM)**
- Related software management/deployment software

These software packages can all be applied any time prior to the migration of these users.

Performing a migration from the Exchange Admin Center

Performing a migration from the EAC is relatively simple, as long as the Exchange Hybrid configuration has been validated and is functional.

Let's start off by recapping what we learned from Chapter 6, *Performing for a Simple Migration*, and define different parts of the migration process and the terminology used. This will help to make the next instructions a lot easier to follow.

Migration batches

When we migrate user mailboxes into Office 365, we create a migration batch that lets us define the type of migration, select the users to migrate, and define what we want to happen once the migration completes. Effectively, this lets us migrate the users in manageable batches and use different settings if required.

When we create a batch, we have an option to suspend the migration just before it completes. This enables us to migrate the mailboxes of several users but not actually transfer the mailboxes to Office 365 until we are ready. Once you are ready to finish the migration and move the mailboxes, you simply complete the migration batch and the remaining data is transferred. This means we can sync mailbox data over several hours or days and pause until our next maintenance window, when we can finish the migration without causing any interruption to the users.

Even if you use to automatically complete the migration batch, users' mailboxes will continue to synchronise once every 24 hours while the migration batch is active in the portal.

Endpoints

During the setup of a migration batch, we define our migration type and select the mailboxes to migrate, but we also need to configure an endpoint. An endpoint is a set of options that Office 365 uses to connect to our on-premises Exchange servers. These options include the server location, the connection type, and what credentials to use to extract data from the user's mailboxes.

Now that we have a better understanding of the terminology, let's get started!

1. Connect to the Exchange Hybrid server you set up for Office 365. Open the EAC on this server. You should see both your on-premises organization and the Office 365 organization you created for the Hybrid configuration. In the following screenshot, I have highlighted the links that you use to switch between the on-premises and Office 365 portals:

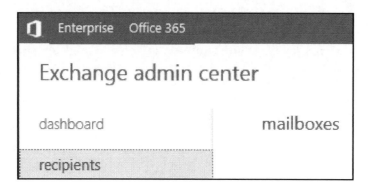

2. Now navigate to the Office 365 organization, go to **recipients** and then go to **migration**. Click on the + sign and select **Migrate to Exchange Online,** as shown in the following screenshot:

3. The migration batch wizard will open. You must now select what type of migration you would like to perform. Since we are performing a Hybrid move, select **Remote move migration**. Click **next**, as shown in the following screenshot:

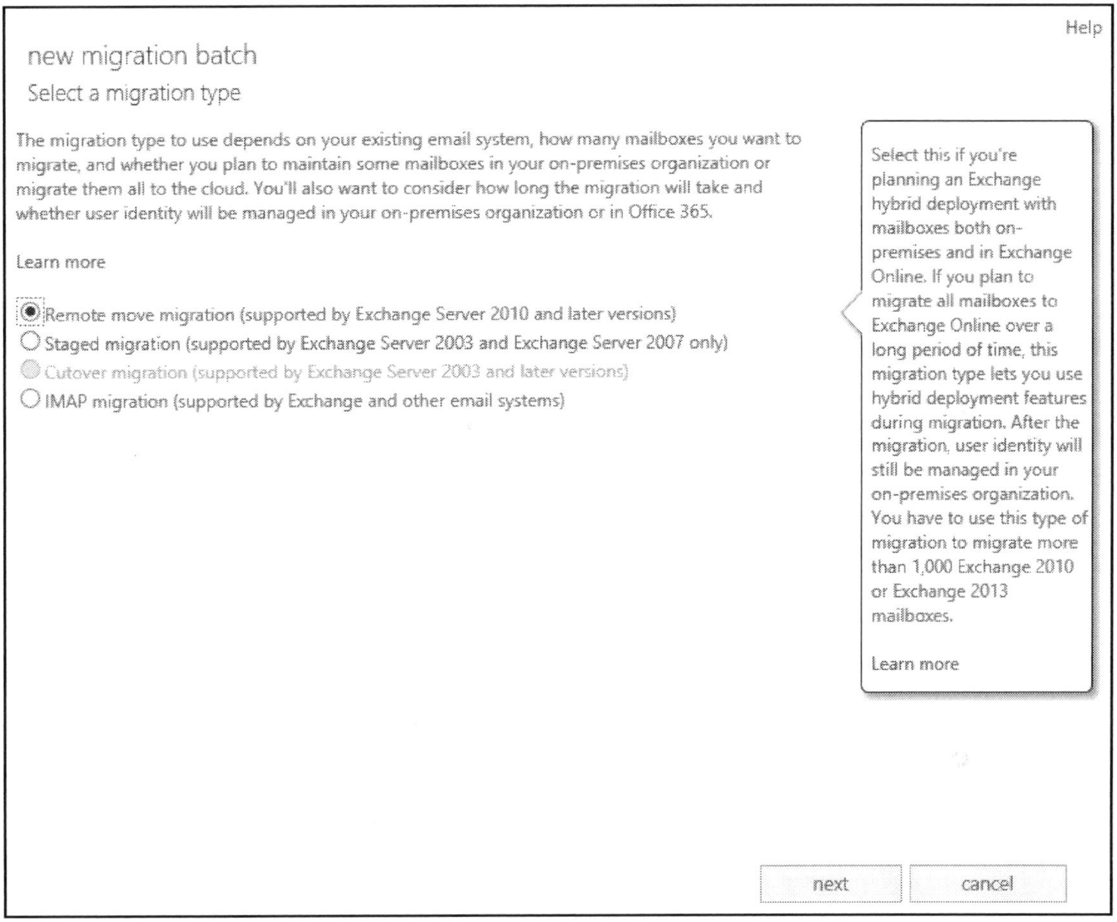

Help

new migration batch

Select a migration type

The migration type to use depends on your existing email system, how many mailboxes you want to migrate, and whether you plan to maintain some mailboxes in your on-premises organization or migrate them all to the cloud. You'll also want to consider how long the migration will take and whether user identity will be managed in your on-premises organization or in Office 365.

Learn more

- ⦿ Remote move migration (supported by Exchange Server 2010 and later versions)
- ○ Staged migration (supported by Exchange Server 2003 and Exchange Server 2007 only)
- ○ Cutover migration (supported by Exchange Server 2003 and later versions)
- ○ IMAP migration (supported by Exchange and other email systems)

Select this if you're planning an Exchange hybrid deployment with mailboxes both on-premises and in Exchange Online. If you plan to migrate all mailboxes to Exchange Online over a long period of time, this migration type lets you use hybrid deployment features during migration. After the migration, user identity will still be managed in your on-premises organization. You have to use this type of migration to migrate more than 1,000 Exchange 2010 or Exchange 2013 mailboxes.

Learn more

next   cancel

4. At this point, you can select to move one mailbox or multiple mailboxes. Select the mailbox you plan to move to Exchange Online. Click **next**, as shown in the following screenshot:

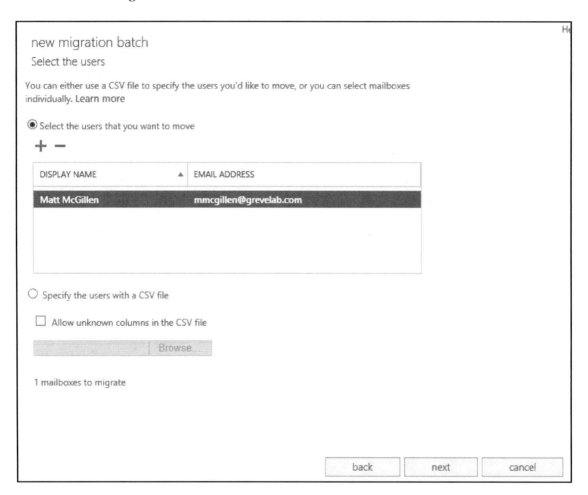

5. When you set up Exchange Hybrid, the endpoints were automatically created and selected as part of the migration process. The on-premises credentials used during the hybrid configuration wizard are set on the endpoint. If the password requires updating, you can edit the existing endpoint and set a new password. If everything is correct and the hybrid was set up properly, you should be able to click **next,** as shown in the following screenshot:

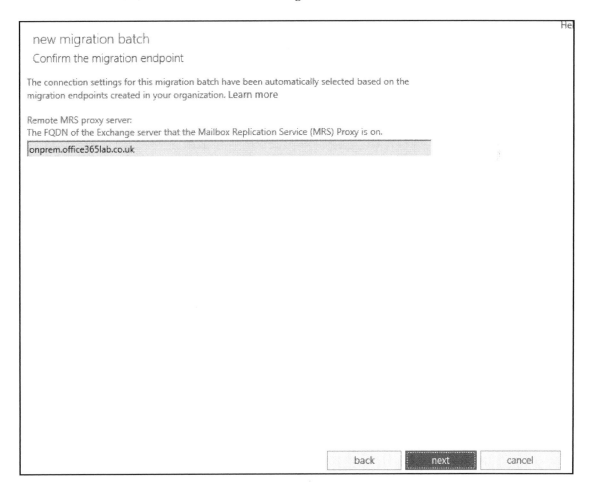

6. Now name the migration batch with a familiar name related to the user(s) you selected. If the user has an archive, the archive will automatically be moved with the user. If you want to only migrate the user's archive, select that option. The migration process will also skip 10 bad messages by default. If you are moving a known problematic mailbox or the mailbox has large attachments, you can also define how many it will skip before cancelling the migration. Then click **next**, as shown in the following screenshot:

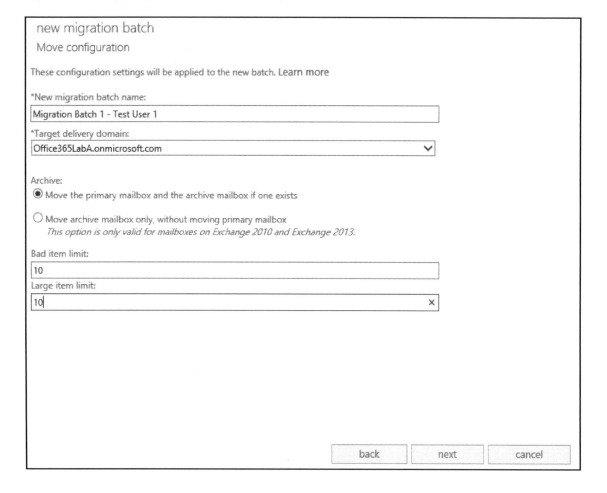

7. At this point, you can select who to send a report to as the batch completes. You can also choose to manually start this batch later. In addition, you can select to migrate the majority of the mailbox now, but put the mailbox migration in a hold state before it completes. Only select this option if you have large mailboxes and want to complete their migration at a later time. Now click **new**, as shown in the following screenshot:

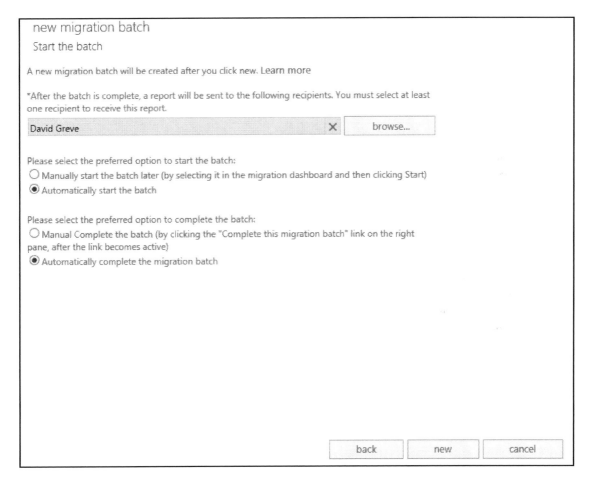

8. To view the move process, go to Office 365 organization in EAC, click on **recipients**, and then click on **migration**. In this window, you can view the migration process and check whether it is complete.

9. Once the move request is complete, as shown in the following screenshot, you can validate that the end user was migrated properly by having them log on to Outlook or Outlook Web Access:

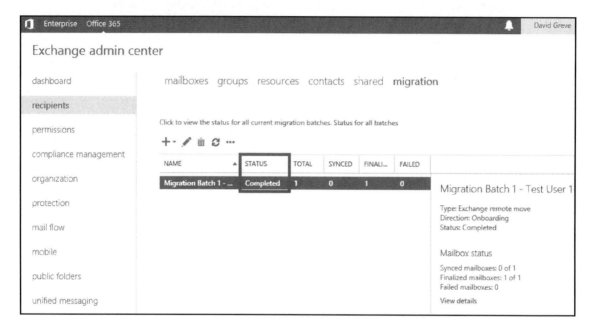

10. When the user next opens Outlook, they will receive the following message. Once the user restarts Outlook, they will automatically connect to Office 365 and be prompted to authenticate their mailbox, as shown in the following screenshot. It's critical they enter their UPN to log on (for AD FS) and their Active Directory password:

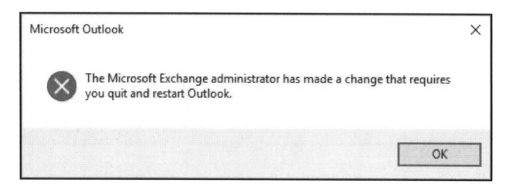

11. Finally, if you have not already done so, apply the appropriate Exchange licenses to the mailboxes you migrated. The mailboxes will function in Office 365 for a short period of time without these licenses. However, it is very important that you apply the appropriate licenses right away, so the users receive the services they expect in Office 365 and are not locked out.

Summary

In this chapter, we reviewed how to both license and migrate the users in an Exchange Hybrid configuration, from on-premises Exchange to Exchange Online. We learned about migrations from on-premises while leveraging the Exchange Admin Center from within Office 365.

In next chapter, we will learn about the clean-up activities we can perform after we complete all migrations to Office 365, from Exchange on-premises.

12
Post Migration Considerations

By now, we have a good understanding of how to prepare for, deploy, and start the process of migrating mailboxes. Before we get too far down the path of migrations, let's consider some additional changes that may be required to either support a complete move to Office 365 or a long-term coexistence strategy.

As we approach finalizing our migrations to Office 365, let's review some on-premises changes that may be necessary. These changes may include:

- On-premises resources changes
- Changing your MX record in a hybrid configuration

On-premises resource changes

With most Exchange Organizations, we may be leveraging various types of resource mailboxes or Public Folders. When you start migrating users to Office 365, your Office 365 users will lose access to these delegated resources. If the resource is a conference room, the user will still be able to book time in that conference room and view the existing schedules; however, that's the extent of management for those resource objects. Public Folders are inaccessible, unless we connect the on-premises Public Folders to Exchange Online.

While you migrate on-premises mailboxes, you may need to consider moving these resources with the users moving to Office 365. Let's cover these various resources and how you need to prepare for their moves to Office 365. We will cover are the following resources:

- Shared mailboxes
- Conference rooms
- Public Folders

Shared mailboxes

If you are leveraging shared mailboxes on-premises today, then you may want or need to migrate them to Office 365. Typically, if the shared mailbox is accessed by other users, and not an application, you should consider moving the shared mailboxes with the users accessing them. Before you move the mailbox, it's important that we confirm the shared mailbox is actually listed as a shared mailbox and not a standard user mailbox. It is also worth noting that shared mailboxes have a 50 GB size limit within Office 365. To set an on-premises mailbox as a shared mailbox, simply run the following PowerShell cmdlet from an Exchange 2013 management shell:

```
Set-mailbox <Alias> -type:shared
```

Once you have confirmed, the mailbox is set to shared, perform a standard mailbox move to Office 365, as you would with any other user mailbox. The reason why this step is important is so that the shared mailbox will not require a license. If you move a shared mailbox to Office 365 as user mailbox, then it will require a license to be used. If you move a user mailbox and realize later that it should be shared, it can be converted within the EAC after the migration.

Alternatively, you can create a shared mailbox directly in Office 365, but bear in mind that in a hybrid configuration this won't be visible in the Global Address List. You can do so through either PowerShell or the EAC. The following is an example of creating a room object directly in the EAC.

Go to **recipients**, then **shared**, and then click on the + sign for a new shared mailbox, as shown in the following screenshot:

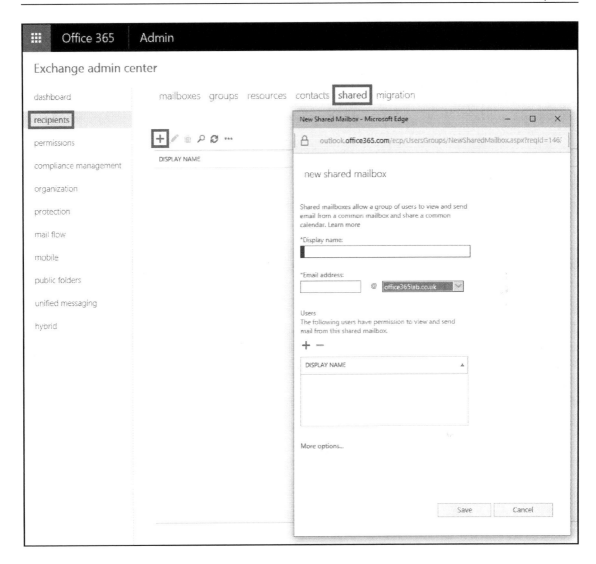

After creating the shared mailbox, you can now manage and assign users from PowerShell or the Exchange Admin Center.

Conference rooms

Conference rooms are very much like shared mailboxes. It's important that we ensure the conference room is listed as a room object prior to migrating the mailbox. Room mailboxes are free within Office 365, so if you do not list the conference room as a room object, it will require a license. To set the conference room as a room object, simply run the following PowerShell cmdlet from an Exchange 2013 management shell:

```
Set-mailbox <Alias> -type:room
```

Once you have confirmed that the mailbox is set to room, perform a standard mailbox move to Office 365, as you would with any other user mailbox.

Alternatively, you can create a conference room directly in Office 365. As before, with shared mailboxes, doing this will not make it visible in the Global Address List in a hybrid configuration. You can do so through either PowerShell or the EAC. The following is an example of creating a room object directly in the EAC:

1. Go to **recipients**, then **resources**, and then click on the + sign for a new **Room mailbox**, as shown in the following screenshot:

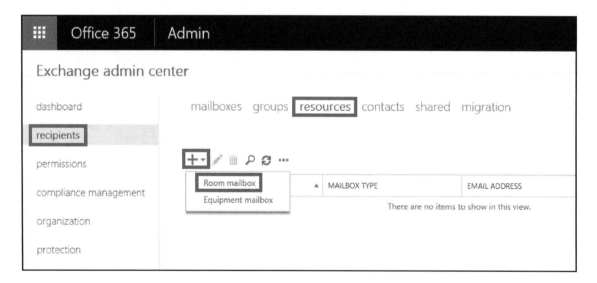

2. Enter all the details for this room. If you plan to receive e-mail on a specific domain for this room, be sure to select the correct domain alias, as shown in the following screenshot:

At this point, you have a bit of flexibility in how you want to configure the room, from the number of attendees in the room, to who can book it and how meetings get approved. Be sure to set the appropriate settings for your organization.

Public Folders

Public Folders can be challenging to manage and govern. Optimally, remediating Public Folders may be the best path for most organizations. It's important that you evaluate how Public Folders are used within your environment, to determine how to convert them. Often, organizations convert Public Folders to shared mailboxes or migrate them to a structure within SharePoint Online. If you are unable to remediate your Public Folders, moving them to Exchange Online may be your next best option.

While you move your organization to Exchange Online, you may not want your users to lose access to Public Folders on-premises. Microsoft offers an option to enable a Public Folder hybrid, which essentially redirects the user to the *remote* Public Folders on-premises.

When you have completed your last mailbox move to Exchange Online, you should then consider moving your Public Folders to Exchange Online. If you have Exchange 2007 or 2010 with the latest updates, use the Public Folder batch process migration, which can be found at

`https://technet.microsoft.com/en-us/library/dn87417(v=exchg.15).aspx`.

If you are using Exchange 2013 or 2016 on-premises, then there is no native way to migrate your Public Folders to Office 365. Your best bet is to use hybrid Public Folders until Microsoft provides a native way to migrate them. The second option is to use a third-party solution from companies such as `www.messageops.com`, `www.bittital.com`, or `www.skykick.com`.

Configuring hybrid Public Folders

In our lab we are using Exchange 2013, which supports hybrid Public Folders, as does Exchange 2016; both allow cloud-based users to access our Public Folders on-premises. This is a good temporary solution until a native method to migrate them is available. The downside is that we must maintain our Exchange servers on-premises until this functionality is available. Setting up a Public Folder hybrid requires us to follow these three steps:

- Download and prepare scripts
- Configure synchronization

- Configure Office 365 Public Folder access

We will have a look at them in the following sections.

Downloading and preparing scripts

Download the synchronizationscripts to one of your internal Exchange servers from
`https://www.microsoft.com/en-us/download/details.aspx?id=46381`.

Configuring synchronization

Since mail-enabled Public Folders are not synchronized to Office 365 via Azure AD
Connect, we need to run the downloaded PowerShell script. From an Exchange PowerShell
console, run the following:

```
Sync-MailPublicFolders.ps1 -Credential (Get-Credential) -
CsvSummaryFile:sync_summary.csv
```

This script will prompt you for your Office 365 admin credentials and ask you to confirm its
actions by pressing *Y* and *Enter*. The script will synchronize all your on-premises Public
Folders into Office 365, making them available in the GAL, as shown in the following
screenshot:

Because this script will synchronize the Public Folders, you will have to manually run this
script every time you add, remove, or change the Public Folders. If you want, you can set
up a scheduled task to automatically run this script at a set interval.

Configuring Office 365 Public Folder access

Now we must instruct Office 365 to redirect the user's Public Folders and point them to the on-premises exchange servers. We do this by connecting a PowerShell session to Exchange Online and configuring remote Public Folders.

Open up PowerShell and type the following commands in sequence. When prompted for log on credentials, enter the details for your cloud admin account:

```
$UserCredential = Get-Credential

$Session = New-PSSession -ConfigurationName Microsoft.Exchange -
ConnectionUri https://outlook.office365.com/powershell-liveid/ -Credential
$UserCredential -Authentication Basic -AllowRedirection

Import-PSSession $Session
```

The following screenshot shows the expected output from these cmdlets. Once connected, you have direct control over Exchange Online via the PowerShell window:

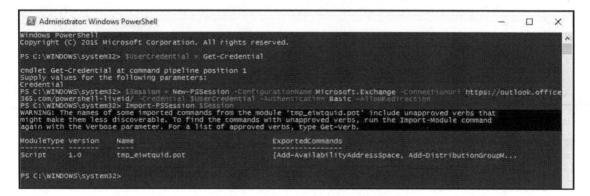

Now we instruct Office 365 to enable remote Public Folders and specify the Public Folder mailbox. If you have multiple Public Folder mailboxes, then separate them using a comma:

```
Set-OrganizationConfig -PublicFoldersEnabled Remote -
RemotePublicFolderMailboxes PFMailbox1
```

Now run the following cmdlet to confirm that the **PublicFoldersEnabled** attribute is set to **Remote** and that the Public Folder mailboxes are listed next to **RemotePublicFolderMailboxes,** as shown in the screenshot following the cmdlet:

```
Set-OrganizationConfig | fl *public*
```

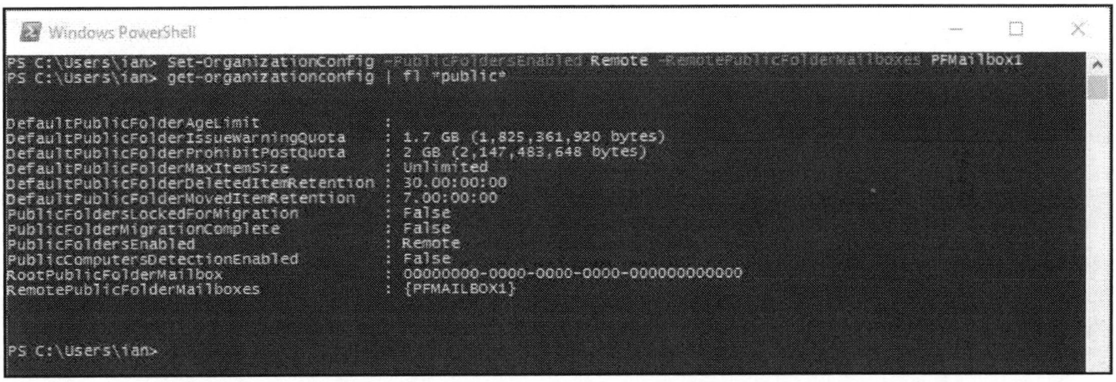

If all runs correctly, all the users who have had their mailboxes migrated to Office 365 will be able to see the Public Folders from the on-premises environment, as shown in the following screenshot. The users won't need to do anything; they will automatically appear after a few minutes after running the preceding commands.

One major downside to hybrid Public Folders is that Public Folder permissions can't be managed from one location; they must be managed from both as, cross-premises permissions are not supported:

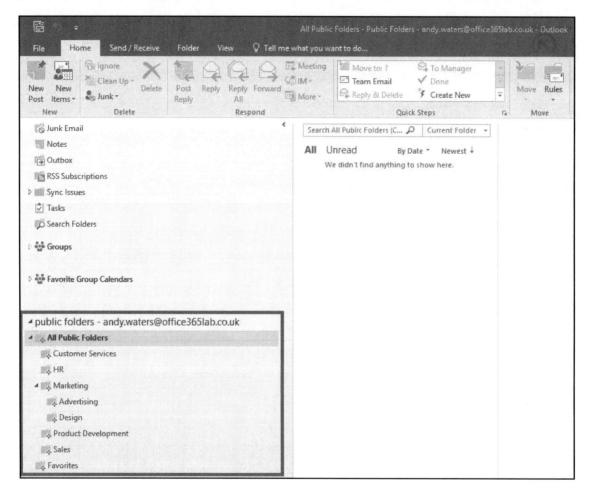

This is a great step in the right direction by Microsoft, because as you have seen, it is relatively straightforward to configure hybrid Public Folders and this allows our on-premises and cloud hosted users to operate on the same set of folders. You can now wait until a native method for migrating these folders to Exchange Online becomes available or later decide to use a third-party solution. While in hybrid mode, you will have to maintain your on-premises exchange environment until you have fully migrated.

Changing your MX record in a hybrid configuration

At some point, you will want to consider moving your inbound mail routing from your on-premises mail system to Office 365's **Exchange Online Protection(EOP)** for Exchange. If you do not have any on-premises gateway mail routing requirements, you may want to consider this move when most of your mailboxes are in Office 365. If you plan to do a flash cut-over, then you may want to consider the MX change right away.

Moving your MX record does not mean that on-premises mailboxes will stop receiving e-mail. This is why the hybrid option is available for Exchange on-premises organizations. You may have other on-premises mail routing requirements, which should be evaluated before changing your MX record.

To get started, we first need to set up your MX record to route mail to Office 365 EOP:

1. Go to the **Domains** section within the Office 365 admin portal (`https://portal.office.com`) and click on the domain you would like to change the MX record for, as shown in the following screenshot:

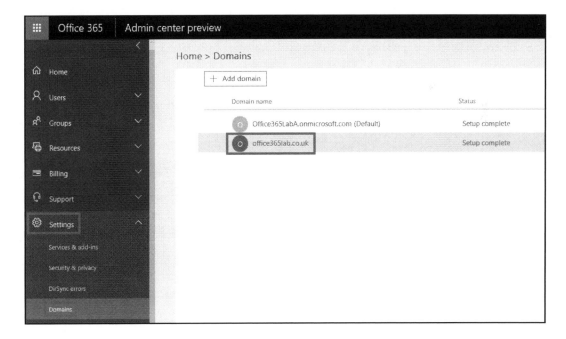

2. Update your MX record according to the settings listed on the DNS records page, as shown in the following screenshot:

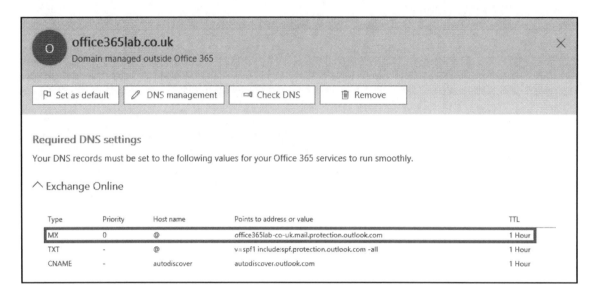

Once you have changed your MX record, all inbound mails will start to be redirected to Exchange Online; however, the hybrid connector will also allow mail to continue to be delivered on-premises. The MX record change is only one part of the change necessary to shift the inbound/outbound mail flow in Office 365. If you would like the outbound mail flow to go directly out of Exchange Online for Exchange Online mailboxes, you will need to change the outbound hybrid connector. If you choose to do this, ensure you update the SPF record according to the preceding DNS record. Failing to do so may result in mail sent out from Office 365 being seen as spam.

The existing hybrid connector is capturing all the outbound mail and directing it to the on-premises servers. To validate this, let's go to the Office 365 Exchange Admin Center at `http s://portal.office.com`:

1. Click on **Exchange**, under **Admin centers**, as shown in the following screenshot:

2. Now go to **mail flow** and click on **connectors**, as shown in the following screenshot:

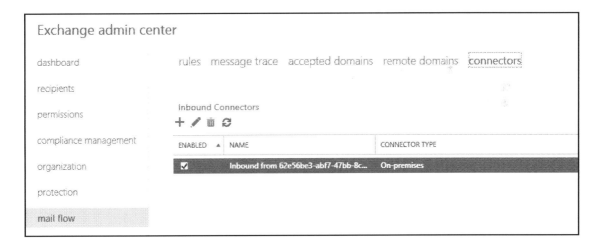

3. To start, we need to review how the hybrid outbound connector was created. Click on the **Outbound Hybrid connector** under **Outbound Connectors**. If the **Outbound domains** on the right is set to *****, we will have to limit the scope of this connector. In this example, shown in the following screenshot, our domain shows *****, which means all the outbound mail will use the hybridconnector:

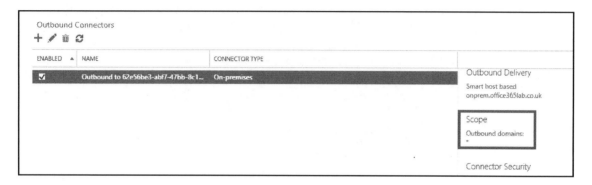

4. Edit the outbound connector so that we can change the outbound domains. Go to the **scope** section of the connector and change the **Recipient domains** to all the domains you host in your on-premises Exchange Organization. See the following example, as a way you may create yours:

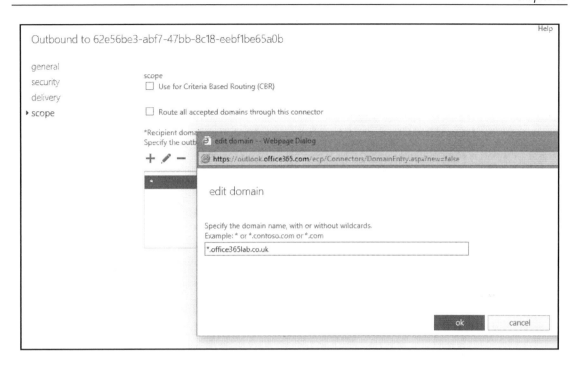

5. The scope should no longer have *, as shown in the following screenshot:

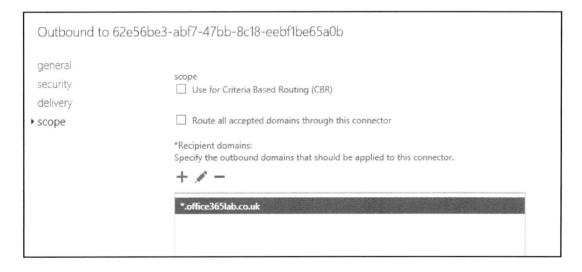

6. Once you have completed your change, click **save**. Outbound hybrid mail flow should still be functional, if you added all the appropriate domains. Any outbound mail going directly to non-hybrid domains will automatically go out to the internet by DNS lookup.

After your update your MX record, wait for DNS to replicate, which can take up to 72 hours to complete. Then start to test the mail flow from internet e-mail accounts to your Office 365 and on-premises mailboxes. If you set up the connectors properly and DNS has had a chance to replicate, all mail should be going through Office 365 and either delivered to an Office 365 mailbox or traverse over the hybrid connectors and to your on-premises mailboxes.

Summary

Resources play an important role in any migration or move to Office 365. This role includes how the users leverage these resources. We learned how to migrate these resources to Office 365, allowing the users to continue to leverage these resources, while minimizing down-time when the users are in transition.

In the next chapter, we will summarize the planning, preparation, and migration process to Office 365.

13
Additional Hybrid Solution – Lync Online/Skype for Business

If you have deployed Communicator, Lync Server, or Skype for Business on your network and invested lot of time migrating e-mail or setting up an Exchange Hybrid, then it makes sense to look at the options for configuring a hybrid setup with Office 365 Skype for Business, formally known as Lync Online.

In this chapter, we will explore the benefits and restrictions we can expect from this type of configuration. Using this information, you can decide the best path to hybrid cloud success for your organization.

Overview of a Skype for Business hybrid

A hybrid configuration between on-premises Lync Server 2010, 2013, or Skype for Business server 2015 to Office 365 gives you the ability to move users from your local pools into the cloud with a single PowerShell command and then back again with another. This simple act opens up a multitude of possibilities we can use to expand our networks and give our organisations the edge over the competition. Let's take a closer look at a few of these benefits in more detail.

Benefits

Configuring a Skype for Business hybrid gives us greater flexibility and opens up more options so we can expand our networks and empower our users to work more efficiently and increase collaboration between our users and partners.

Let's look at a few of the benefits we can expect from deploying a basic hybrid configuration:

- **Reduce or maintain existing connectivity requirements**: By hosting our user accounts in the cloud, we no longer need to provide VPN connectivity between sites or deploy clustered edge pools to support growing demands.
- **Subscription-based licensing**: Cloud hosted accounts reduce capital outlay by paying a small monthly fee.
- **Easy expansion and access across the world**: We no longer need to worry about providing good data connections to on-premises servers. Microsoft operates the most secure and reliable data centers all over the world.
- **Reduced on-premises server requirements**: By offloading users into the cloud, we no longer need to expand on-premises server-farms to keep up with growth.
- **Perform a staged migration to Office 365**: Moving departments into the cloud at a controlled pace ensures success.
- **Deploy users on demand**: We can deploy hundreds of new user accounts within minutes without having to plan, purchase, and deploy any new server hardware.

Restrictions

We have taken a look at many of the benefits of a hybrid configuration, but we must fully understand the restrictions before deciding if this is the right move for us:

- Third-party applications used on-premises may not be compatible with cloud-based users
- Skype for Business hybrid requires Active Directory Synchronization to be deployed
- User management is performed on-premises and in the cloud portal
- AD FS is required for SSO to provide the best user experience
- Office 365 supports a maximum of 250 contacts per user; all others will not be migrated into the cloud environment

- Unless you are using an Office 365 E5 plan, no voice capabilities are available to cloud-based users, which includes: **Public Switched Telephone Network (PSTN)** calling, emergency dialing, voice mail, call hold, transfer, forwarding, delegation and team calling, common area phones, private line, call parking, response groups, and PSTN dial-in meetings
- No detailed reporting capabilities
- No persistent chat
- A full deployment utilizing Skype for Business server 2015 or Lync Server 2013

Lync Server 2010 can be used with all the latest updates installed, however Lync Server 2013 or Skype for Business server 2015 administrative tools must be installed on a separate server with access to the other servers on the network. This is required to run the `Move-CSUser` cmdlet we will see later.

 We have said that there are no enterprise voice capabilities in SFB Online, but at the time of writing however, Microsoft is rapidly expanding their services. So although there are still no enterprise voice features available, they are moving in the right direction.

Considerations

Now that we have looked at the benefits and restrictions, we know if we use Lync voice in our organisation we cannot extend that functionality to our cloud-based users. We know that to set up a hybrid we require the **Azure Active Directory Connect** (**AAD Connect**) tool to be deployed to synchronize our Active Directory user accounts and SFB attributes into the cloud, and we need AD FS to provide SSO. All of this means we may have to invest in new server hardware and software to support the hybrid configuration. User management is no longer restricted to the Lync administration tools and we now have to connect to the SFB Online to manage our cloud-based users, which may result in additional training for our internal support staff.

Supported clients

SFB Online supports the following client applications but it is highly recommended that you install the latest client available, which can be downloaded as part of your Office 365 subscription:

- Skype for Business
- Lync 2013

- Lync 2010
- Lync Windows store app
- Lync web app
- Lync mobile
- Lync for Mac 2011
- Lync room system and Skype for Business room system
- Lync basic 2013

Configuring a Skype for Business hybrid

Enabling a hybrid deployment is a relatively straightforward process and if your organisation has is already using or planning an Exchange hybrid, then some of the requirements will likely be already in place, such as Directory Synchronization and AD FS for the best user experience. Let's take a look at the SFB-specific configuration steps:

- Check firewall access rules and open ports
- Check required DNS records
- Configure on-premises SFB servers
- Configure Skype for Business Online within Office 365
- Move users from on-premises to cloud
- Move users from cloud to on-premises

In our lab environment we will be using Lync Server on-premises but all the PowerShell scripts presented here will work if you are using Skype for Business server in your on-premises network.

Firewall ports

To enable a hybrid deployment, we only have to open one more additional port `5061` to the access edge external IP address. This enables federation communication with SFB Online.

You should already have the other required ports open in your existing infrastructure, but we have listed them all in the following table for you to review:

Port	Protocol	Direction	Usage	Target
5061	TCP	Inbound/outbound	Federation communication	Access edge external IP
443	SIP/TLS	Inbound	Client signalling	Access edge external IP
443	PSOM / TLS	Inbound/outbound	Data sharing	WebCon edge external IP
443	STUN / TCP	Inbound/outbound	Audio video and application sharing	AV edge external IP
3478	STUN / UDP	Inbound/outbound	Audio and video	AV edge external IP
500000-59999	RTP / TCP / UDP	Inbound/outbound	Audio and video	AV edge external IP

DNS records

A prerequisite for deploying a hybrid with SFB Online is to have a fully deployed Lync or Skype for Business server, which includes 2013 or greater edge servers.

Knowing this, you should already have all the required DNS records in place, but there are three important records you need to ensure are available and pointing to the on-premises deployment to enable federation and edge server discovery.

It is common to see administrators point these records to Office 365, but they should actually point to the on-premises edge servers. These will allow Office 365 to automatically detect and locate your federated deployment, and allow your on-premises servers to handle the redirection of cloud-based users back to Office 365.

This is a good point that needs highlighting because our on-premises SFB/Lync Servers handle client authentication and redirection, so they must be up at all times for our cloud users to function, that is unless they are manually configured with the correct server settings to connect directly with Office 365:

- **Type**: A
- **Record**: sip
- **Target**: `sip.<yourdomain>` (for example: `sip.office365lab.co.uk`)

- **Type**: SRV
- **Service**: _sip
- **Protocol**: _tls
- **Port**: 443
- **Weight**: 1
- **Priority**: 100
- **Target**: `sip.<yourdomain>` (for example: `sip.office365lab.co.uk`)

These settings allow external Skype for Business clients to locate the networks edge servers:

- **Type**: SRV
- **Service**: _sipfederationtls
- **Protocol**: _tcp
- **Port**: 5061
- **Weight**: 1
- **Priority**: 100
- **Target**: `sip.<yourdomain>` (for example: `sip.office365lab.co.uk`)

This allows external servers to automatically discover your federation. We will see later in this chapter how we secure access to our federated domain.

Skype for Business on-premises server configuration

We have checked our DNS records and ensured that our firewalls will allow access. Now let's run through the steps required to enable a hybrid configuration to SFB Online on our on-premises servers:

- Check that the correct version of SFB Online PowerShell module is installed
- Identify the tenant's SFB Online admin URL
- Configure access edge policy
- Configure the SIP federated domains list
- Define a new hosting provider

Checking for installation of correct version of Skype for Business Online PowerShell module

Let's start by checking we have the correct version of the Skype for Business online PowerShell tool set and the correct `OCSCore.msi` files installed.

Log in to the frontend server you will be configuring your hybrid from and open up programs and features. If you don't have version 6 or above of the PowerShell module, then download it from

`https://www.microsoft.com/en-us/download/details.aspx?id=39366.`

In the following screenshot, we can see the PowerShell module now installed on our lab environment:

Microsoft Visual C++ 2013 Redistributable (x64) - 12.0.21005	Microsoft Corporation	09/08/2015	20.5 MB	12.0.21005.1
Microsoft VSS Writer for SQL Server 2012	Microsoft Corporation	15/08/2015	3.12 MB	11.2.5058.0
Skype for Business Online, Windows PowerShell Module	Microsoft Corporation	09/08/2015	114 MB	6.0.9276.0
SQL Server Browser for SQL Server 2012	Microsoft Corporation	15/08/2015	12.6 MB	11.2.5058.0
Windows Fabric	Microsoft Corporation	01/08/2015	67.6 MB	1.0.1008.0

If you don't see the Skype for Business PowerShell module, then you probably have the old Lync Online module instead. Uninstall the Lync Online module before installing the new Skype for Business version.

You should have already installed all the available updates for your Lync Servers, but download and install the following cumulative update to ensure that all the commands run without error:

`http://www.microsoft.com/en-us/download/details.aspx?id=3682`

Identifying the tenant's SFB admin URL

We need to log in to the SFB admin center to find our tenant's admin URL which we will need later to pass into some PowerShell commands.

Log in to the 365 portal `https://portal.office.com` and go to **Admin center**. From there, click on **Admin center** on the left-hand panel, expand it, and then select **Skype for Business**. This will take you to the Skype for Business admin center:

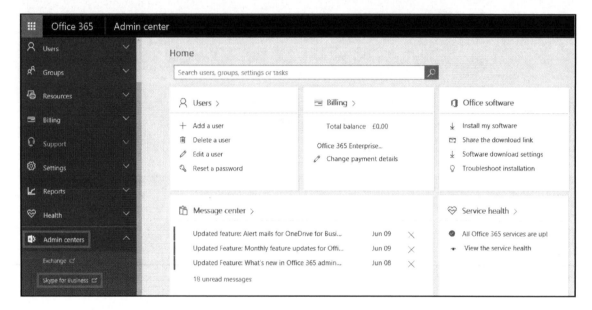

Copy the URL from your browser's address bar and save it for later. In the following screenshot, we can see the URL starts with `https://admin1e.online.lync.com` and it's this part we need for later:

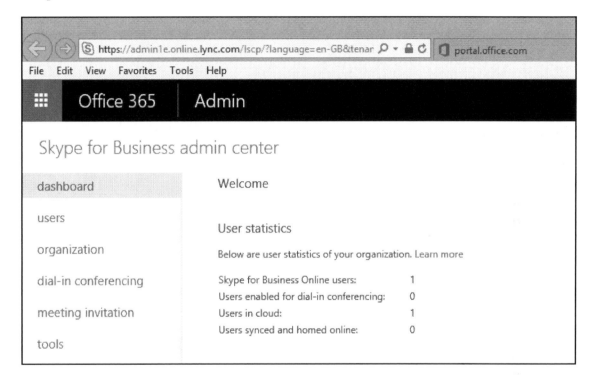

Configuring access edge policy

To configure our edge servers, we need to set a few attributes to allow remote access and to define how we want to discover our federated partners, which in this case is SFB online.

There are two ways to do this and the first is by using PowerShell and the command `Set-CSAccessEdgeConfiguration`. This commandlet is used to configure how our edge servers behave. There are four parameters that need setting, so let's take a close look at what each does:

- `-AllowOutsideUsers`: This simply enables access to the on-premises servers remotely from the Internet.

- -AllowFederatedUsers: This lets our internal users communicate with other federated domains. Just in case you are wondering, a federated domain is just where another system allows accesses to its users. It is managing and controlling access, and in this case we call it federation.
- -UseDnsSrvRouting: Remember those DNS SRV records we configured and checked earlier? Well, this parameter tells our edge servers to use those DNS SRV records to send and receive federation request.
- -EnablePartnerDiscovery: This lets our configuration know that we want to restrict who our on-premises servers can federate with. Normally we have to set an entry in the allowed domains list to specify who we will federate with, but because we are going to share our SIP domain with SFB online, this is not needed.

Ok, let's fire up a PowerShell window on our Lync Server and enter the following command:

```
Set-CSAccessEdgeConfiguration -AllowOutsideUsers 1 -AllowFederatedUsers 1 -
UseDnsSrvRouting -EnablePartnerDiscovery $false
```

You can see the PowerShell command being run in the following screenshot. There are no confirmation messages or anything. So long as it doesn't throw any errors, you can move on:

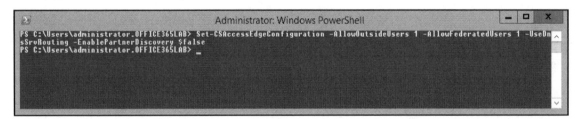

Before we jump ahead, there are those that prefer to use the GUI to make changes. So let's take a look at where we set them.

Open up the Lync Server control panel on one of our frontend servers. Then browse to **Federation and External Access** | **Access Edge Configuration** | **Edit** | **Show details**, as shown in the following screenshot:

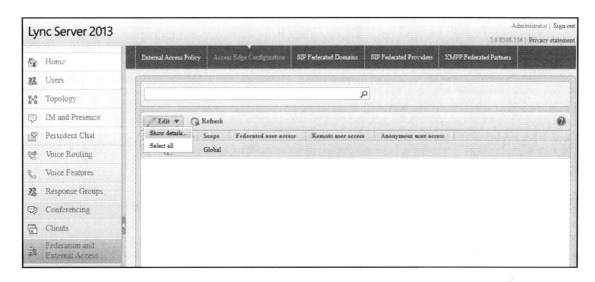

In our lab network, each of these options was disabled beforehand, so we can see that after running the PowerShell command, **Enable federation and public IM connectivity** and **Enable remote user access** have been checked. If you are configuring these options via the GUI, then check them and press **Commit,** as shown in the following screenshot:

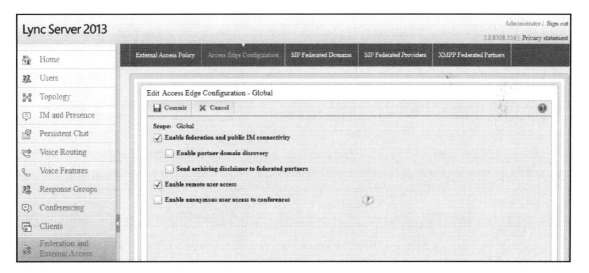

Defining new hosting provider

A hosting provider needs to be created because it defines a remote system we can talk to and share information with. In our case, we need to define a new Lync Online provider with all the required options to allow a hybrid setup using our own SIP domain.

Let's start off by removing any old Lync Online providers that may be on the system, loading up PowerShell on one of our frontend servers, and running the following command:

```
Remove-CsHostingProvider -Identity LyncOnline -force
```

You can see there is no output from our lab environment, so no errors indicates success:

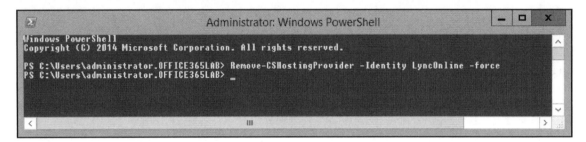

Now we need to enter a long command into PowerShell using the `New-CSHostingProvider` commandlet, but first let's break down which each parameter we will need and look at what each is doing:

- `Identity`: Specifies the name for the provider he we use Lync Online but it could be Skype Online.
- `ProxyFqdn`: The publicly accessible server used by the hosting provider.
- `Enabled`: Specifies if the provider is in use or not. We can go ahead and enable it in our lab.
- `EnabledSharedAddressSpace`: This is where we tell our frontend servers that the provider will be sharing our SIP domain, which in our case is `office365lab.co.uk`. This allows us to host users within the hosting provider and allows the users with the same address space on-premises.

- `HostsOCSUsers`: This specifies whether the provider is hosting Lync user accounts or not. Office Communications Server (**OCS**), which is showing its age here because OCS was the name used before Lync Server came along and now we have Skype for Business server.

- `VerficationLevel`: Specifies whether the users can communicate with anyone using this provider or whether they can communicate only with people on their contacts list.

- `IsLocal`: Specifies whether the provider is within our own topology.

- `AutodiscoverUrl`: Defines the service which returns user-specific pool configurations and service URLs.

Here is the full PowerScript command, along with all the parameter settings. Open up PowerShell on your Lync frontend servers and run the following:

```
New-CSHostingProvider -Identity LyncOnline -ProxyFqdn
"sipfed.online.lync.com" -Enabled $true -EnabledSharedAddressSpace $true -
HostsOCSUsers $true  -VerificationLevel UseSourceVerification -IsLocal
$false -AutodiscoverUrl
https://webdir.online.lync.com/Autodiscover/AutodiscoverService.svc/root
```

When you run the command it will feed back your options, giving you a chance to verify what's been entered. No errors here, so let's take a look at where we can configure a hosting provider using the GUI:

Log in to the Lync Server control panel, and go to **Federation and Exernal Access** and then **SIP Federated Providers**. If you already have a Lync Online provider specified, then highlight it, click **Edit**, and then click **Delete,** as shown in the following screenshot:

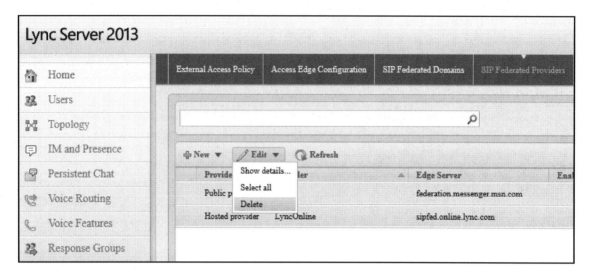

Now create the new provider and click on **New**, and then click on **Public Provider**:

Click on **Enable communications with this provider** and enter a **Provider name**, which can be anything you wish. Enter the **Access Edge service (FQDN)** address as `sipfed.online.lync.com` and then select the verification level that suits your business's policies. Here we have selected so that users can only communicate with people on their contact list. This stops people randomly sending messages to anyone, as shown in the following screenshot:

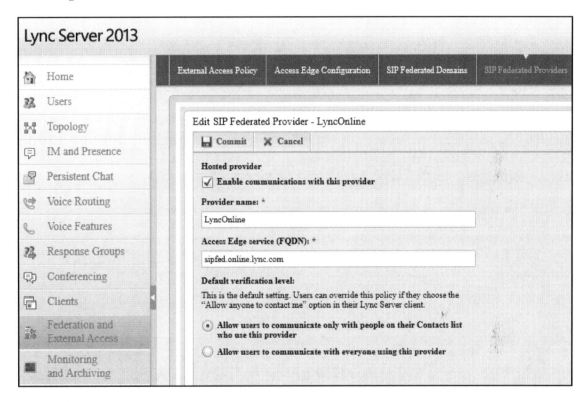

Let us now move on to the next section.

Skype for Business Online configuration

Now that we have our on-premises configuration in place, all we need to do is enable shared SIP address space in our SFB Online tenant. What's that, you say? As the name suggests, we are sharing our SIP domain name, which in our case is office365lab.co.uk. We are configuring a hybrid because we are going to have users both on-premises and hosted in SFB, so by enabling shared SIP address space, we are telling SFB that it won't know about all the users in the space. Knowing this, it should communicate with its federated partner to discover the users and direct communication between the clients correctly.

Fire up a PowerShell window on your frontend 2013 server, or if you have a 2010 deployment, use the 2013 tools that you have installed onto a separate server, and enter each of these following commands, pressing *Enter* after each. The second line will prompt you for your Office 365 admin account credentials. Enter them into the window and press **Ok**, and then continue entering the lines:

```
Import-Module LyncOnlineConnector
$cred = Get-Credential

$CSSession = New-CsOnlineSession -Credential $cred
Import-PSSession $CSSession -AllowClobber

Set-CsTenantFederationConfiguration -SharedSipAddressSpace $true
```

In this next screenshot, we can see the results of these commands being run from our lab frontend server:

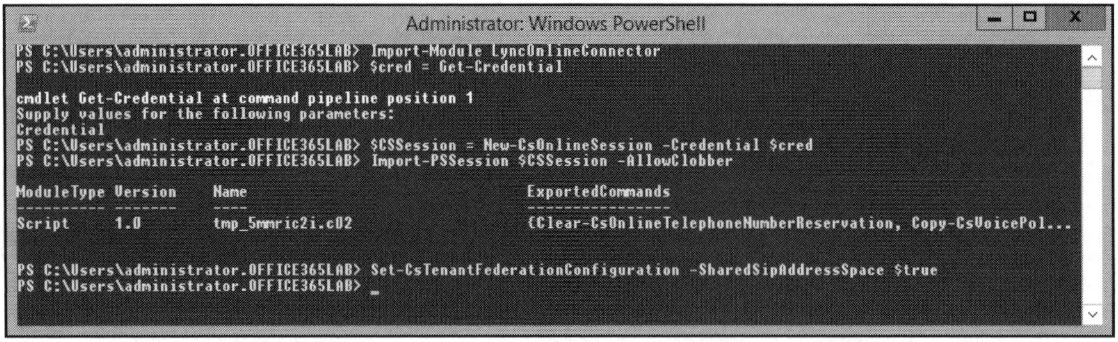

We can verify that shared SIP address space has been enabled by running the following command:

```
Get-CsTenantFederationConfiguration
```

Verify that **SharedSipAddressSpace** is set to **True**, as shown in the following screenshot:

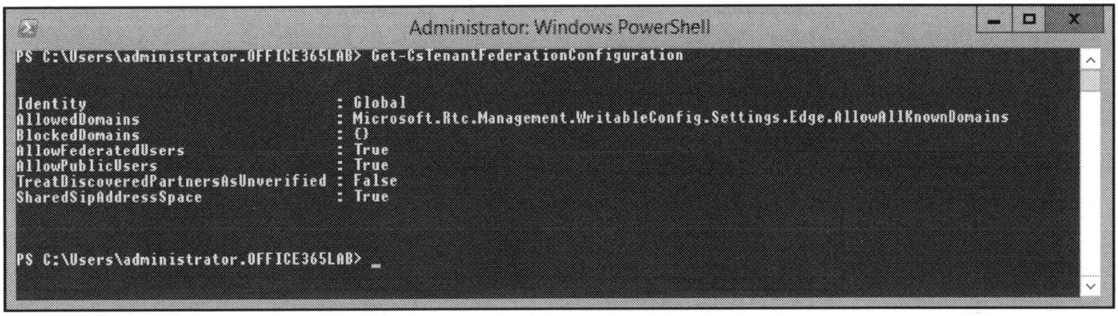

Moving users

We are finally ready to try and move a test user from our on-premises deployment into the cloud, but let's first look at how we identify where the user is currently homed. From a PowerShell session on one of our frontend servers, run the following command, specifying the user's SIP address:

```
Get-CSUser ian@office365lab.co.uk
```

In the following screenshot, we can see the results from our lab environment. We use `RegistrarPool` to identify which pool the user belongs to. We can use this to see whether a specific user is hosted locally or in the cloud:

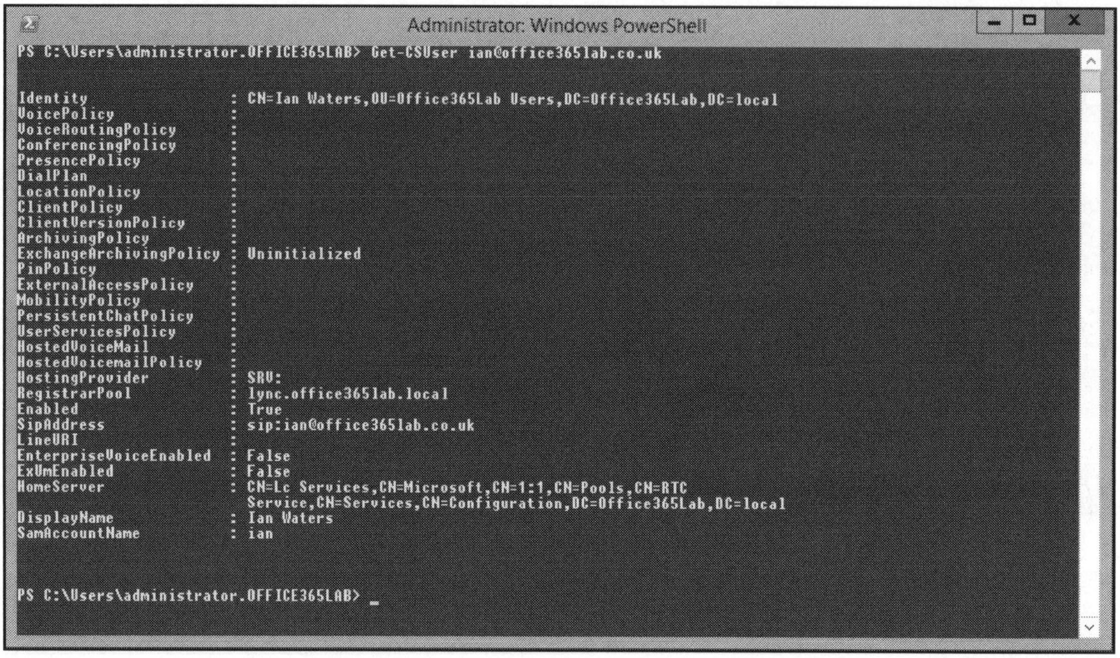

Okay, let's get down to business! Let's move one of our on-premises accounts into the cloud. Load up a PowerShell window on a frontend server and enter the commands listed next, pressing *Enter* after each. After you enter the first command, it will ask you for a username and password. Here you should enter your cloud administrator account credentials.

Remember that administrator URL we noted down earlier in this chapter? Here is where we need to use it. When we call the `Move-CSUser` commandlet, it requires us to pass in `HostedMigrationOverrideUrl`, which must be adjusted to match our tenant's administrative URL, which in our case was `admin1e.online.lync.com`. The admin URL should be in the following format:

```
https://<Admin URL>/HostedMigration/hostedmigrationservice.svc
```

```
$creds=Get-Credential

Move-CSUser -Identity ian@office365lab.co.uk -Target sipfed.online.lync.com
-Credential $creds -HostedMigrationOverrideUrl
https://admin1e.online.lync.com/HostedMigration/hostedmigrationservice.svc
```

After running these commands, it will ask us to confirm our action. Here we enter `y` to confirm. If we see no error messages, then everything should have worked as expected:

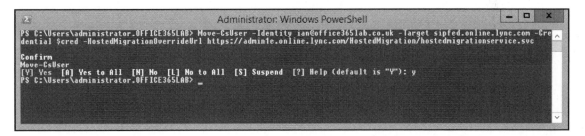

We have now moved the user. We can verify this by running the `Get-CSUser` commandlet again, and as you can see in the following screenshot, the `HostingProvider` now shows `sipfed.online.lync.com`, meaning that the user account is now hosted in the cloud:

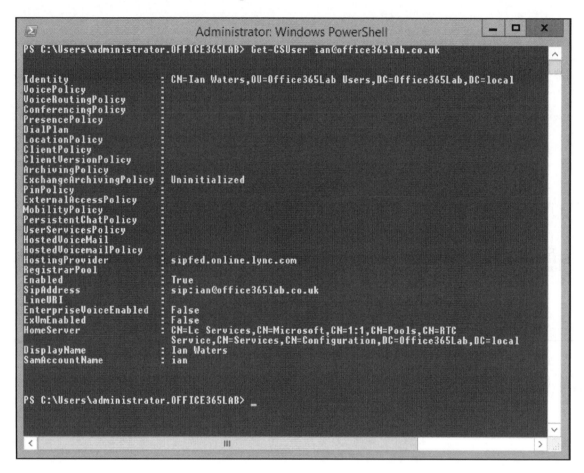

For those of us who prefer to use the GUI, open up the Lync Server control panel on one of the frontend servers. Click on Users and as we can see here in our lab environment, we can look at the **Homed** column to determine which users are hosted on-premises or in the cloud:

Now let's log into Lync and see what happens now that we have moved this user into the cloud. As you can see, the user is informed that changes have been made and that they need to log out and back in again:

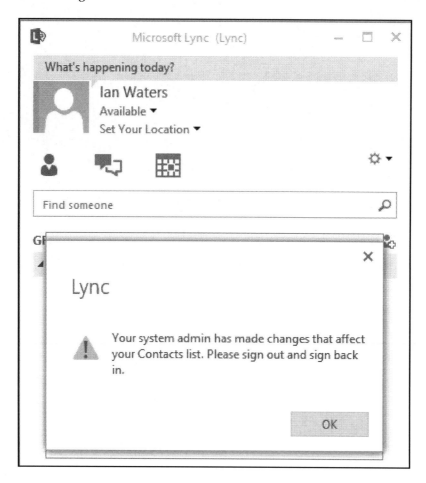

Even after logging out and back in again, we don't notice any differences. Everything looks as it should to the user; they have all their existing contacts and groups. However, in only a few steps we can now begin to offload the users from our on-premises servers:

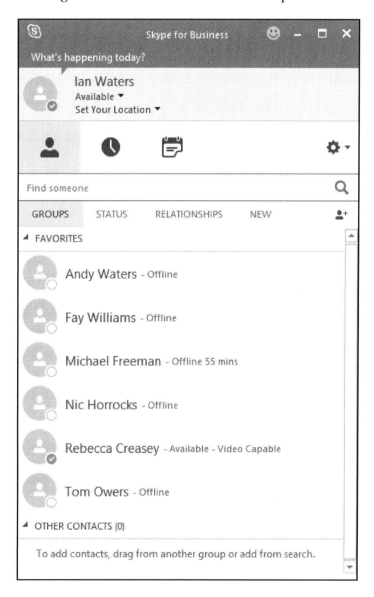

Office 365 to on-premises

At times we still need to move the cloud-based users back to on-premises management for a number of reasons, which can include:

- We need a user to make use of our on-premises enterprise voice features
- The user may require use of a third-party application that is not currently compatible with Office 365
- There may be an extended outage within Office 365

Load up PowerShell on a frontend server and run the following PowerShell commands, pressing *Enter* after each:

```
$creds=Get-Credential

Move-CsUser -Identity ian@office365lab.co.uk -Target
lync.office365lab.local -Credential $creds -HostedMigrationOverrideUrl
https://admin1e.online.lync.com/HostedMigration/hostedmigrationservice.svc
```

Like before, we are prompted to confirm the move, so we press y to accept and continue. If the move completes, no error messages will be displayed:

Managing users in the cloud

Before any users are moved into the cloud, it is a good idea to match the SFB online policies and settings with your on-premises configuration, settings such as presence privacy mode, mobile notifications, meeting invitation disclaimers, and logo URLs.

Once we have prepared the cloud environment and we have users in the cloud, we need to manage them. Unfortunately, we can't do this from our on-premises servers. We must log in to the SFB admin center to make configuration changes to the users hosted online.

In the following screenshot, we can see the user account we moved earlier, ready to make configuration changes as required. Move a test user account and master all the settings available before moving your live users:

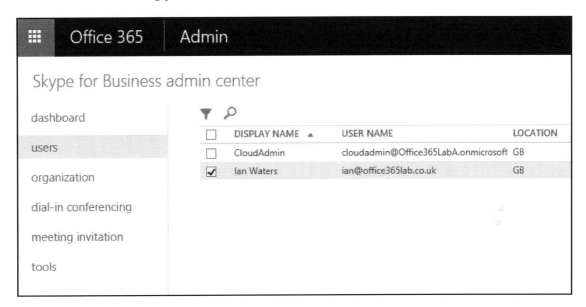

Summary

In this chapter, we explored the benefits and restrictions of a Skype for Business hybrid and also considered how these will affect our organisation. We successfully configured a hybrid configuration between Lync Server 2013 and Skype for Business online, and saw how we can move users in and out with ease. If you have Skype for Business Server 2015 deployed on-premises, all the PowerShell scripts shown are up to date and correct to configure a hybrid for your network too. SFB Online is set for some exciting new features, including enterprise voice capabilities. It's well worth keeping an eye on the roadmap to see when these will be made available so you can take advantage as soon as possible. Let's move on to Chapter 14, *Additional Hybrid Solution – SharePoint Online*; and start exploring setting up a SharePoint hybrid.

14
Additional Hybrid Solution – SharePoint Online

In this chapter, we explore our options and see what's involved in configuring a SharePoint hybrid. In this chapter, we will cover the following topics:

- Overview of a SharePoint hybrid
- Benefits
- Supported topologies
- Restrictions
- Considerations
- Overview of a SharePoint hybrid configuration

Overview of a SharePoint hybrid

The popularity of SharePoint is growing all the time, increasing our user's efficiency and allowing businesses to grow rapidly. Configuring a SharePoint hybrid allows us to build on our existing implementation and expand out to the cloud. However, there are still a lot of improvements Microsoft could make and new features they could implement to make it a smoother and richer experience. You may find that after reading this chapter you will need to engage with and investigate third-party services, depending on what you need to achieve.

You may be surprised by what you do and don't get with a hybrid configuration. You may find it's actually not the best way forward, but there are lots of benefits you can leverage to make the transition to SharePoint Online a smoother experience. So what do we actually get?

- **Hybrid search**: Allows the users to search both the on-premises SharePoint farm and SharePoint Online, giving them easy access to files regardless of their location
- **OneDrive for Business hybrid**: Redirects on-premises OneDrive users to SharePoint Online, allowing you to quickly expand your user base and storage capacity
- **Business Connectivity Services (BCS)**: Securely publishes internal data to remote users
- **Hybrid duet enterprise online**: If you use SAP in your enterprise, duet allows data to be published to the remote users

Benefits

There are lots of benefits to businesses, both large and small, in implementing a SharePoint hybrid. Let's take a look at the most commonly talked about benefits:

- Increase user base quickly
- Increase storage capacity
- Utilize new features not available on-premises
- Support for phased migrations to the cloud
- Search across SharePoint Online and on-premises from either location
- Sites can be hosted in SharePoint Online by using redirection with on-premises user accounts
- Access data from on-premises servers in SharePoint Online
- Duet integration, making it possible to access data in on-premises SAP from SharePoint Online

Supported topologies

Search is one of the major selling points of a hybrid configuration. Users can log on to the on-premises SharePoint servers or log in to SharePoint Online externally and search for files, and the magic of a hybrid returns all the search results from either system or both, depending on how you configure the search topology. There are three search topologies available to us, so let's take a look at each and decide which is going to work best for our business and which complies with our security policies.

When we talk about topologies, they are defined from the position of SharePoint Online.

Outbound hybrid

Searches performed in our on-premises environment pulls results from SharePoint Online. The search topology is outbound from SharePoint on-premises:

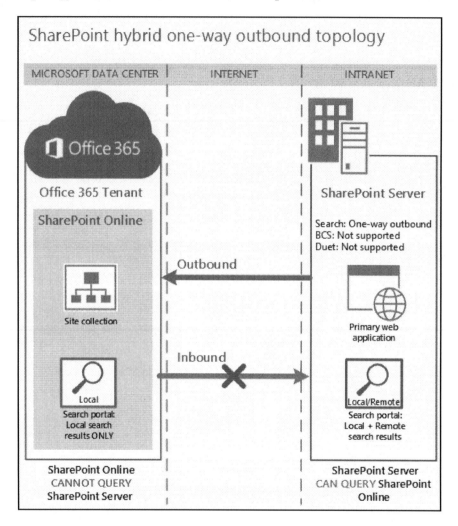

Inbound hybrid

Searches performed in SharePoint Online pulls results from our on-premises environment. The search topology is inbound from SharePoint Online:

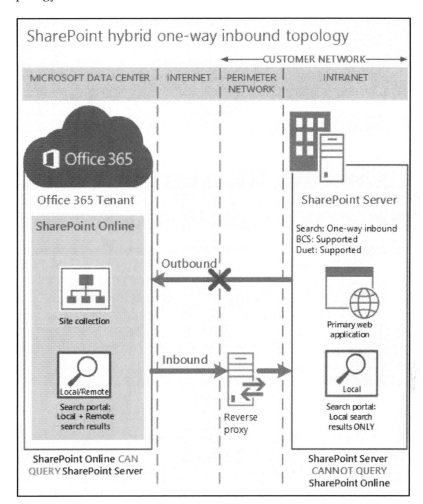

Two-way hybrid

Searches performed in either environment pulls results from the other.

By defining our search topology, we can control what our users have access to and what they can search for, depending on their location. You may have security policies that prevent your on-premises information to be accessible from outside of the network, in which case we would choose an outbound hybrid search topology. This means that search queries performed on-premises would show results from our local environment and SharePoint Online. Searches performed in SharePoint Online will only show results from files hosted online and not from our on-premises environment.

A two-way search topology is usually the best choice when our goal is to extend our on-premises environment out to the cloud and our external users:

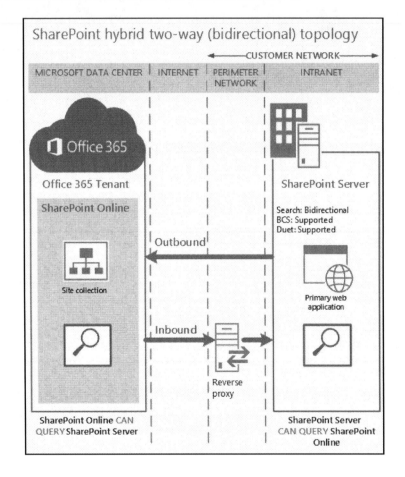

Restrictions

We have looked at some of the benefits a SharePoint Online can give us, but we must consider the restrictions before we can be sure a hybrid is right for us:

- Requires Active Directory Synchronization to be deployed
- AD FS is recommended for a good user experience
- Reduced scope for customizations

Considerations

SharePoint hybrid gives us some great features but, there are lots of issues we need to consider while developing our hybrid and migration plans.

From a user perspective, there will be differences in the user interface and items such as comments, followed sites, and documents will not be synced between both the environments.

Also, sites are not synchronised between environments; sites live in either location but never both. Documents accessed remotely from the on-premises servers will put more strain on your upload bandwidth.

Site branding will not replicate between environments, so you will need to invest time in matching the on-premises branding with SharePoint Online or you may wish to create a brand new look.

A public certificate for on-premises servers will be required to publish your internal SharePoint farm to avoid any problem with untrusted certificate warnings.

If you are considering a SharePoint Online hybrid, then it's probable you already have some kind of reverse proxy in place. If you already publish AD FS or other web-based services then you should be all set, but if not, check whether your current firewall is capable of publishing multiple internal websites because you will be publishing SharePoint on-premises and likely AD FS.

Implementing a SharePoint hybrid configuration

Implementing a hybrid SharePoint can be a daunting task because there is so much PowerShell involved and even skipping the smallest step can cause nothing to work as expected. Take your time and test everything as you go and you can achieve success. Let's dive in and configure a hybrid in our lab environment. We will break down the configuration and look at the following topics in order:

- Software requirements
- Certificates
- Reverse proxy
- Configure trust relationship
- OneDrive for Business
- Hybrid sites
- Hybrid search
- Hybrid business connectivity services

Software requirements

Your internal domain must be running 2008 R2, and theWindows Server 2012, Windows Server 2012 R2 forest functional level.

SharePoint Server 2013 must be deployed on all on-premises servers and it is recommended that each has all the latest updates installed before you begin to configure your hybrid.

To configure a SharePoint hybrid, you will need an E3, E4, or E5 Office 365 plan. Unfortunately for many smaller businesses, the business premium plan is not compatible.

Reverse proxy

To configure a SharePoint hybrid, search and to publish data externally using **Business Connectivity Services** (**BCS**) and Duet Enterprise, we will need to utilize a reverse proxy device. A reverse proxy secures our internal network by pre-authenticating the search queries coming from SharePoint Online, as well as allowing us to publish additional internal services, such as AD FS.

Microsoft recommends and supports the following proxy servers, but any enterprise level reverse proxy should do the job, although it won't be supported:

- Windows Server 2012 R2 **Web Application Proxy** (**WAP**)
- Forefront **Threat Management Gateway** (**TMG**)
- F5 BIG-IP
- Citrix NetScaler

Configuring trust relationship

To allow SharePoint Online and SharePoint on-premises to communicate securely, we need to configure a trust between them and we secure that trust using certificates. We can use a simple self-signed certificate and you can use a CA generated one, but actually it's preferable for it to be self-signed. Let's move on and begin setting up our hybrid by generating an STS certificate.

Certificates

Before we can start the process for setting up a **server to server** (**STS**) trust, we need to create a new self-signed certificate to use with the security token service between the on-premises server and the SharePoint Online tenant:

1. Begin by opening **Internet Information Server** (**IIS**) on your chosen SharePoint server and click on the root server node, in this case **SHAREPOINT**. Select **Server Certificates** and then click on **Create Self-Signed Certificate,** as shown in the following screenshot:

2. Choose an appropriate name for the certificate file and select **Personal** from the drop down menu. Then press **OK,** as shown in the following screenshot:

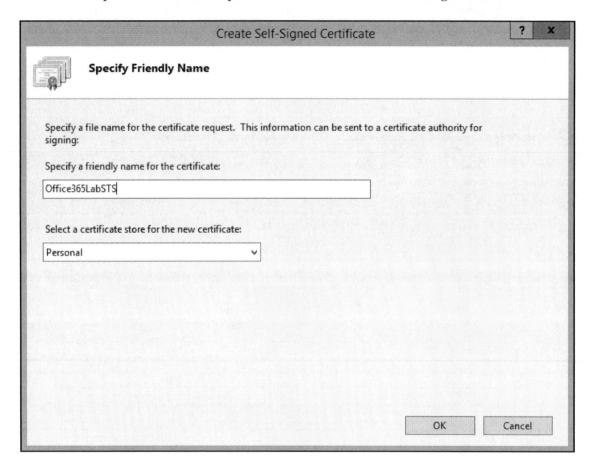

3. Refresh the certificate list and ensure the new certificate is listed, as shown in the following screenshot:

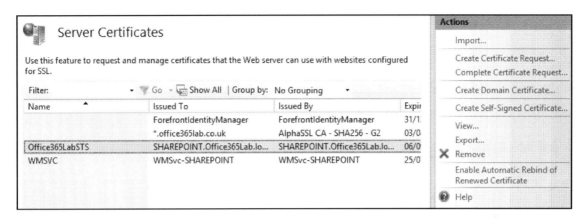

4. Next we need to export the certificate into two formats, CER and PFX, which includes the private key. Left-click on the certificate and select **Export** from the **Actions** menu. Choose a name and location for the file and set a password to secure the file. Then press **OK,** as shown in the following screenshot:

5. Now we need to export the public certificate into its own certificate file, ready for use later when we run the PowerShell STS setup commands.

6. Right-click the certificate and click on **View,** as shown in the following screenshot:

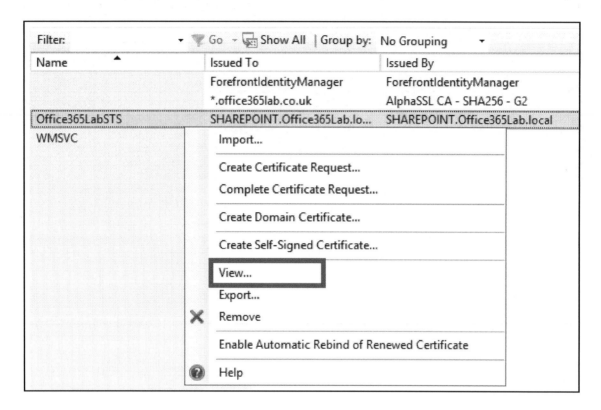

7. Click on the **Details** tab and then click on **Copy to File**, as shown in the following screenshot:

8. Choose the **Base 64 encoded** option and press **Next**, as shown in the following screenshot:

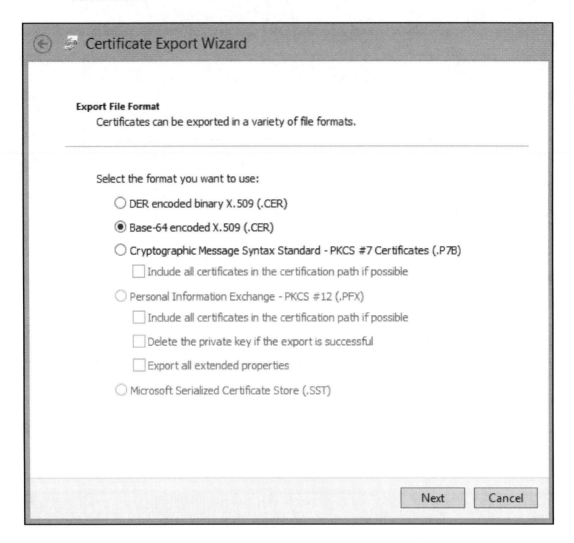

9. Select an appropriate name and location to save the file and press **Next,** as shown in the following screenshot:

10. Once the export has completed verified, check you have both the PFX and CER files ready before continuing, as shown in the following screenshot:

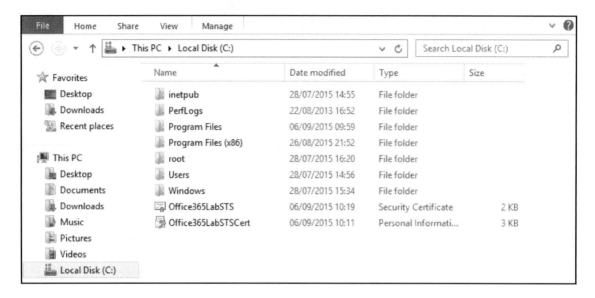

That's it for certificates!

OneDrive for Business

If you have deployed OneDrive in your on-premises environment, then you can make use of another hybrid feature called OneDrive for Business hybrid. You can configure SharePoint to redirect all the users, or by using an Active Directory group a selection of them, to OneDrive for Business hosted in the cloud.

This then allows the users to access their personal storage from anywhere in the world without having to connect to the corporate network using a VPN or remote desktop services. It means you no longer have to expand your on-premises server farms to increase storage and also you can quickly and easily expand the user base when needed with very little effort.

From the users' perspective, they can work more efficiently, work from anywhere, and the experience is much the same regardless of their location. They can also now access documents on their mobile phones utilising Microsoft Office apps and can even share documents with users outside of your organisation.

Luckily, this feature is very easy to configure but it does require you to have Active Directory synchronization deployed. Also, the users in your online tenant need to have a SharePoint license assigned to their account, and for the best user experience, AD FS is recommended.

That being said, let's deploy it in our lab environment!

To deploy OneDrive for Business hybrid, we need to perform the following actions:

- Create a group in Active Directory that will contain the users we want to redirect to SharePoint Online
- Identify our OneDrive site collection URL in SharePoint Online
- Configure OneDrive for Business hybrid settings in our on-premises server farm

If you want to go ahead and redirect everyone to SharePoint Online, you don't need to configure a new group in Active Directory, but if you have already deployed OneDrive internally, then users will have lots of documents stored locally. Knowing this, you will likely want to perform a staged migration to OneDrive for Business online so a new AD group will be required. In our lab environment, I created a new security group called **OneDrive Online Users**, but you can call yours whatever you want. I then added a test user account to the group, which is recommended so you can fully test the changes before rolling them out to other users.

We now log into **SharePoint admin center** and note down the URL for the My Site collection, as shown in the following screenshot. The part before – `my.sharepoint.com` will be specific to your tenant but, note down the full URL because we will need it later:

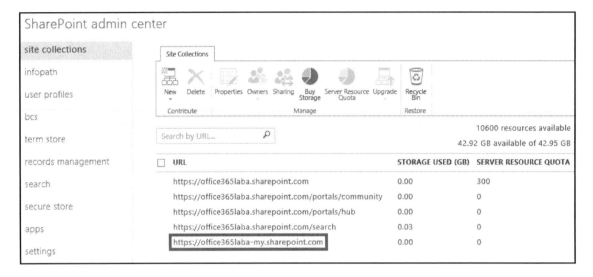

Now let's log in to our primary SharePoint server on-premises and open up the **Central Administration** page. From the menu on the left, click on **Office 365** and then on **Configure OneDrive and Sites links**, as shown in the following screenshot:

If you have chosen to enable this feature for only a few users, then the first job is to configure an audience. Click on **Create an Audience** as shown in the following screenshot to begin setting one up:

Give the audience a name and select a suitable owner. Select to include users who **Satisfy all of the rules** and press **OK**, as shown in the following screenshot:

Now we create an audience rule; we configure to select a user who is a **Member Of** the **OneDrive Online Users** group and click **OK**, as shown in the following screenshot:

At this point, we will return to the OneDrive for Business configuration page and it is here we need to enter the URL for our **My Site URL** collection we located earlier. It is also possible to redirect the sites link so the users can follow sites in SharePoint Online. Once all the options are set, click the **OK** button, as shown in the following screenshot:

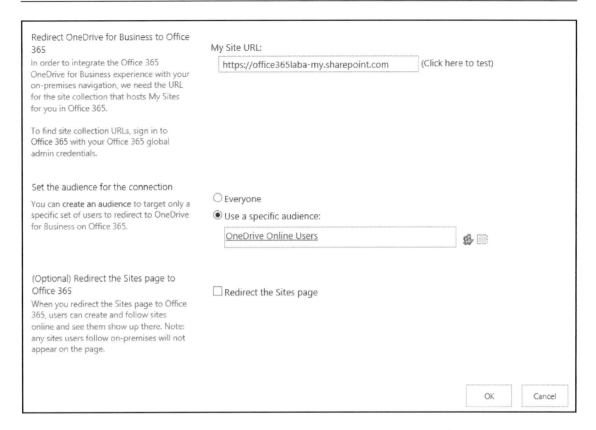

Now everything should be configured correctly. Let's log in as our test user to **SharePoint** on-premises and click on the **OneDrive** link, as shown in the following screenshot:

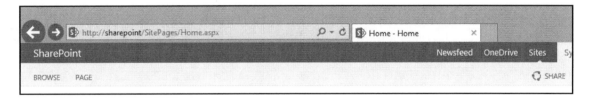

As shown in the following screenshot, we have successfully been redirected to OneDrive for Business online! Now this is where things can get a bit tricky for us and our users but, that is where we benefit from a good migration plan. Documents stored locally will not automatically migrate online, so before we start moving the users into the cloud, we need to give our users clear instructions on how to move the local documents into the new online system. It's unfortunate that it has to be done manually by them or by members of your team visiting each user and guiding them through the process:

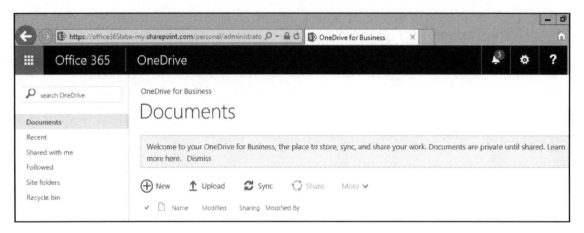

Hybrid search

Hybrid search is one of the features that tries to blur the lines between your on-premises and SharePoint Online environments. As you begin to migrate more data into the cloud, the users will require hybrid search functionality to quickly and easily find the files they require. The setup process is relatively long and complicated, and there are plenty of things that can and probably will go wrong. The best advice I can give is to test as much as possible at every stage and ensure you don't try to skip any steps or assume that services have been set up correctly in the past. There are six steps that we will go through in our lab environment and as usual I encourage you to do the same in yours before attempting any configuration changes in your production environment.

Let's dive in and look at the steps involved, and look at the potential issues to watch out for:

- Enable services
- Configure AD sync
- Configure STS trust
- Configure server-to-server authentication
- Configure result sources
- Configure query rules

Fasten your seatbelts, because here we go!

Enabling services

First we must ensure our chosen on-premises SharePoint server has the required services running. Open up SharePoint central administration and browse to **Application Management** and then **Manage services on server**. You will see the following screenshot:

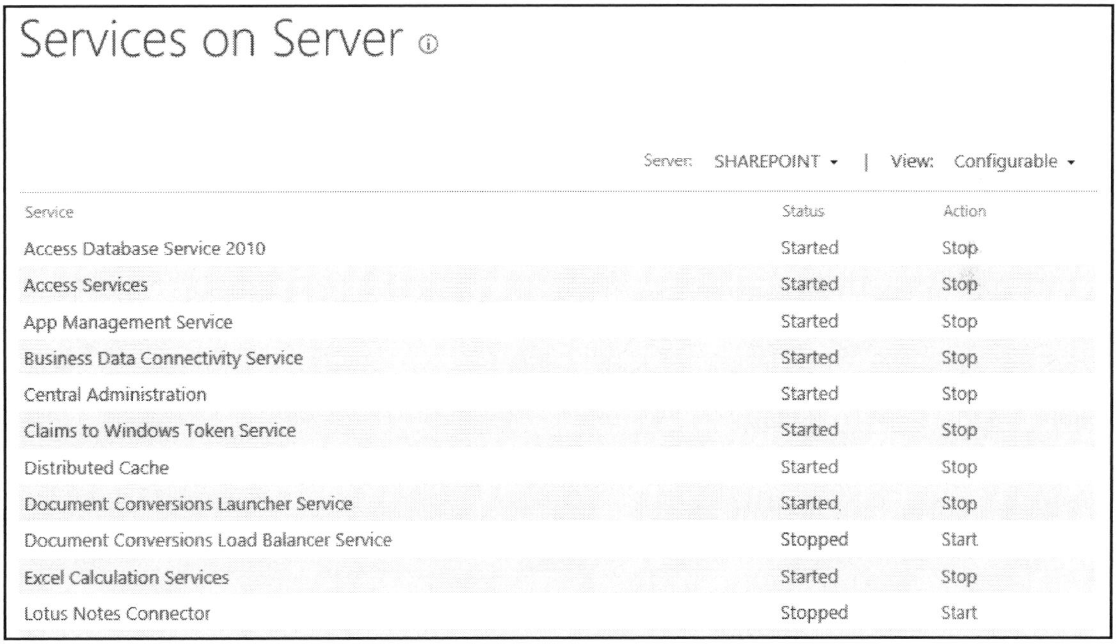

Services on Server ⓘ

	Server: SHAREPOINT ▾	View: Configurable ▾
Service	**Status**	**Action**
Access Database Service 2010	Started	Stop
Access Services	Started	Stop
App Management Service	Started	Stop
Business Data Connectivity Service	Started	Stop
Central Administration	Started	Stop
Claims to Windows Token Service	Started	Stop
Distributed Cache	Started	Stop
Document Conversions Launcher Service	Started	Stop
Document Conversions Load Balancer Service	Stopped	Start
Excel Calculation Services	Started	Stop
Lotus Notes Connector	Stopped	Start

Go down the list of services and start the following if they are in a stopped state:

- Managed metadata web service
- User profile service
- Microsoft SharePoint foundation subscription settings service

Configuring AD sync

Let's continue and configure SharePoint AD synchronisation, which is needed to map user properties such as the **User Principle Name (UPN)** and e-mail addresses.

Open up the SharePoint **Central Administration** page and click on **Application Management** and then **Manage service applications**. Locate **User Profile Synchronization Service** and click on it to open up the **Manage Profile Service** page. First, we need to set the type of synchronization we are going to be configuring. Click on **Configure Synchronizaion Settings,** as shown in the following screenshot:

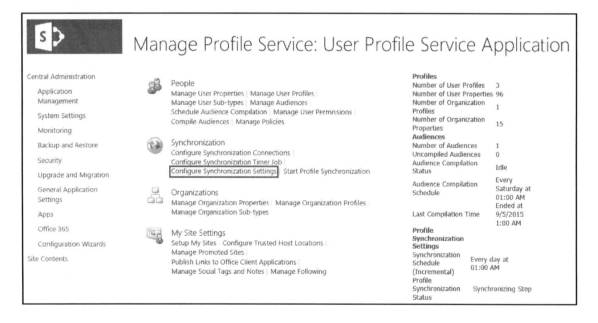

In our lab environment, we want to make use of Active Directory group, so select **Users and Groups** and choose the option to **Use SharePoint Active Directory Import,** as shown in the following screenshot. Then click **Save:**

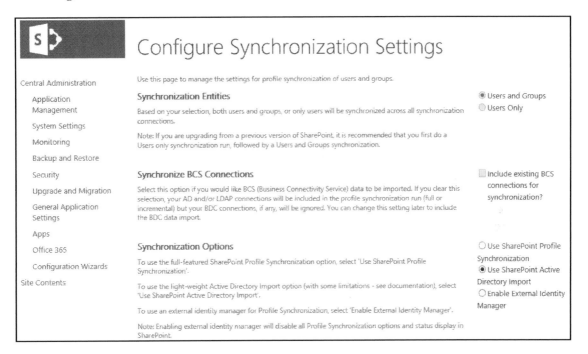

Now we need to configure a synchronization connection that specifies which AD organizational groups or individual users will be synchronized. From the **Manage Service Profile** page, click **Configure Synchronization Connections** and then **Create new connection,** as shown in the following screenshot:

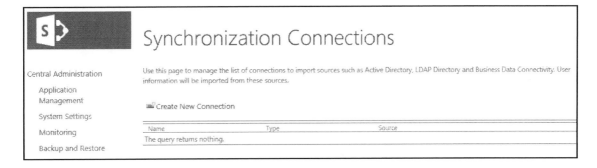

Give the connector a suitable name and select the type as **Active Directory**. Enter the name of your forest, select the provider type as **Windows Authentication**, and enter the username and password of a suitable domain administrator account, as shown in the following screenshot:

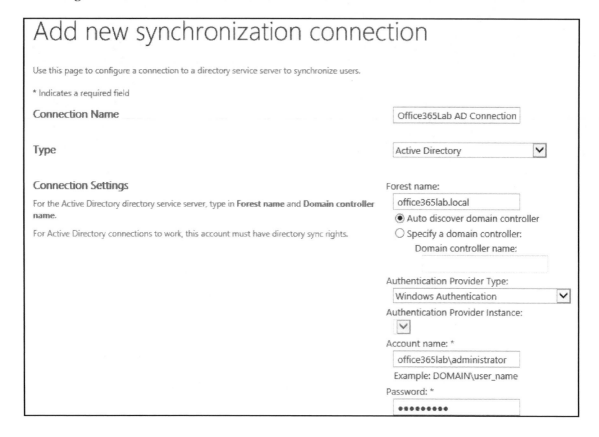

Next, click on **Populate Containers**, and if the settings defined previously are correct, it will show your Active Directory domain structure. Select the OU that contains the user accounts which use SharePoint on-premises. In our lab environment, we **Select All** and press **Ok,** as shown in the following screenshot:

If the settings are successful, then you should now see the connection profile in the **Synchronization Connections** list, as shown in the following screenshot:

Now that we have our AD connection configured, we need to ensure the user properties are mapped correctly.

Navigate to **Central Administration**, **Application management**, **Manage service applications**, **User Profile Synchronization Service**, and then **Manage User Properties**. We need to ensure that the following user properties are set:

Property name	Mapped attribute
User principal name	`userPrincipalName`
Work e-mail	`Mail`

On the **Manage User Properties** screen, locate these user properties and ensure they are mapped to the correct attribute. If not, then you can right-click a property and edit it to configure the mapped attribute, as shown in the following screenshot:

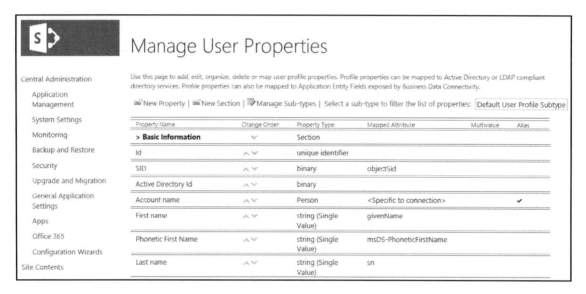

Now that we have our AD connection configured and our user properties mapped, we can start a full user synchronization.

From **Central Administration,** browse to **Application Management** | **Manage service applications** | **User Profile Synchronization Service** and then click **Start Profile Synchronization**. Select **Start Full Synchronization** and then press **OK,** as shown in the following screenshot:

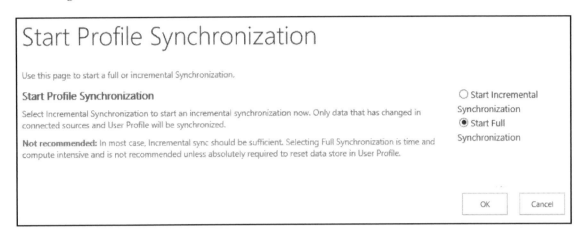

After a minute or two, the user profiles will have synchronized and you can check it has completed from the **User Profile Synchronization** page.

Configuring site-to-site trust

Now we must configure a site to site trust so that our on-premises server and SharePoint Online can communicate securely. First we must ensure the search center site is configured to use integrated windows authentication with NTLM.

From **Central Administration** | **Application Management** and open up **Manage web applications**. In our lab environment, we select **SharePoint- 80** and then click on **Authentication Providers,** as shown in the following screenshot:

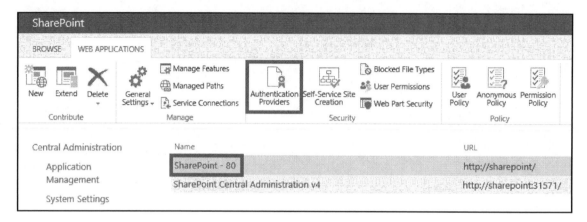

Click on **Default** to configure the default zone, as shown in the following screenshot:

Now ensure **Enable Windows Authentication** and **Integrated Windows authentication** are checked and select **NTLM** from the drop-down list, as shown in the following screenshot. Then press the **Save** button to make the changes:

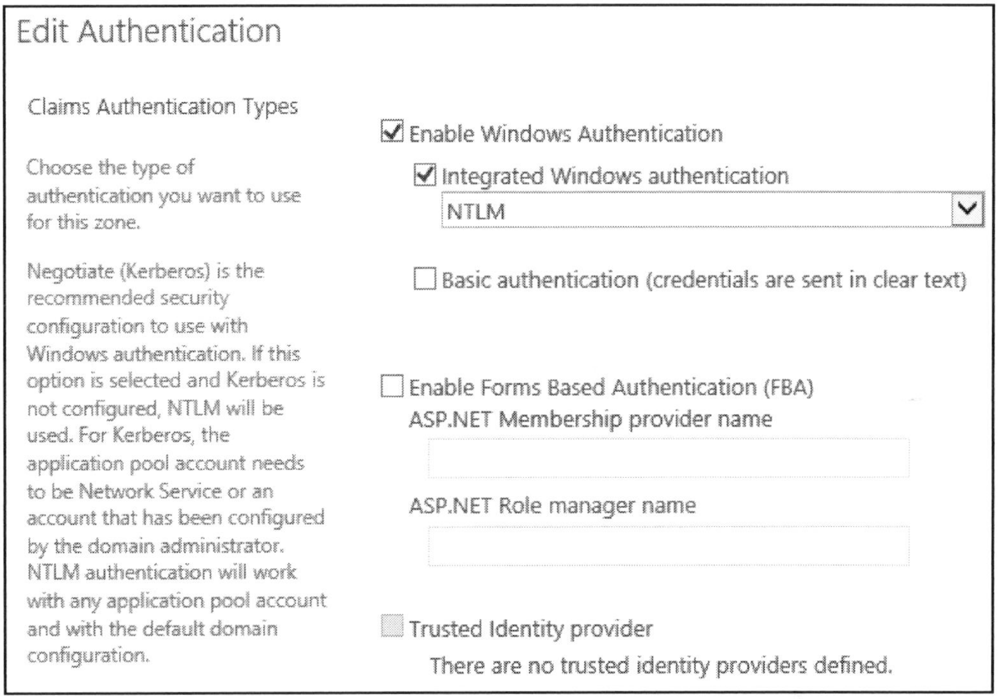

```
Edit Authentication

Claims Authentication Types              ☑ Enable Windows Authentication

Choose the type of                           ☑ Integrated Windows authentication
authentication you want to use
for this zone.                                   NTLM                                              ⌄

Negotiate (Kerberos) is the
recommended security                     ☐ Basic authentication (credentials are sent in clear text)
configuration to use with
Windows authentication. If this
option is selected and Kerberos is
not configured, NTLM will be         ☐ Enable Forms Based Authentication (FBA)
used. For Kerberos, the                   ASP.NET Membership provider name
application pool account needs
to be Network Service or an
account that has been configured
by the domain administrator.
NTLM authentication will work        ASP.NET Role manager name
with any application pool account
and with the default domain
configuration.                               ☐ Trusted Identity provider
                                                 There are no trusted identity providers defined.
```

Okay, so all the work so far has been about laying the groundwork for the following mammoth PowerShell scripts. I hope you like PowerShell, because there's no other method to do this!

Replacing default Security Token Service (STS) certificate

Open up the **SharePoint 2013 Management Shell** and run the following commands in order, but first you will need to change the $pfxPath and $pfxPass variables to match your own name and certificate password to match your own:

```
$pfxPath = "c:\Office365LabSTSCert.pfx"
$pfxPass = "DJ989we..wefds908*"
$stsCertificate = New-Object
System.Security.Cryptography.X509Certificates.X509Certificate2 $pfxPath,
$pfxPass, 20
Set-SPSecurityTokenServiceConfig -ImportSigningCertificate $stsCertificate
certutil -addstore -enterprise -f -v root $stsCertificate
```

```
iisreset
net stop SPTimerV4
net start SPTimerV4
```

The output will be as shown in the following screenshot:

Configuring server-to-server authentication

Earlier in the chapter, I said that I hope you like PowerShell. Well, here is why. Unfortunately, we don't have the space here to go through every command in detail. However, open up PowerShell and enter each line, pressing enter after each, and if all goes well you will be ready to start configuring hybrid search. You will need to change the following variables to match your environment:

```
$spcn="*.office365lab.co.uk"
$spsite=Get-Spsite http://sharepoint
$cerPath = "c:\Office365LabSTS.cer"
$pfxPath = "c:\Office365LabSTSCert.pfx"
$pfxPass = "DJ989we..wefds908*"
```

Once you have updated the variables, you are ready to run the script:

```
//IMPORT MODULES
Add-PSSnapin Microsoft.SharePoint.PowerShell
Import-Module Microsoft.PowerShell.Utility
Import-Module MSOnline -force
Import-Module MSOnlineExtended -force
Import-Module Microsoft.Online.SharePoint.PowerShell -force
enable-psremoting
//CONNECT TO TENANT
new-pssession
$cred=Get-Credential
Connect-MsolService -Credential $cred
//SET TENANT VARIABLES
$spcn="*.office365lab.co.uk"
$spsite=Get-Spsite http://sharepoint
$site=Get-Spsite $spsite
$spoappid="00000003-0000-0ff1-ce00-000000000000"
$spocontextID = (Get-MsolCompanyInformation).ObjectID
$metadataEndpoint = "https://accounts.accesscontrol.windows.net/" +
$spocontextID + "/metadata/json/1"
//SETUP CERTIFICATES
$cerPath = "c:\Office365LabSTS.cer"
$pfxPath = "c:\Office365LabSTSCert.pfx"
$pfxPass = "DJ989we..wefds908*"
$cer = New-Object
System.Security.Cryptography.X509Certificates.X509Certificate2 -
ArgumentList $pfxPath, $pfxPass
$cer.Import($cerPath)
$binCert = $cer.GetRawCertData()
$credValue = [System.Convert]::ToBase64String($binCert);
New-MsolServicePrincipalCredential -AppPrincipalId $spoappid -Type
asymmetric -Usage Verify -Value $credValue
```

```
//SET SERVICE PRINCIPLE
$msp = Get-MsolServicePrincipal -AppPrincipalId $spoappid
$spns = $msp.ServicePrincipalNames
$spns.Add("$spoappid/$spcn")
Set-MsolServicePrincipal -AppPrincipalId $spoappid -ServicePrincipalNames
$spns
//VERIFY THE SPN BY CHECKING THE OUTPUT INCLUDES YOUR PUBLIC DOMAIN
$msp = Get-MsolServicePrincipal -AppPrincipalId $spoappid
$spns = $msp.ServicePrincipalNames
$spns
//REGISTER SHAREPOINT ONLINE ID WITH ON-PREMISES SERVER
$spoappprincipalID = (Get-MsolServicePrincipal -ServicePrincipalName
$spoappid).ObjectID
$sponameidentifier = "$spoappprincipalID@$spocontextID"
$appPrincipal = Register-SPAppPrincipal -site $site.rootweb -nameIdentifier
$sponameidentifier -displayName "SharePoint Online"
//VERIFY THE OUTPUT
$appPrincipal | fl
//SET SHAREPOINT REALM
Set-SPAuthenticationRealm -realm $spocontextID
//ENSURE THE GUIDS MATCH IN THE FOLLOWING COMMANDS
$spocontextID
Get-SPAuthenticationRealm
//CONFIGURE AN ON-PREMISES PROXY FOR AZURE AD
New-SPAzureAccessControlServiceApplicationProxy -Name "ACS" -
MetadataServiceEndpointUri $metadataEndpoint -DefaultProxyGroup
New-SPTrustedSecurityTokenIssuer -MetadataEndpoint $metadataEndpoint -
IsTrustBroker:$true -Name "ACS"
//VERIFY OUTPUT
Get-SPTrustedSecurityTokenIssuer
```

When we go back to the SharePoint **TRUST RELATIONSHIPS** window, we will see the new certificates set up by the script, as shown in the following screenshot:

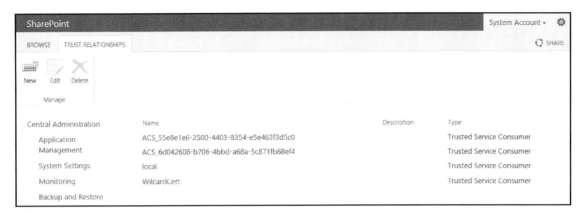

Configuring result source

Now we are set to configure where the search results from SharePoint Online will be collected from.

From **Central Administration** | **Application Management** | **Manage Service Applications**, click on the first **Search Service Application** link, as shown in the following screenshot:

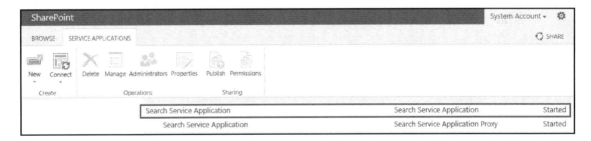

On the **Search Service Application** page, select **Result Sources** from the left-hand menu, which will open the **Search Service Application: Manage Result Sources** page.

Click **New Result Source** to configure where our SharePoint Online search results will be collected from, as shown in the following screenshot:

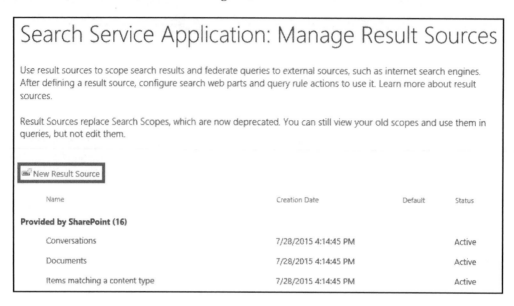

Give the result source a suitable name, in this case SharePoint Online. Select **Remote SharePoint** in the **Protocol** section, and then enter the URL for SharePoint Online in the **Remote Service URL** box, as shown in the following screenshot. Press the **OK** button to save the result source:

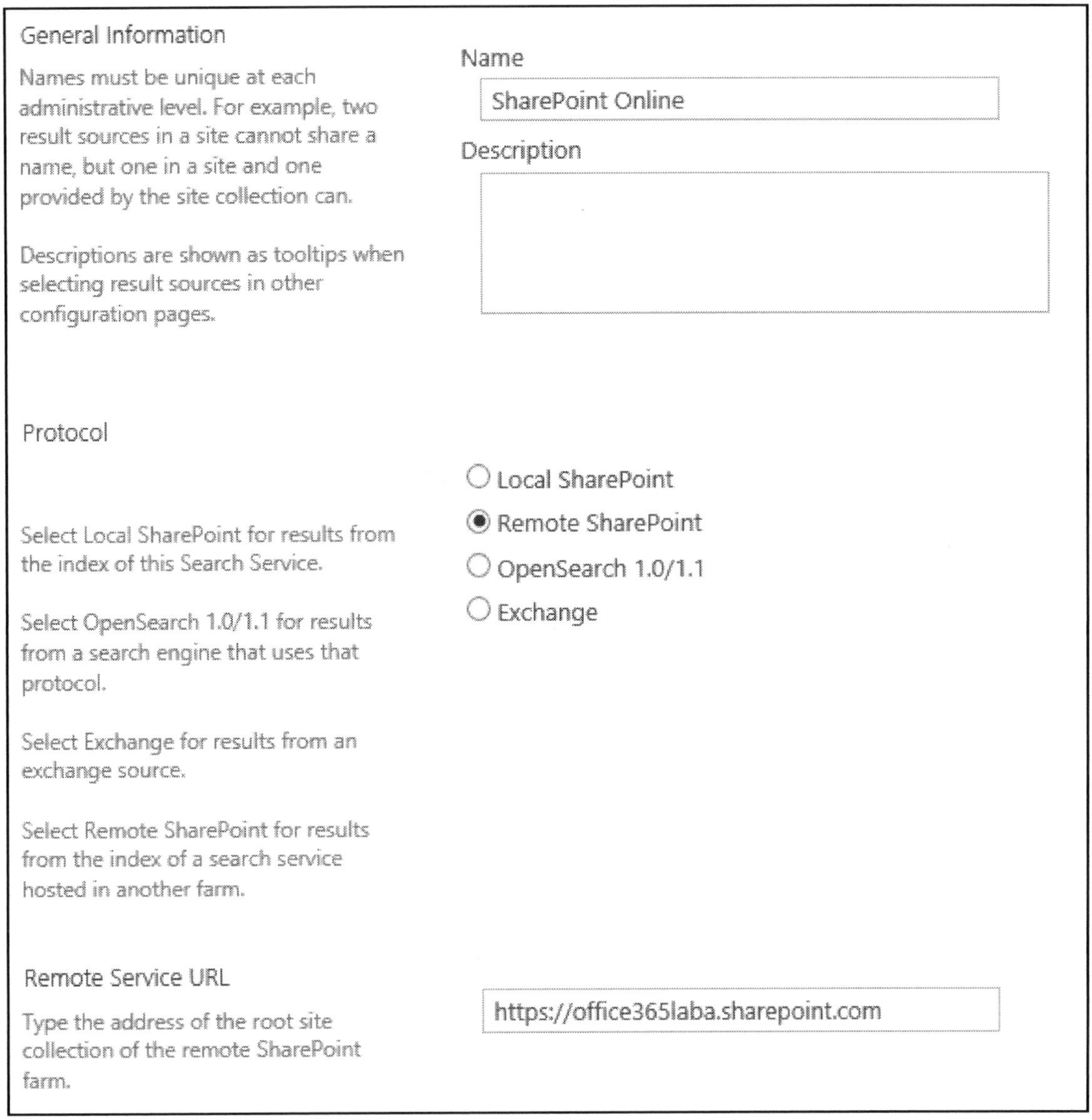

General Information

Names must be unique at each
administrative level. For example, two
result sources in a site cannot share a
name, but one in a site and one
provided by the site collection can.

Descriptions are shown as tooltips when
selecting result sources in other
configuration pages.

Name

SharePoint Online

Description

Protocol

Select Local SharePoint for results from
the index of this Search Service.

Select OpenSearch 1.0/1.1 for results
from a search engine that uses that
protocol.

Select Exchange for results from an
exchange source.

Select Remote SharePoint for results
from the index of a search service
hosted in another farm.

○ Local SharePoint
◉ Remote SharePoint
○ OpenSearch 1.0/1.1
○ Exchange

Remote Service URL

Type the address of the root site
collection of the remote SharePoint
farm.

https://office365laba.sharepoint.com

The result sources are now seen, as shown in the following screenshot:

Search Service Application: Manage Result Sources

Use result sources to scope search results and federate queries to external sources, such as internet search engines. After defining a result source, configure search web parts and query rule actions to use it. Learn more about result sources.

Result Sources replace Search Scopes, which are now deprecated. You can still view your old scopes and use them in queries, but not edit them.

New Result Source

Name	Creation Date	Default	Status
Defined for this search service (1)			
SharePoint Online	9/6/2015 12:49:59 PM		Active
Provided by SharePoint (16)			
Conversations	7/28/2015 4:14:45 PM		Active

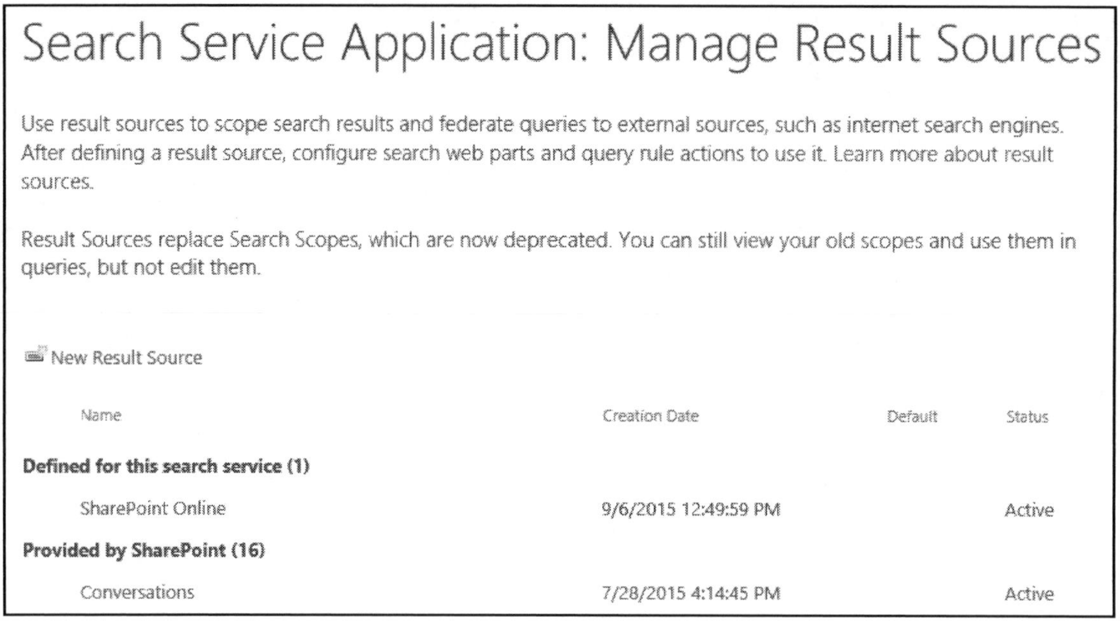

Now that the result source has been configured, right-click on it and select **Test Source**. If everything is working correctly, you should see the following screenshot, but if not it should give you some helpful error messages so you can begin troubleshooting the problem. In our lab environment, everything is working as expected. Let's continue and create a query rule that will define how the results from our source will display to the users:

Configuring query rules

Query rules define how and what results are displayed to the end user. In our lab environment, we want to show search results from SharePoint Online above any local results when they search using the enterprise search centre. My logic here is that there will be far fewer files held in SharePoint Online to start with, and also if there are no results they won't be displayed.

Open up the **Manage Query Rules** page from **Central Administration | Application Management | Manage Service Applications | Search Service Application** and then click on **Query Rules** on the left-hand menu.

First we select a contact for our new rule, and in our case we want our rule to fire when the users search for **Local SharePoint Results**. This might sound wrong because we are trying to display results from SharePoint Online, but this is okay because the users will be searching locally, we are simply expanding the search for them.

Click on **New Query Rule** to begin configuring our SharePoint Online rule, as shown in the following screenshot:

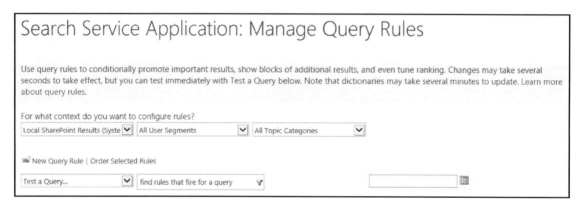

Give the rule a suitable name, such as SharePoint Online. Next, click on **Remove Condition** so that the searches are performed against SharePoint Online no matter what the user searches for. If you want, you can configure special words which trigger these results to show, such as "search online," which would then return the online results rather than returning them all of the time. In our lab, let's make it easy and return the online results at all times by clicking on **Remove Condition**.

We now need to set up how our results are going to display to the user, so click on **Add Result Block,** as shown in the following screenshot:

General Information

Rule name

SharePoint Online

Fires only on source Local SharePoint Results.

▷ Context

Query Conditions

Define when a user's search box query makes this rule fire. You can specify multiple conditions of different types, or remove all conditions to fire for any query text. Every query condition becomes false if the query is not a simple keyword query, such as if it has quotes, property filters, parentheses, or special operators.

Query Matches Keyword Exactly ⌄

    Query exactly matches one of these phrases (semi-colon separated)

Remove Condition

Add Alternate Condition

Actions

When your rule fires, it can enhance search results in three ways. It can add promoted results above the ranked results. It can also add blocks of additional results. Like normal results, these blocks can be promoted to always appear

Promoted Results

Add Promoted Result

Result Blocks

Add Result Block

Change ranked results by changing the query

Using a result block, we can define how the results are displayed. We can have them show up after the local results or before, and we can add helpful text that tells the server where the results are coming from. In our lab, SharePoint Online results are going to show up at the top of all the results. We only need to make three changes here: the block title, the result source, and the location of the results.

To the **Block Title**, I added the text from SharePoint Online, so the users know it's a file found in the cloud. In the **Search this Source** dropdown, we select the result source we configured earlier; in this case it was SharePoint Online. Finally, we select **This block is always shown above core results**, as shown in the following screenshot, to display the online results first:

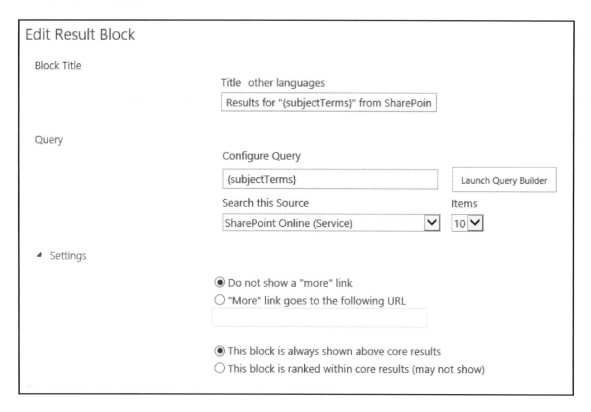

Press **OK** to save the result block and then do the same to save the result query.

Finally, let's open the enterprise search page and find out whether all our hard work has paid off! Bingo! Our lab environment successfully retrieved the search results from SharePoint Online and returned them along with our on-premises SharePoint results, as shown in the following screenshot:

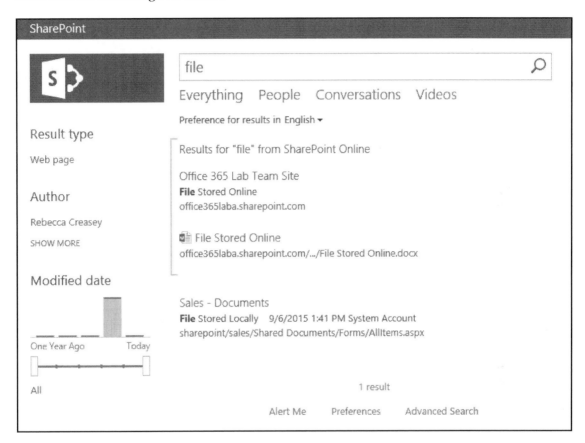

Hybrid Business Connectivity Services

Business Connectivity Services (**BCS**) allows us to publish data from our on-premises SharePoint environment into SharePoint Online using lists or SharePoint apps. One common use of this is to publish sales or performance data held in Excel sheets on-premises to sales employees that connect to SharePoint Online.

Sales people often work out of the office, visiting clients and travelling, so being able to edit sensitive information locally within your organisation and to share that data securely with remote users is an extremely powerful feature to utilize.

Configuring hybrid BCS is beyond the scope of this book but, it was well worth mentioning so you can investigate this feature further yourself. A good place to start is the Technet site *Deploy a Business Connectivity Services hybrid solution in SharePoint* found at `https://techne` `t.microsoft.com/en-us/library/dn197239.aspx`.

Summary

Configuring SharePoint hybrid features can be a daunting task and require a lot of planning and testing at every step along the way, but the results are well worth the effort. We have seen how configuring hybrid search allows us to extend our on-premises SharePoint environment into the cloud by making it easy to locate files regardless of their location. We have seen how we can expand our storage requirements without having to invest in new hardware or software by using OneDrive for Business hybrid and redirecting local users to SharePoint Online to access their personal files. Finally, we briefly looked at an example of using BCS, which allows us to securely publish sensitive data to external users.

Just remember that it's not just about implementing these features successfully, it's also about giving our users the best training possible so they can make use of them. This in turn results in more efficiency and productivity, and ultimately less calls to your helpdesk!

Index

B

bandwidth, migration process
  migration bandwidth 202, 204
  user bandwidth 205, 206, 207
Billing
  Bills 44
  Licenses 45
  Purchase Services 45
  Subscriptions 41, 42, 44
Business Connectivity Services (BCS) 380
  about 386, 422
  reference link 422
business scenarios
  about 61
  ageing servers 62
  remote workforce 62
  staff expansion 62

C

calculator
  URL 202
centralized Exchange Organization 113
Certificate Revocation List (CRL) 198, 201
Cloud Solutions Provider (CSP) 8
comma-separated values (CSV) file 133
conference rooms
  setting 340, 341, 342
cutover migration
  about 123
  requisites 129

D

deployment considerations, Exchange Hybrid
  about 110
  Exchange schedule free/busy store 111
  Hybrid server, scaling 111
  location and version, of existing messaging
    system 110, 111
  migration bandwidth, for Hybrid server 111
  Public Folder Hybrid 112
Directory Synchronization server 196
Directory Synchronization
  about 89
  advanced filtering options, configuring 295, 296

Azure AD Connect, installing 282, 283, 284,
    285, 286, 287, 288, 291
  checking tools 188
  deploying 272
  DirSync readiness wizard 273, 274, 275, 276,
    278, 279, 280
  IdFix tool 188, 190, 191
  manual syncing 298, 299
  readiness wizard, using 191, 192, 193, 194
  scheduling 297, 298
  specifications 272, 273
  verifying 292, 293, 294
disconnected Exchange Organization 115
distributed Exchange Organization 114
distribution list management
  cons 94
  pros 94
Domain Keys Identified Mail (DKIM) 57
domain
  adding 29
  DNS requisites 30
  setting up 31, 32, 34, 36

E

end users
  preparing 321
  self-deployment 322, 323, 324, 325
  software deployment service, for distribution 326
Enterprise Agreement (EA) 16
environment, preparing for migration
  Gmail 126
  Hosted Exchange 126
  IMAP 126
  on-premise Exchange 2003 127, 128, 129
Exchange admin center interface
  about 55
  Compliance Management 56
  Mail flow 57
  Mobile 58
  Organization 57
  Permissions 56
  Protection 57
  Public Folders 58
  Recipients 56
  unified messaging 58